Introduction to

Introduction to Post-Tonal Theory

third edition

Joseph N. Straus

Graduate Center
City University of New York

PEARSON

Prentice
Hall

Upper Saddle River, New Jersey 07458

Library of Congress Cataloging-in-Publication Data
Straus, Joseph Nathan.
    Introduction to post-tonal theory / Joseph N. Straus.—3rd ed.
      p.   cm.
    ISBN 0-13-189890-6
      1. Music theory.   2. Atonality.   3. Twelve-tone system.   4. Musical analysis.   I. Title.

MT40.S96 2005
781.2'67—dc22

2004050370

Editor-in-Chief: Sarah Touborg
Senior Acquisitions Editor: Christopher T. Johnson
Editorial Assistant: Evette Dickerson
Marketing Manager: Sheryl Adams
Marketing Assistant: Cherron Gardner
Managing Editor: Joanne Riker
Production Editor: Laura A. Lawrie
Manufacturing and Prepress Buyer: Benjamin D. Smith
Cover Designer: Bruce Kenselaar
Composition: This book was set in 10/12 Times by Stratford Publishing Services
Printer/Binder: Interior printed by Courier Companies, Inc. The cover was printed by Phoenix Color Corp.

Credits and acknowledgments borrowed from other sources and reproduced, with permission, in this textbook appear on appropriate page within text.

Pearson Education LTD.
Pearson Education Singapore, Pte. Ltd
Pearson Education, Canada, Ltd
Pearson Education-Japan

Pearson Education Australia PTY, Limited
Pearson Education North Asia Ltd
Pearson Educación de Mexico, S.A. de C.V.
Pearson Education Malaysia, Pte. Ltd

10 9 8 7 6 5 4
ISBN 0-13-189890-6

Contents

Preface

Compared to tonal theory, now in its fourth century of development, post-tonal theory is in its infancy. But in the past three decades, it has shown itself to be an infant of prodigious growth and surprising power. A broad consensus has emerged among music theorists regarding the basic musical elements of post-tonal music—pitch, interval, motive, harmony, collection—and this book reports that consensus to a general audience of musicians and students of music. Like books on scales, triads, and simple harmonic progressions in tonal music, this book introduces basic theoretical concepts for the post-tonal music of the twentieth and twenty-first centuries.

Beyond basic concepts, the third edition of this book also contains information on many of the most recent developments in post-tonal theory, including expanded or new coverage of the following topics:

- Transformational networks and graphs
- Contour theory
- Composing-out
- Atonal voice leading
- Atonal pitch space
- Triadic post-tonality (including voice-leading parsimony)
- Inversional symmetry and inversional axes
- Interval cycles
- Diatonic, whole-tone, octatonic, and hexatonic collections

As a result, this book is not only a primer of basic concepts but also an introduction to the current state of post-tonal theory, with its rich array of theoretical concepts and analytical tools.

Although this book can make no pretense to comprehensiveness either, either chronologically or theoretically—there is just too much great music and fascinating theory out there—this third edition explores a much wider range of composers and musical styles than its predecessors. Although the "classical" prewar repertoire of music by Schoenberg, Stravinsky, Bartók, Webern, and Berg still comprises the musical core, theoretical concepts are now also illustrated with music by Adams, Babbitt, Berio, Boulez, Britten, Cage, Carter, Cowell, Crawford, Crumb, Debussy, Feldman, Glass, Gubaidulina, Ives, Ligeti, Messiaen, Musgrave, Reich, Ruggles, Sessions, Shostakovich, Stockhausen, Varèse, Wolpe, Wuorinen, and Zwilich.

As with the previous editions of this book, I received invaluable advice from many friends and colleagues based on their teaching experience. I am grateful to Wayne Alpern, Jonathan Bernard, Claire Boge, Ricardo Bordini, Scott Brickman, Michael Buchler, Uri Burstein, James Carr, Patrick Fairfield, Michael Friedmann, Edward Gollin, Dave Headlam, Gary Karpinski, Rosemary Killam, Bruce Quaglia, Daniel Mathers, Carolyn Mullin, Catherine Nolan, Jay Rahn, Nancy Rogers, Steven Rosenhaus, Art Samplaski, Paul Sheehan, Stephen Slottow, David Smyth, Harvey Stokes, Dmitri Tymoczko, and Joyce Yip. My thanks go also to Chris Johnson and Laura Lawrie at Prentice Hall for their expert editorial work at every stage. Michael Berry provided additional editorial assistance. Closer to home, in matters both tangible and intangible, Sally Goldfarb has offered continuing guidance and support beyond my ability to describe or repay. Adam and Michael helped, too.

Joseph N. Straus
Graduate Center
City University of New York

The publishers are gratefully acknowledged for permission to use the following musical examples:

John Adams, HARMONIUM Words by Emily Dickinson. Copyright © 1981 by Associated Music Publishers, Inc. (BMI) International Copyright Secured. All Rights Reserved. Reprinted by Permission.

Milton Babbitt, STRONG QUARTET NO. 2 Copyright © 1967 (Renewed) by Associated Music Publishers, Inc. (BMI). International Copyright Secured. All rights Reserved. Reprinted by Permission.

Babbitt, SEMI-SIMPLE VARIATIONS. © 1957 Theodore Presser Company. Used by permission of the Publisher.

Music of Bela Bartók

PIANO SONATA NO. 1 © Copyright 1927 by Boosey & Hawkes, Inc. for the USA. Copyright Renewed. Reprinted by permission.

STRING QUARTET NO. 4 © Copyright 1929 by Boosey & Hawkes, Inc. for the USA. Copyright Renewed. Reprinted by permission.

SONATA FOR TWO PIANOS AND PERCUSSION © Copyright 1942 by Hawkes & Son (London) Ltd. Copyright Renewed. Revised version © Copyright 1970 by Hawkes & Son (London) Ltd. Copyright Renewed. Reprinted by permission of Boosey & Hawkes, Inc.

Alban Berg, Violin Concerto © 1936 by Universal Edition A.G., Vienna. © Renewed. All Rights Reserved. Used by permission of European American Music Distributors Corporation, sole U.S. and Canadian agent for Universal Edition A.G., Vienna.

Luciano Berio, Flute SEQUENZE © 1958 (Renewed 1985) SUGAR SRL and EXTRAVAGANZA PUBLISHING. All Rights in the United States Administered by EMI APRIL MUSIC INC. All rights Reserved International Copyright Secured Used by Permission.

Pierre Boulez, LE MARTEAU SANS MAîTRE © 1954, 1957 by Universal Edition Ltd., London. Poèmes de René Char: © 1954 by José Corti Editur, Paris. All Rights Reserved. Used by permission of European American Music Distributors Corporation, sole U.S. and Canadian agent for Universal Edition Ltd., London.

Pierre Boulez, STRUCTURES 1A © 1955 by Universal Edition Ltd., London. All Rights Reserved. Used by permission of European American Music Distributors Corporation, sole U.S. and Canadian agent for Universal Edition Ltd., London.

John Cage, FOR PAUL TAYLOR AND ANITA DENECKS, © 1978 by Henmar Press Inc., New York. All rights reserved. Used by permission.

Elliott Carter, STRING QUARTET NO. 2 © Copyright 1961 (Renewed) by Associated Music Publishers, Inc. (BMI) International Copyright Secured. All Rights Reserved. Reprinted by Permission.

Henry Cowell, THE BANSHEE © Copyright 1930 (Renewed) by Associated Music Publishers, Inc. (BMI). International Copyright Secured. All Rights Reserved. Reprinted by Permission.

Crawford (Seeger), DIAPHONIC SUITE NO. 1 Copyright © 1972 Continuo Music Press, Inc. International Copyright Secured. Made in U.S.A. All rights reserved. Reprinted by permission.

Crawford (Seeger), STRING QUARTET. © Merion Music, Inc. Used by permission.

Sofia Gubaidulina, STRING TRIO. © Copyright Chante Du Monde. Sub-published in the United States, Canada and Mexico by G. Schirmer, Inc. (ASCAP) International Copyright Secured. All Rights Reserved. Reprinted by Permission.

George Crumb, ANCIENT VOICES OF CHILDREN, © Copyright 1971 by C. F. Peters Corporation Inc., New York. All Rights Reserved. Used by permission.

George Crumb, MAKROKOSMOS, VOL 1, No. 1, © Copyright 1973 by C. F. Peters Corporation, New York. All Rights Reserved. Used by permission.

George Crumb, MAKROKOSMOS, VOL 2, No. 8 ("Gargoyles"), © Copyright 1973 by C. F. Peters Corporation, New York. All Rights Reserved. Used by permission.

Morton Feldman, DURATIONS III, No. 3, © Copyright 1962 by C. F. Peters Corporation, New York. All Rights Reserved. Used by permission.

Morton Feldman, PROJECTION No. 1 FOR SOLO CELLO, © Copyright 1962 by C. F. Peters Corporation, New York. All Rights Reserved. Used by permission.

THE RAKE'S PROGRESS © Copyright 1951 by Hawkes & Son (London), Ltd. Copyright Renewed. Reprinted by permission of Boosey & Hawkes, Inc.

SYMPHONY OF PSALMS © Copyright 1931 by Hawkes & Son (London), Ltd. Copyright Renewed. Revised version © Copyright 1948 by Hawkes & Son (London), Ltd. Copyright Renewed. Reprinted by permission of Boosey & Hawkes, Inc.

SERENADE IN A © Copyright 1926 by Hawkes & Son (London), Ltd. Copyright Renewed. Reprinted by permission of Boosey & Hawkes, Inc.

A SERMON, A NARRATIVE, AND A PRAYER © Copyright 1961 by Hawkes & Son (London), Ltd. Copyright Renewed. Reprinted by permission of Boosey & Hawkes, Inc.

REQUIEM CANTICLES © Copyright 1967 by Hawkes & Son (London), Ltd. Copyright Renewed. Reprinted by permission of Boosey & Hawkes, Inc.

THREE PIECES FOR STRING QUARTET © Copyright 1928 by Hawkes & Son (London), Ltd. Copyright Renewed. Reprinted by permission of Boosey & Hawkes, Inc.

SYMPHONY IN C © Copyright 1948 by Schott Musik International. © Renewed. All Rights Reserved. Used by permission of European American Music Distributors Corporation, sole U.S. and Canadian agent for Schott Musik International.

Edgard Valese, DENSITY 21.5, © 1946 G. Ricordi & Company (SIAE). All All rights for the world obo G. Ricordi & Company (SIAE) administered by BMG Ricordi S.P.A.—Milan (SIAE). All rights for the U.S. obo BMG Ricordi S.P.A.— Milan (SIAE) administered by Careers-BMG Music Publishing, Inc. (BMI).

Edgard Valese, HYPERPRISM, © 1946 G. Ricordi & Company (SIAE). All All rights for the world obo G. Ricordi & Company (SIAE) administered by BMG Ricordi S.P.A.—Milan (SIAE). All rights for the U.S. obo BMG Ricordi S.P.A.—Milan (SIAE) administered by Careers-BMG Music Publishing, Inc. (BMI).

Anton Webern, 5 LIEDER, OP. 3, Used by permission of European American Music Distributors LLC, US and Canadian agent for Universal Edition.

Anton Webern, MOVEMENTS FOR STRING QUARTET OP. 5 © 1922 by Universal Edition A.G., Vienna. © renewed 1949 by Anton Webern's Erben. All Rights Reserved. Used by permission of European American Music Distributors Corporation, sole U.S. and Canadian agent for Universal Edition A.G., Vienna.

Anton Webern, STRING QUARTET, OP. 28 © 1955 by Universal Edition A.G., Vienna. All Rights Reserved. Used by permission of European American Music Distributors Corporation, sole U.S. and Canadian agent for Universal Edition A.G., Vienna.

Anton Webern, THREE SONGS, OP. 25 © 1956 by Universal Edition A.G., Vienna. All Rights Reserved. Used by permission of European American Music Distributors Corporation, sole U.S. and Canadian agent for Universal Edition A.G., Vienna.

Anton Webern, VARIATIONS, OP. 27 © 1937 by Universal Edition A.G., Vienna. © renewed. All Rights Reserved. Used by permission of European American Music Distributors Corporation, sole U.S. and Canadian agent for Universal Edition A.G., Vienna.

Anton Webern, SONGS, OP. 14 © 1924 by Universal Edition A.G., Vienna. © renewed 1952 by Anton Webern's Erben. All Rights Reserved. Used by permission of European American Music Distributors Corporation, sole U.S. and Canadian agent for Universal Edition A.G., Vienna.

Anton Webern, CONCERTO, OP. 24 © 1948 by Universal Edition A.G., Vienna. All Rights Reserved. Used by permission of European American Music Distributors Corporation, sole U.S. and Canadian agent for Universal Edition A.G., Vienna.

Stefan Wolpe, "FORM FOR PIANO," MM. 1–4 © Copyright 1962 by Tonos Musikverlags GmbH, Darmstadt/Germany.

Charles Wuorinen, TWELVE SHORT PIECES. NO. 3, © Copyright 1980 by C. F. Peters Corporation, New York. All Rights Reserved. Used by permission.

Chapter 1
Basic Concepts and Definitions

Octave Equivalence

There is something special about the octave. Pitches separated by one or more octaves are usually perceived as in some sense *equivalent*. Our musical notation reflects that equivalence by giving the same name to octave-related pitches. The name A, for example, is given not only to some particular pitch, like the A a minor third below middle C, but also to all the other pitches one or more octaves above or below it. Octave-related pitches are called by the same name because they sound so much alike and because Western music usually treats them as functionally equivalent.

Equivalence is not the same thing as identity. Example 1–1 shows a melody from Schoenberg's String Quartet No. 4, first as it occurs at the beginning of the first movement and then as it occurs a few measures from the end.

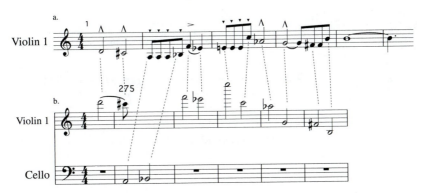

Example 1–1 Two equivalent melodies (Schoenberg, String Quartet No. 4).

The two versions are different in many ways, particularly in their rhythm and range. The range of the second version is so wide that the first violin cannot reach all of the

1

notes; the cello has to step in to help. At the same time, however, it is easy to recognize that they are basically the same melody—in other words, that they are octave equivalent.

In Example 1–2, the opening of Schoenberg's Piano Piece, Op. 11, No. 1, compare the first three notes of the melody with the sustained notes in measures 4–5.

Example 1–2 Two equivalent musical ideas (Schoenberg, Piano Piece, Op. 11, No. 1).

There are many differences between the two collections of notes (register, articulation, rhythm, etc.), but a basic equivalence also. They are equivalent because they both contain a B, a G♯, and a G.

We find the same situation in the passage shown in Example 1–3, from a string quartet movement by Webern. The first three notes of the viola melody—G, B, and C♯—return as the cadential chord at the end of the phrase. The melody and the chord are octave equivalent.

Example 1–3 Two equivalent musical ideas (Webern, Movements for String Quartet, Op. 5, No. 2).

When we assert octave equivalence, and other equivalences we will discuss later, our object is not to smooth out or dismiss the variety of the musical surface. Rather, we seek to discover the relationships that underlie the surface and lend unity and coherence to musical works.

Pitch Class

We will distinguish between a *pitch* (a tone with a certain frequency) and a *pitch class* (a group of pitches with the same name). Pitch-class A, for example, contains all the pitches named A. To put it the other way around, any pitch named A is a member of pitch-class A. Sometimes we will speak about specific pitches; at other times we will talk, more abstractly, about pitch classes. When we say that the lowest note on the cello is a C, we are referring to a specific pitch. We can notate that pitch on the second ledger line beneath the bass staff. When we say that the tonic of Beethoven's Fifth Symphony is C, we are referring not to some particular pitch C, but to *pitch-class* C. Pitch-class C is an abstraction and cannot be adequately notated on musical staves. Sometimes, for convenience, we will represent a pitch class using musical notation. In reality, however, a pitch class is not a single thing; it is a class of things, of pitches one or more octaves apart.

The passage shown in Example 1–4 consists of seventeen three-note chords. The pitches change as the instruments jump around, but each chord contains the same three pitch classes: F♯, G, and A♭ (notice that the violin is playing harmonics that produce a pitch two octaves higher than the filled-in notehead).

Example 1–4 Many pitches, but only three pitch classes: F♯, G, and A♭ (Feldman, *Durations III,* No. 3).

Enharmonic Equivalence

In common-practice tonal music, a B♭ is not the same as an A♯. Even on an equal-tempered instrument like the piano, the tonal system gives B♭ and A♯ different functions and different meanings, representing different degrees of the scale. In G major, for example, A♯ is ♯2̂ whereas B♭ is ♭3̂, and scale-degrees 2̂ and 3̂ have very different musical roles both melodically and harmonically. These distinctions are largely

abandoned in post-tonal music, however, where notes that are enharmonically equivalent (like B♭ and A♯) are also functionally equivalent. For example, the passage in
Example 1–5 involves three repetitions: the A returns an octave higher, the B returns
two octaves lower, and the A♭ returns three octaves higher as a G♯. A♭ and G♯ are
enharmonically equivalent.

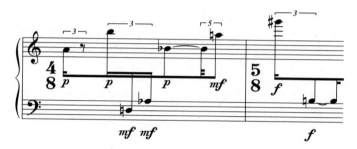

Example 1–5 Enharmonic equivalence (Stockhausen, *Klavierstuck III*).

There may be isolated moments where a composer notates a pitch in what
seems like a functional way (sharps for ascending motion and flats for descending,
for example). For the most part, however, the notation is functionally arbitrary, determined by simple convenience and legibility. The melodies in Example 1–6 are enharmonically equivalent (although the first one is much easier to read).

Example 1–6 Enharmonic equivalence.

Integer Notation

Octave equivalence and enharmonic equivalence leave us with only twelve different
pitch classes. All the B♯s, C♯s, and D♭♭s are members of a single pitch class, as are all
the C♯s and D♭s, all the C✕s, Ds, and E♭♭s, and so on. We will often use integers from 0
through 11 to refer to the pitch classes. Figure 1–1 shows the twelve different pitch
classes and some of the contents of each.

integer name	pitch-class content
0	B♯, C, D♭♭
1	C♯, D♭
2	C×, D, E♭♭
3	D♯, E♭
4	D×, E, F♭
5	E♯, F, G♭♭
6	F♯, G♭
7	F×, G, A♭♭
8	G♯, A♭
9	G×, A, B♭♭
10	A♯, B♭
11	A×, B, C♭

Figure 1–1

We will use a "fixed *do*" notation: the pitch class containing the Cs is arbitrarily assigned the integer 0 and the rest follows from there.

Integers are traditional in music (figured-bass numbers, for example) and useful for representing certain musical relationships. We will never do things to the integers that don't have musical significance. We won't divide integers, because, while dividing 7 into 11 makes numerical sense, dividing G into B doesn't make much musical sense. Other arithmetical operations, however, will prove musically useful. We will, for example, subtract numbers, because, as we will see, subtraction gives us a simple way of talking about intervals. Computing the distance between 7 and 11 by subtracting 7 from 11 makes numerical sense, and the idea of computing the distance between G and B makes musical sense. We will use numbers and arithmetic to model interesting aspects of the music we study. The music itself is not "mathematical" any more than our lives are "mathematical" just because we count our ages in integers. In this book, we will identify pitch classes with either traditional letter notation or integers, whichever seems clearest and easiest in a particular context.

Mod 12

Every pitch belongs to one of the twelve pitch classes. Going up an octave (adding twelve semitones) or going down an octave (subtracting twelve semitones) will just produce another member of the same pitch class. For example, if we start on the E♭ above middle C (a member of pitch class 3) and go up twelve semitones, we end up back on pitch class 3. In other words, in the world of pitch classes, $3 + 12 = 15 = 3$. More generally, any number larger than 11 or smaller than 0 is equivalent to some integer from 0 to 11 inclusive. To figure out which one, just add or subtract 12 (or any multiple of 12). Twelve is called the *modulus,* and our theoretical system frequently will rely upon arithmetic *modulo 12,* for which *mod 12* is an abbreviation. In a mod 12 system, $-12 = 0 = 12 = 24$, and so on. Similarly, -13, -1, 23, and 35 are all equivalent to 11 (and to each other) because they are related to 11 (and to each other) by adding or subtracting 12.

It is easiest to understand these (and other) mod 12 relationships by envisioning a circular clockface, like the one in Figure 1–2.

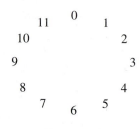

Figure 1–2

In a mod 12 system, moving 12 (or a multiple of 12) in either direction only brings you back to your starting point. As a result, we will generally be dealing only with integers between 0 and 11 inclusive. When we are confronted with a number larger than 11 or smaller than 0, we will usually write it, by adding or subtracting 12, as an integer between 0 and 11. We will sometimes use negative numbers (for example, when we want to suggest the idea of descending), and we will sometimes use numbers larger than 11 (for example, when discussing the distance between two widely separated pitches), but in general we will discuss such numbers in terms of their mod 12 equivalents.

We locate pitches in an extended *pitch space,* ranging in equal-tempered semitones from the lowest to the highest audible tone. We locate pitch classes in a modular *pitch-class space,* as in Figure 1–2, which circles back on itself and contains only the twelve pitch classes. It's like the hours of the day or the days of the week. As our lives unfold in time, each hour and each day are uniquely located in linear time, never to be repeated. But we can be sure that, if it's eleven o'clock now, it will be eleven o'clock again in twelve hours (that's a mod 12 system), and that if it's Friday today, it will be Friday again in seven days (that's a mod 7 system). Just as our lives unfold simultaneously in linear and modular time, music unfolds simultaneously in pitch and pitch-class space.

Intervals

Because of enharmonic equivalence, we will no longer need different names for intervals with the same absolute size—for example, diminished fourths and major thirds. In tonal music, such distinctions are crucial; intervals are defined and named according to their tonal function. A third, for example, is an interval that spans three steps of the diatonic scale, while a fourth spans four steps. A major third is consonant, while a diminished fourth is dissonant. In music that doesn't use diatonic scales and doesn't systematically distinguish between consonance and dissonance, it seems cumbersome and even misleading to use traditional interval names. It will be easier and more accurate musically just to name intervals according to the number of semitones they contain. The intervals between C and E and between C and F♭ both contain four semitones and are both instances of interval 4, as are B♯–F♭, C–D×, and so on.

Example 1–7 extracts a series of seven harmonic intervals played in rhythmic unison by the second violin and viola in a passage from Elliott Carter's String Quartet No. 3, a piece in which two instrumental duos often play distinct intervals. The first six intervals are spelled as major thirds while the seventh is spelled as a diminished fourth, but in this musical context it is clear that all seven intervals are to be understood as enharmonically equivalent.

Example 1–7 Enharmonically equivalent intervals (Carter, String Quartet No. 3, mm. 245–62).

Figure 1–3 gives some traditional interval names and the number of semitones they contain.

traditional name	no. of semitones	traditional name	no. of semitones
unison	0	major 6th, diminished 7th	9
minor 2nd	1	augmented 6th, minor 7th	10
major 2nd, diminished 3rd	2	major 7th	11
minor 3rd, augmented 2nd	3	octave	12
major 3rd, diminished 4th	4	minor 9th	13
augmented 3rd, perfect 4th	5	major 9th	14
augmented 4th, diminished 5th	6	minor 10th	15
perfect 5th, diminished 6th	7	major 10th	16
augmented 5th, minor 6th	8		

Figure 1–3

Pitch Intervals

A pitch interval is simply the distance between two pitches, measured by the number of semitones between them. A pitch interval, which will be abbreviated *ip,* is created when we move from pitch to pitch in pitch space. It can be as large as the range of our hearing or as small as a semitone. Sometimes we will be concerned about the direction of the interval, whether ascending or descending. In that case, the number will be preceded by either a plus sign (to indicate an ascending interval) or a minus sign (to indicate a descending interval). Intervals with a plus or minus sign are called *directed* or *ordered intervals.* At other times, we will be concerned only with the absolute space between two pitches. For such *unordered intervals,* we will just provide the number of semitones between the pitches.

Whether we consider the interval ordered or unordered depends on our particular analytical interests at the time. Example 1–8 shows the opening melody from Schoenberg's String Quartet No. 3, and identifies both its ordered and unordered pitch intervals.

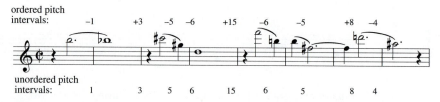

Example 1–8 Ordered and unordered pitch intervals (Schoenberg, String Quartet No. 3).

The ordered pitch intervals focus attention on the contour of the line, its balance of rising and falling motion. The unordered pitch intervals ignore contour and concentrate entirely on the spaces between the pitches.

Ordered Pitch-Class Intervals

A pitch-class interval is the distance between two pitch classes. A pitch-class interval, which will be abbreviated *i,* is created when we move from pitch class to pitch class in modular pitch-class space. It can never be larger than eleven semitones. As with pitch intervals, we will sometimes be concerned with ordered intervals and sometimes with unordered intervals. To calculate pitch-class intervals, it is best to think again of a circular clockface as in Figure 1–2. We will consider clockwise movement to be equivalent to movement upward, and counterclockwise movement equivalent to movement downward. With this in mind, the ordered interval from C♯ to A, for example, is −4 or +8. In other words, from pitch-class C♯, one can go either up eight semitones or down four semitones to get to pitch-class A. This is because +8 and −4 are equivalent (mod 12). It would be equally accurate to call that interval 8 or

−4. By convention, however, we will usually denote ordered pitch-class intervals by an integer from 0 to 11. To state this as a formula, we can say that the ordered interval from pitch class x to pitch class y is y − x (mod 12). Notice that the ordered pitch class interval from A to C♯ (1 − 9 = −8 (mod 12) = 4) is different from that from C♯ to A (8), since, when discussing ordered pitch-class intervals, order matters. Four and 8 are each other's *complement mod 12,* because they add up to 12, as do 0 and 12, 1 and 11, 2 and 10, 3 and 9, and 5 and 7. Six is its own complement mod 12.

Figure 1–4 calculates some ordered pitch-class intervals using the formula.

The ordered pitch-class interval from C♯ to E♭ is 3 − 1 = 2
from E♭ to C♯ is 1 − 3 = 10
from B to F is 5 − 11 = 6
from D to B♭ is 10 − 2 = 8
from B♭ to C♯ is 1 − 10 = 3

Figure 1–4

You will probably find it faster just to envision a musical staff, keyboard, or a clock-face. To find the ordered pitch-class interval between C♯ and A, just envision the C♯ and then count the number of half-steps you will need to go upward (if you are envisioning a staff or keyboard) or clockwise (if you are envisioning a clockface) to the nearest A.

Unordered Pitch-Class Intervals

For unordered pitch-class intervals, it no longer matters whether you count upward or downward. All we care about is the space between two pitch classes. Just count from one pitch class to the other by the shortest available route, either up or down. The formula for an unordered pitch-class interval is x − y (mod 12) *or* y − x (mod 12), whichever is smaller. The unordered pitch-class interval between C♯ and A is 4, because 4 (1 − 9 = −8 = 4) is smaller than 8 (9 − 1 = 8). Notice that the unordered pitch-class interval between C♯ and A is the same as that between A and C♯. It is 4 in both cases, since from A to the nearest C♯ is 4 and from C♯ to the nearest A also is 4. Including the unison, 0, there are only seven different unordered pitch-class intervals, because, to get from one pitch class to any other, one never has to travel farther than six semitones. Figure 1–5 calculates some unordered pitch-class intervals using the formula. The correct answer is underlined.

The unordered pitch-class interval between C♯ and E♭ is 3 − 1 = 2 or 1 − 3 = 10
E♭ and C♯ is 1 − 3 = 10 or 3 − 1 = 2
B and F is 5 − 11 = 6 or 11 − 5 = 6
D and B♭ is 10 − 2 = 8 or 2 − 10 = 4
B♭ and C♯ is 1 − 10 = 3 or 10 − 1 = 9

Figure 1–5

Again, you will probably find it faster just to envision a clockface, musical staff, or keyboard. To find the unordered pitch-class interval between B♭ and F♯, for example, just envision a B♭ and count the number of semitones to the nearest available F♯ (4).

In Example 1–9a (again the opening melody from Schoenberg's String Quartet No. 3), the first interval is ordered pitch-class interval 11, to be abbreviated as i11.

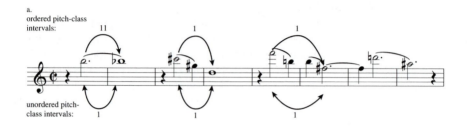

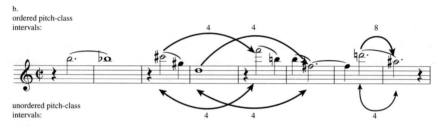

Example 1–9 Ordered and unordered pitch-class intervals (Schoenberg, String Quartet No. 3).

That's because to move from B to B♭ one moves −1 or its mod 12 equivalent, i11. Eleven is the name for descending semitones or ascending major sevenths or their compounds. If the B♭ had come before the B, the interval would have been i1, which is the name for ascending semitones or descending major sevenths or their compounds. And that is the interval described by the two subsequent melodic gestures, C♯–D and F–F♯. As ordered pitch-class intervals, the first is different from the second and third. As unordered pitch-class intervals, all three are equivalent. In Example 1–9b, two statements of i4 are balanced by a concluding i8; all three represent unordered pitch-class interval 4.

Interval Class

An unordered pitch-class interval is also called an *interval class.* Just as each pitch-class contains many individual pitches, so each interval class contains many individual pitch intervals. Because of octave equivalence, compound intervals—intervals larger than an octave—are considered equivalent to their counterparts within the octave. Furthermore, pitch-class intervals larger than six are considered equivalent to their complements mod 12 (0 = 12, 1 = 11, 2 = 10, 3 = 9, 4 = 8, 5 = 7, 6 = 6). Thus, for example, intervals 23, 13, 11, and 1 are all members of interval class 1. Figure 1–6 shows the seven different interval classes and some of the contents of each.

interval class	0	1	2	3	4	5	6
pitch intervals	0,12,24	1,11,13	2,10,14	3,9,15	4,8,16	5,7,17	6,18

Figure 1–6

We thus have four different ways of talking about intervals: ordered pitch interval, unordered pitch interval, ordered pitch-class interval, and unordered pitch-class interval. If in some piece we come across the musical figure shown in Example 1–10, we can describe it in four different ways.

ordered pitch interval: +19
unordered pitch interval: 19
ordered pitch-class interval: 7
unordered pitch-class interval: 5

Example 1–10 Four ways of describing an interval.

If we call it a +19, we have described it very specifically, conveying both the size of the interval and its direction. If we call it a 19, we express only its size. If we call it a 7, we have reduced a compound interval to its within-octave equivalent. If we call it a 5, we have expressed the interval in its simplest, most abstract way. None of these labels is better or more right than the others—it's just that some are more concrete and specific while others are more general and abstract. Which one we use will depend on what musical relationship we are trying to describe.

It's like describing any object in the world—what you see depends upon where you stand. If you stand a few inches away from a painting, for example, you may be aware of the subtlest details, right down to the individual brushstrokes. If you stand back a bit, you will be better able to see the larger shapes and the overall design. There is no single "right" place to stand. To appreciate the painting fully, you have to be willing to move from place to place. One of the specially nice things about music is that you can hear a single object like an interval in many different ways at once. Our different ways of talking about intervals will give us the flexibility to describe many different kinds of musical relationships.

Interval-Class Content

The quality of a sonority can be roughly summarized by listing all the intervals it contains. To keep things simple, we will generally take into account only interval classes (unordered pitch-class intervals). The number of interval classes a sonority contains depends on the number of distinct pitch classes in the sonority. The more pitch classes, the greater the number of interval classes. Figure 1–7 summarizes the number of interval classes in sonorities of all sizes. (We won't bother including the occurrences of interval class 0, which will always be equal to the number of pitch classes in the sonority.)

no. of pitch classes	no. of interval classes
1	0
2	1
3	3
4	6
5	10
6	15
7	21
8	28
9	36
10	45
11	55
12	66

Figure 1–7

For any given sonority, we can summarize the interval content in scoreboard fashion by indicating, in the appropriate column, the number of occurrences of each of the six interval classes, again leaving out the occurrences of interval class 0. Such a scoreboard conveys the essential sound of a sonority. Notice that now we are counting all of the intervals in the sonority, not just those formed by notes that are right next to each other. That is because all of the intervals contribute to the overall sound.

Example 1–11 refers to the same passage and the same three-note sonority discussed back in Example 1–2.

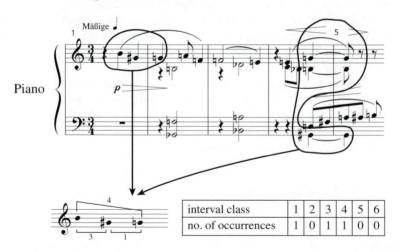

interval class	1	2	3	4	5	6
no. of occurrences	1	0	1	1	0	0

Example 1–11 Interval-class content of a three-note motive (Schoenberg, Piano Piece, Op. 11, No. 1).

Like any three-note sonority, it contains three intervals, in this case one occurrence each of interval classes 1, 3, and 4 (no 2s, 5s, or 6s). How different this is from the sonorities preferred by Stravinsky in the passage from his opera *The Rake's Progress,* shown in Example 1–12 or by Varèse in the passage from his solo flute piece *Density 21.5* shown in Example 1–13! Stravinsky's chords contain only 2s and 5s and Varèse's melodic cells contain only 1s, 5s, and 6s. The difference in their sound is a reflection of the difference in their interval content.

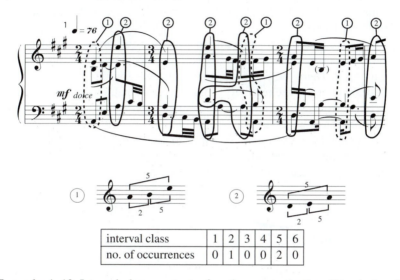

interval class	1	2	3	4	5	6
no. of occurrences	0	1	0	0	2	0

Example 1–12 Interval-class content of a three-note motive (Stravinsky, *The Rake's Progress,* Act I).

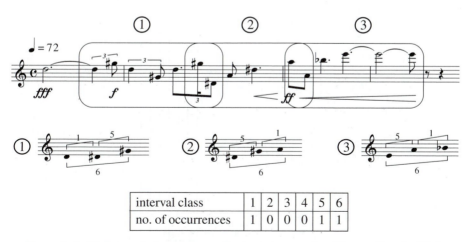

interval class	1	2	3	4	5	6
no. of occurrences	1	0	0	0	1	1

Example 1–13 Interval-class content of a three-note motive (Varese, *Density 21.5,* mm. 11–14).

Interval-Class Vector

Interval-class content is usually presented as a string of six numbers with no spaces intervening. This is called an *interval-class vector*. The first number in an interval-class vector gives the number of occurrences of interval class 1; the second gives the number of occurrences of interval class 2; and so on. The interval-class vector for the sonority in Example 1–11 is 101100, the interval-class vector for the sonority in Example 1–12 is 010020, and the interval-class vector for the sonority in Example 1–13 is 100011.

We can construct a vector like this for sonorities of any size or shape. A tool like the interval-class vector would not be nearly so necessary for talking about traditional tonal music. There, only a few basic sonorities—four kinds of triads and five kinds of seventh chords—are regularly in use. In post-tonal music, however, we will confront a huge variety of harmonies. The interval-class vector will give us a convenient way of summarizing their basic sound.

Even though the interval-class vector is not as necessary a tool for tonal music as for post-tonal music, it can offer an interesting perspective on traditional formations. Example 1–14 calculates the interval-class vector for the major scale.

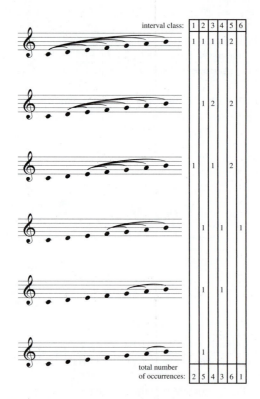

Example 1–14 Interval-class vector for the major scale.

Notice our methodical process of extracting each interval class. First, the intervals formed with the first note are extracted, then those formed with the second note, and so on. This ensures that we find all the intervals and don't overlook any. As with any seven-note collection, there are 21 intervals in all.

Certain intervallic properties of the major scale are immediately apparent from the interval-class vector. It has only one tritone (fewer than any other interval) and six occurrences of interval-class 5, which contains the perfect fourth and fifth (more than any other interval). This probably only confirms what we already knew about this scale, but the interval-class vector makes the same kind of information available about less familiar collections. The interval-class vector of the major scale has another interesting property—it contains a different number of occurrences of each of the interval classes. This is an extremely important and rare property (only three other collections have it) and it is one to which we will return. For now, the important thing is the idea of describing a sonority in terms of its interval-class content.

BIBLIOGRAPHY

The material presented in Chapter 1 (and in much of Chapters 2 and 3 as well) is also discussed in three widely used books: Allen Forte, *The Structure of Atonal Music* (New Haven: Yale University Press, 1973); John Rahn, *Basic Atonal Theory* (New York: Longman, 1980); and George Perle, *Serial Composition and Atonality,* 6th ed., rev. (Berkeley and Los Angeles: University of California Press, 1991). Two important books offer profound new perspectives on this basic material, and much else besides: David Lewin, *Generalized Musical Intervals and Transformations* (New Haven: Yale University Press, 1987); and Robert Morris, *Composition with Pitch Classes* (New Haven: Yale University Press, 1987). Ambitious students will be interested in Robert Morris, *Class Notes for Atonal Music Theory* (Hanover, N.H.: Frog Peak Music, 1991) and *Class Notes for Advanced Atonal Music Theory* (Hanover, N.H.: Frog Peak Music, 2001). For an aural skills approach to post-tonal theory, see Michael Friedmann, *Ear Training for Twentieth-Century Music* (New Haven: Yale University Press, 1990).

Exercises

THEORY

I. Integer Notation: Any pitch class can be represented by an integer. In the commonly used "fixed *do*" notation, C = 0, C♯ = 1, D = 2, and so on.

1. Represent the following melodies as strings of integers:

2. Show at least two ways each of the following strings of integers can be notated on a musical staff:
    a. 0 1 3 9 2 11 4 10 7 8 5 6
    b. 2 4 1 2 4 6 7 6 4 2 4 2 1 2
    c. 0 11 7 8 3 1 2 10 6 5 4 9
    d. 11 8 7 9 5 4

II. Pitch Class and Mod 12: Pitches that are one or more octaves apart are equivalent members of a single pitch class. Because an octave contains twelve semitones, pitch classes can be discussed using arithmetic modulo 12 (mod 12), in which any integer larger than 11 or smaller than 0 can be reduced to an integer from 0 to 11 inclusive.

1. Using mod 12 arithmetic, reduce each of the following integers to an integer from 0 to 11 inclusive:
    a. 15
    b. 27
    c. 49
    d. 13
    e. −3
    f. −10
    g. −15

2. List at least three integers that are equivalent (mod 12) to each of the following integers:
    a. 5
    b. 7
    c. 11

3.   Perform the following additions (mod 12):
  a. $6 + 6$
  b. $9 + 10$
  c. $4 + 9$
  d. $7 + 8$

4.   Perform the following subtractions (mod 12):
  a. $9 - 10$
  b. $7 - 11$
  c. $2 - 10$
  d. $3 - 8$

III. Intervals: Intervals are identified by the number of semitones they contain.

  1.   For each of the following traditional interval names, give the number of semitones in the interval:
    a. major third
    b. perfect fifth
    c. augmented sixth
    d. diminished seventh
    e. minor ninth
    f. major tenth

  2.   For each of the following numbers of semitones, give at least one traditional interval name:
    a. 4
    b. 6
    c. 9
    d. 11
    e. 15
    f. 24

IV. Ordered Pitch Intervals: A pitch interval is the interval between two pitches, counted in semitones. + indicates an ascending interval; − indicates a descending interval.

  1.   Construct the following ordered pitch intervals on a musical staff, using middle C as your starting point.
    a. +15
    b. −7
    c. −4
    d. +23

2. For the following melodies, identify the ordered pitch interval formed by each pair of adjacent notes.

a.

b.

c.

d.

V. Unordered Pitch Intervals: An unordered pitch interval is simply the space between two pitches, without regard to the order (ascending or descending) of the pitches.

1. Construct the following unordered pitch intervals on a musical staff, using middle C as the lowest note.
    a. 15
    b. 4
    c. 7
    d. 11
    e. 23

2. For the melodies in Exercise IV/2, identify the unordered pitch interval formed by each pair of adjacent notes.

VI. Ordered Pitch-Class Intervals: A pitch-class interval is the interval between two pitch classes. On the pitch-class clockface, always count clockwise from the first pitch class to the second.

1. For each of the melodies in Exercise IV/2, identify the ordered pitch-class interval formed by each pair of adjacent notes.

2. Which ordered pitch-class intervals are formed by the following ordered pitch intervals?
    a. +7
    b. −7

      c. +11
      d. +13
      e. −1
      f. −6

VII. Unordered Pitch-Class Intervals: An unordered pitch-class interval is the shortest distance between two pitch classes, regardless of the order in which they occur. To calculate an unordered pitch-class interval, take the shortest route from the first pitch class to the second, going either clockwise or counterclockwise on the pitch-class clockface.

    1. For each of the melodies in Exercise IV/2, identify the unordered pitch-class interval formed by each pair of adjacent notes.

    2. An unordered pitch-class interval is also called an interval class. Give at least three pitch intervals belonging to each of the six interval classes.

VIII. Interval-class Vector: Any sonority can be classified by the intervals it contains. The interval content is usually shown as a string of six numbers called an interval-class vector. The first number in the interval-class vector gives the number of occurrences of interval class 1; the second number gives the number of occurrences of interval class 2; and so on.

    1. For each of the following collections of notes, give the interval-class content, expressed as an interval-class vector.
       a. 0, 1, 3, 4, 6, 7, 9, 10
       b. 0, 2, 4, 6, 8, 10
       c. 2, 3, 7
       d. the augmented triad
       e. the pentatonic scale
       f. 1, 5, 8, 9

    2. For each of the following interval-class vectors, try to construct the collection that it represents.
       a. 111000
       b. 004002
       c. 111111
       d. 303630

ANALYSIS

I. Webern, Symphony Op. 21, Thema, mm. 1–11, clarinet melody: How is this melody organized? What patterns of recurrence do you notice? Begin by identifying all of the ordered and unordered pitch and pitch-class intervals. (*Hint:* Consider not only the intervals formed between adjacent notes of the melody, but also the intervals that frame it, for example, the interval between the first note and the last, between the second note and the second-to-last, and so on.)

II.   Schoenberg, Piano Concerto, mm. 1–8, right-hand melody: Are there any inter-
        vals or motives that recur? (*Hint:* The melody is framed by its first note, E♭,
        which also is its highest note, its lowest note, A♭, and its final note, G. Are there
        varied repetitions of this three-note motive directly within the melody?)

III.   Stravinsky, "Musick to heare" from *Three Shakespeare Songs,* mm. 1–8, flute
        melody: What patterns of intervallic recurrence do you see? (*Hint:* Think of the
        first four notes as a basic motivic/intervallic structure.)

IV.   Crawford, *Diaphonic Suite* No. 1 for Oboe or Flute, mm. 1–18: How is this
        melody organized? The composer thought of this melody as a kind of musical
        poem and indicated the lines of the poem with double bars (at the end of mm. 5,
        9, 14, and 18). Describe the musical "rhymes" and any other intervallic or
        motivic recurrences. (*Hint:* Take the first three notes, ip +2 followed by ip –1,
        as a basic motive.)

V.   Varèse, *Octandre,* mm. 1–5, oboe melody: How is this melody organized?
        (*Hint:* Consider both the first four notes, G♭–F–E–D♯, and the highest three of
        those, G♭–E–D♯, as basic motivic units.)

VI.   Babbitt, "The Widow's Lament in Springtime," mm. 1–6, vocal melody: How
        is this melody organized intervallically and motivically? How many different
        ordered pitch-class intervals are used? Amid this variety, what are the sources
        of unity? (*Hint:* Consider the framing intervals—first to last, second to second-
        to-last, etc., as well as the direct melodic intervals.)

EAR-TRAINING AND MUSICIANSHIP

I.   Webern, Symphony Op. 21, Thema: Sing the clarinet melody, accurately and in
        tempo, using pitch-class integers in place of the traditional solfege syllables.
        To maintain a single syllable for each note, sing "oh" for 0, "sev" for 7, and
        "lev" for 11.

II.   Schoenberg, Piano Concerto, mm. 1–8, right-hand melody: Sing the melody,
        accurately and in tempo, using pitch-class integers.

III.   Stravinsky, "Musick to heare" from *Three Shakespeare Songs,* mm. 1–8, flute
        melody: Sing the melody, accurately and in tempo, using pitch-class integers.

IV.   Crawford, *Diaphonic Suite* No. 1 for Oboe or Flute, mm. 1–18: Play this
        melody, accurately and in tempo, on any appropriate instrument.

V.   Varèse, *Octandre,* mm. 1–5, oboe melody: Play this melody, accurately and in
        tempo, on any appropriate instrument.

VI.   Babbitt, "The Widow's Lament in Springtime," mm. 1–6, vocal melody: Sing
        the melody, accurately and in tempo, using either the words of the text (by
        William Carlos Williams) or pitch-class integers.

VII.   Identify melodic and harmonic intervals played by your instructor as ordered
        and unordered pitch and pitch-class intervals.

VIII.   From a given note, learn to sing above or below by a specified pitch interval
        (within the constraints of your vocal range).

COMPOSITION

I. Write two short melodies of contrasting character for solo flute or oboe that make extensive use of one of the following motives: ip<+3, –11>, ip<+3, –4>, i<8, 2, 1>, or i<2, 11>.

II. Write brief duets for soprano and alto that have the following characteristics:

    1. Begin with middle C in the alto and the B eleven semitones above it in the soprano.

    2. Use whole notes only, as in first-species counterpoint.

    3. The interval between the parts must be a member of ic1, ic2, or ic6.

    4. Each part may move up or down only by ip1, ip2, ip3, or ip4.

    5. End on the notes you began with.

    6. Try to give an attractive, purposeful shape to both melodies.

Analysis 1

Webern, "Wie bin ich froh!" from Three Songs, Op. 25
Schoenberg, "Nacht," from *Pierrot Lunaire,* Op. 21

Listen several times to a recording of "Wie bin ich froh!"—a song written by Anton Webern in 1935. We will concentrate on the first five measures, shown in Example A1–1.

Example A1–1 Webern, "Wie bin ich froh!" from Three Songs, Op. 25 (mm. 1–5).

Analysis 1

Here is a translation of the first part of the text, a poem by Hildegarde Jone.

Wie bin ich froh!	How happy I am!
noch einmal wird mir alles grün	Once more all grows green around me
und leuchtet so!	And shines so!

The music may sound at first like disconnected blips of pitch and timbre. A texture that sounds fragmented, that shimmers with hard, bright colors, is typical of Webern. Such a texture is sometimes called "pointillistic," after the technique of painting with sharply defined dots or points of paint. Gradually, with familiarity and with some knowledge of pitch and pitch-class intervals, the sense of each musical fragment and the interrelations among the fragments will come into focus.

The lack of a steady meter may initially contribute to the listener's disorientation. The notated meters, 3/4 and 4/4, are hard to discern by ear, since there is no regular pattern of strong and weak beats. The shifting tempo—there are three ritards in this short passage—confuses matters further. The music ebbs and flows rhythmically rather than following some strict pattern. Instead of searching for a regular meter, which certainly does not exist here, let's focus instead on the smaller rhythmic figures in the piano part, and the ways they group to form larger rhythmic shapes.

The piano part begins with a rhythmic gesture consisting of three brief figures: a sixteenth-note triplet, a pair of eighth-notes, and a four-note chord. Except for two isolated single tones, the entire piano part uses only these three rhythmic figures. But, except for measure 2, the three figures never again occur in the same order or with the same amount of space between them. The subsequent music pulls apart, plays with, and reassembles the opening figures. Consider the placement of the sixteenth-note triplet, which becomes progressively more isolated as the passage progresses. In the pickup to measure 1 and in measure 2, it is followed immediately by the pair of eighth-notes. In measure 3, it is followed immediately, not by a pair of eighth-notes, but by a single note. At the beginning of measure 4, it is again followed by a single note, but only after an eighth-triplet rest. At the end of measure 4, it is even more isolated—it is followed by a long silence. The shifting placement of the rhythmic figures gives a gently syncopated feeling to the piano part. You can sense this best if you play the piano part or tap out its rhythms.

Now let's turn to the melodic line. Begin by learning to sing it smoothly and accurately. This is made more difficult by the wide skips and disjunct contour so typical of Webern's melodic lines. Singing the line will become easier once its organization is better understood. Using the concepts of pitch and pitch class, and of pitch and pitch-class intervals, we can begin to understand how the melody is put together.

There is no way of knowing, in advance, which intervals or groups of intervals will turn out to be important in organizing this, or any, post-tonal work. Each of the post-tonal pieces discussed in this book tends to create and inhabit its own musical world, with musical content and modes of progression that may be, to a significant extent,

Analysis 1

independent of other pieces. As a result, each time we approach a new piece, we will have to pull ourselves up by our analytical bootstraps. The process is going to be one of trial and error. We will look, initially, for recurrences (of notes and intervals) and patterns of recurrence. It often works well to start right at the beginning, to see the ways in which the initial musical ideas echo throughout the line.

In "Wie bin ich froh," it turns out that the first three notes, G–E–D♯, and the intervals they describe play a particularly central role in shaping the melody. Let's begin by considering their ordered pitch intervals (see Figure A1–1).

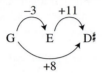

Figure A1–1

The same ordered pitch intervals occur in the voice in two other places, in measure 3 (D–B–B♭) and again in measure 4 (C–A–G♯). (See Example A1–2.)

Example A1–2   Three fragments with the same ordered pitch intervals.

Sing these three fragments, then sing the whole melody and listen to how these fragments help give it shape. The second fragment starts five semitones lower than the first, while the third fragment starts five semitones higher. That gives a sense of symmetry and balance to the melody, with the initial fragment lying halfway between its two direct repetitions. Furthermore, the second fragment brings in the lowest note of the melody, B, while the third fragment brings in the highest note, G♯. These notes, together with the initial G, create a distinctive frame for the melody as a whole, one which replicates the ordered pitch-class intervals of the initial fragment (see Example A1–3).

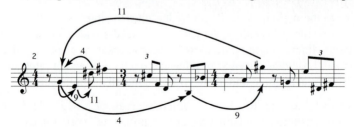

Example A1–3   A melodic frame (first note, lowest note, highest note) that replicates the ordered pitch-class intervals of the initial fragment.

Analysis 1

Composers of post-tonal music often find ways of projecting a musical idea simultaneously on the musical surface and over larger musical spans. This kind of *composing-out* is an important unifying device and it is one to which we will often return.

The three melody notes at the beginning of measure 3, C♯–F–D, also relate to the opening three-note figure, but in a more subtle way. They use the same pitch intervals as the first three notes of the melody (3, 8, and 11), but the intervals occur in a different order. In addition, two of the three intervals have changed direction (see Figure A1–2).

Figure A1–2

In other words, the fragment C♯–F–D has the same unordered pitch intervals as the opening figure, G–E–D♯. The relationship is not as obvious as the one shown in Example A1–2, but it is still not hard to hear. Sing the two fragments, then sing the entire melody and listen for the resemblance (see Example A1–4).

Example A1–4 Two fragments with the same unordered pitch intervals.

The first four pitch classes of the melody are the same, and in the same order, as the last four: G–E–D♯–F♯ (see Example A1–5).

Example A1–5 The first four notes and the last four have the same ordered pitch-class intervals.

Analysis 1

The contours of the two phrases (their successive ordered pitch intervals) are different, but the ordered pitch-class intervals are the same: 9–11–3. This similarity between the beginning and end of the melody is a nice way of rounding off the melodic phrase and of reinforcing the rhyme in the text: "Wie bin ich froh! . . . und leuchtet so!" Sing these two fragments and listen for the intervallic equivalence that lies beneath the change in contour.

By changing the contour the second time around, Webern makes something interesting happen. He puts the E up in a high register, while keeping the G, D♯, and F♯ together in a low register. Consider the unordered pitch-class intervals in that registrally defined three-note collection (G–D♯–F♯). It contains interval classes 1 (G–F♯), 3 (D♯–F♯), and 4 (G–D♯). These are exactly the same as those formed by the first three notes (G–E–D♯) of the figure: E–D♯ is 1, G–E is 3, and G–D♯ is 4 (see Example A1–6).

Example A1–6 A registral grouping and a melodic figure contain the same unordered pitch-class intervals.

The melodic line is thus supercharged with a single basic motive. The entire melody develops musical ideas presented in the opening figure, sometimes by imitating its ordered pitch intervals, sometimes by imitating only its unordered pitch intervals, and sometimes, still more subtly, by imitating its ordered or unordered pitch-class intervals (see Example A1–7).

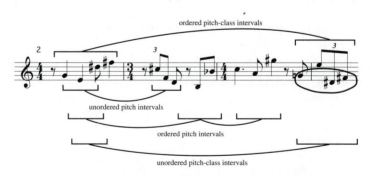

Example A1–7 Development of the initial melodic figure.

Knowledge of the intervallic structure of the melody should make it easier to hear it clearly and to sing it accurately. Sing the melody again, concentrating on the motivic and intervallic interplay shown in Example A1–7.

Analysis 1

The piano accompaniment develops and reinforces the same musical ideas. Rather than trying to deal with every note, let's just concentrate on the sixteenth-note triplet figure that comes five times in the passage. When it occurs in measure 2 (G–E–D♯), it contains the same pitches and thus the same ordered pitch intervals as the beginning of the melody: –3, +11. In measure 3, different pitches are used (C–A–G♯), but the ordered pitch intervals are the same: –3, +11. When it occurs in the pickup to measure 1 (F♯–F–D) and at the end of measure 4 (B–B♭–G), it has the same ordered pitch intervals, but reversed: +11, –3.

The remaining occurrence of the figure, at the beginning of measure 4 (C–A–C♯), is somewhat different from these. Its ordered pitch intervals are –3, +16. It is not comparable to the others in terms of its pitch intervals or even its ordered pitch-class intervals. To understand its relationship to the other figures we will have to consider its interval classes. It contains a 3 (C–A), a 1 (C–C♯), and a 4 (A–C♯). Its interval-class content (the interval-class vector is 101100) is thus the same as the first three notes of the voice melody (see Example A1–8).

Example A1–8 Accompanimental figures derived from the initial melodic idea.

In fact, all of the three-note figures we have discussed in both the vocal and piano parts have this interval-class content. That is one reason the piece sounds so unified. Play each of the three-note figures in the piano part and listen for the ways they echo the beginning of the voice part—sometimes overtly, sometimes more subtly.

So far, we have talked about the voice part and the piano part separately. But, as in more traditional songs, the piano part both makes sense on its own and accompanies and supports the voice. For a brief example, consider the two single notes in the piano part, the F♯ in measure 3 and the G♯ in measure 4. In both cases, the piano note, together with nearby notes in the voice, creates a three-note collection with that familiar interval-class content: 101100 (see Example A1–9).

The passage, at least as far as we have discussed it, is remarkably unified intervallically. It focuses intensively on the pitch intervals 3, 8, and 11 and, more abstractly, on interval classes 1, 3, and 4. The passage is saturated with these intervals and with motivic shapes created from them. Some of the relationships are simple and direct—we can discuss them in terms of shared pitch intervals. Others are subtly concealed

Analysis 1

Example A1–9 Piano and voice together create collections with interval classes 1, 3, and 4 (interval-class vector 101100).

and depend on the more abstract concepts of pitch-class interval and interval-class content. With our knowledge of pitch and pitch-class intervals, we can accurately describe a whole range of motivic and intervallic relationships.

The same sort of intensive intervallic concentration is at work in "Nacht," one of the twenty-one short movements that make up Arnold Schoenberg's *Pierrot Lunaire,* probably the composer's best-known work. Many factors contribute to its stunning effect. The instrumentation is wonderfully varied. The work is scored for a singer and a small instrumental ensemble (piano, flute/piccolo, clarinet/bass clarinet, violin/viola, and cello) in such a way that no two of the twenty-one movements have the same instrumentation.

The singer uses a vocal technique known as *Sprechstimme* (speech-song), a kind of declamation that is halfway between speech and song. The notated pitch should not be sustained but should be slid away from, in the manner of speech. As to whether the notated pitch need be sung accurately in the first place, there is considerable controversy. Some singers lean toward the speech part of speech-song, following only the approximate contours of the notated line; others try to give a clear indication of the actual pitches specified. As we will see, the pitches in the vocal part so consistently reproduce intervals and motives from the instrumental parts that singers should probably touch the notated pitches accurately before sliding away. Listen to a recording of *Pierrot Lunaire,* concentrating on "Nacht," the eighth movement. The score for measures 1–10 is given in Example A1–10, with a translation of the first stanza of the text, itself a German translation of a poem by Albert Giraud.

Finstre, schwarze Riesenfalter	Dark, black giant butterflies
Töteten der Sonne Glanz.	Have obliterated the rays of the sun.
Ein geschlossnes Zauberbuch,	Like an unopened magic-book,
Ruht der Horizont—verschwiegen.	The horizon rests—concealed.

Schoenberg calls this piece a passacaglia. A passacaglia is a continuous variation form that uses a bass ostinato. In this piece, the ostinato consists of the three-note figure E–G–Eb. After the introduction (measures 1–3), this figure occurs once in each measure of this passage. Play this figure as it occurs in each measure, noticing how it moves from voice to voice and register to register. In measures 8 and 9, each tone of

Analysis 1

Example A1–10 Schoenberg, "Nacht," from *Pierrot Lunaire* (mm. 1–10).

Analysis 1

the figure is elaborated, in diminution, by a rapid statement of the same figure transposed (see Example A1–11).

Example A1–11 The head-motive (E–G–E♭) elaborated, in diminution, by transposed versions of itself.

In measure 10, the passage comes to a striking conclusion when the same figure appears in the voice part. This is the only time in the piece that the singer actually *sings*. Her doing so in such a low, dark register and on such musically significant notes adds to the emotional impact of the word *verschwiegen* (concealed), a word that seems to crystallize the ominous, foreboding nature of the entire text.

Let's examine the intervallic makeup of that repeated figure: E–G–E♭. Its ordered pitch intervals are +3, and −4, and (from the first note to the last) −1. These intervals permeate the entire musical fabric. Consider, for example, the tune stated first in the bass clarinet beginning in measure 4, and then imitated in the cello (measure 5), the left hand of the piano (measure 6), and, in part, the right hand of the piano (measure 7) (see Example A1–12).

Example A1–12 The head-motive expanded and developed into a recurring melody.

The tune begins, of course, with E–G–E♭ as its head-motive. It then takes the interval −1, spanned by E–E♭, and extends it into a lengthy chromatic descent. The tune ends with a three-note figure that introduces two new pitch intervals, +9 and +8.

This new figure, B♭–A–G♭, does not have any obvious relationship to the head-motive, E–G–E♭. It has a different contour and different pitch intervals. To understand the relationship, we will have to consider the unordered pitch-class intervals of the two figures. Both have a 1, a 3, and a 4. (Their shared interval-class vector is thus 101100—coincidentally the same as that of the main motive in Webern's song, discussed earlier.) From the perspective of interval class, we can hear the second figure as a development of the first. Sing the tune shown in Example A1–12 and listen for the familiar head-motive, its continuation into a chromatic descent, and its development in the concluding figure.

Analysis 1

In light of these observations, it becomes clear how carefully Schoenberg has notated the pitches of the voice part. Consider its first melodic gesture, shown in Example A1–13.

Example A1–13 Motivic penetration of the *Sprechstimme* part.

In its initial chromatic descent from D♭ to A and the leap upward from A to G♭, it exactly traces the last part of the melody shown in Example A1–12. Then, by moving down to F, it tacks on an additional, overlapping version of the three-note figure involving pitch intervals 8 and 9. Surely these pitches should be clearly indicated by the performer! Try it yourself, first trying to indicate the notated pitches and then mainly chanting. Which do you prefer?

The introduction (measures 1–3) not only sets an appropriately gloomy mood with its use of the lowest, darkest possible register, but also introduces the main intervallic material in a subtle way. To make it easier to see and hear what is going on, the music is written an octave higher in Example A1–14.

Example A1–14 Motivic saturation of the introduction.

Of the six distinct musical lines here, all but one descend by semitone from the initial pitch. The melodic interval of –1, of course, anticipates the many chromatic descents that are coming up later in the music. Even more striking, however, are the relationships between the lines. In the lowest register, the first three notes are E–G–E♭, our familiar head-motive. The second note of the motive, the G, is also the first note of a transposed statement of the motive: G–B♭–G♭. The second note of that statement, the B♭, becomes the first note of a new statement: B♭–D♭–A. This process continues upward until the cello and bass clarinet come in with a restatement, an octave higher, of the original E–G–E♭. One additional statement of the motive, A–C–A♭, begins in

Analysis 1

the middle of the texture on the second beat of measure 2. In all there are six statements of the motive packed into these three measures. The density is extraordinary; the music of the introduction is motivically saturated. Play these measures and listen for each statement of the motive. The music that follows can be heard as an unpacking of material so intensely presented in the introduction.

Chapter 2
Pitch-Class Sets

Pitch-Class Sets

Pitch-class sets are the basic building blocks of much post-tonal music. A pitch-class set is an unordered collection of pitch-classes. It is a motive from which many of the identifying characteristics—register, rhythm, order—have been boiled away. What remains is simply the basic pitch-class and interval-class identity of a musical idea.

In Example 2–1, you see five short excerpts from a piece by Schoenberg, the Gavotte from his Suite for Piano, Op. 25. In each excerpt, a single pitch-class set (D♭, E, F, G) is circled. That pitch-class set is expressed musically in many different ways. It is the melody that begins the piece and that ends the first section (measure 7). It is heard as a pair of dyads at the beginning of the second half of the piece (measure 16) and as a chord (measure 24). Finally, it returns as the last musical idea of the piece (measure 27).

Something similar happens at the beginning of Stefan Wolpe's *Form for Piano* (see Example 2–2). The piece begins with a simple melodic statement of six pitch-classes: A♭–F–B♭–A–G–E. In the music that follows, the same pitch-class set is stated twice more, but with the notes in different registers, rhythms, and order.

The possibility of presenting a musical idea in such varied ways—melodically, harmonically, or a combination of the two—is part of what Schoenberg meant by his well-known statement, "The two-or-more-dimensional space in which musical ideas are presented is a unit." No matter how it is presented, a pitch-class set will retain its basic pitch-class and interval-class identity. A composer can unify a composition by using a pitch-class set (or a small number of different pitch-class sets) as a basic structural unit. At the same time, he or she can create a varied musical surface by transforming that basic unit in different ways. When we listen to or analyze music, we search for coherence. In a great deal of post-tonal music, that coherence is assured through the use of pitch-class sets.

Example 2–1 A single pitch-class set expressed in five different ways (Schoenberg, Gavotte from Suite for Piano, Op. 25).

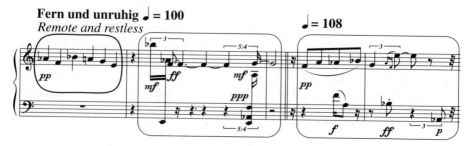

Example 2–2 Three statements of a single pitch-class set (Wolpe, *Form for Piano*).

Normal Form

A pitch-class set can be presented musically in a variety of ways. Conversely, many different musical figures can represent the same pitch-class set. If we want to be able to recognize a pitch-class set no matter how it is presented in the music, it will be helpful to put it into a simple, compact, easily grasped form called the *normal form*. The normal form—the most compressed way of writing a pitch-class set—makes it easy to see the essential attributes of a set and to compare it to other sets.

Consider the first three measures of the third of Schoenberg's Five Orchestral Pieces, Op. 16. Example 2–3 contains a two-piano reduction of a passage that is richly orchestrated and contains thirty-six distinct instrumental attacks.

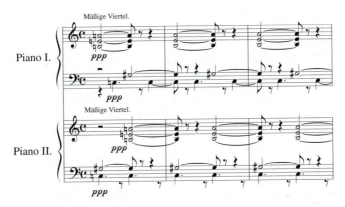

Example 2–3 A complex surface, but only five pitch classes (Schoenberg, Orchestral Piece, Op. 16, No. 3).

Our task is to boil the sonority down into its normal form. First, we eliminate all duplicates and consider only the pitch-class content. There are only five different pitch classes in the passage: C, G♯, B, E, and A. Next, we write those pitch classes as though they were a scale, ascending within an octave. There are five ways of doing this, and our problem is to choose the smallest stack (the most compact and compressed representation of the set). (See Example 2–4.)

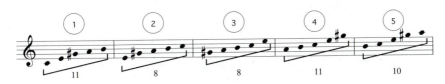

Example 2–4 Finding the normal form.

nd fourth orderings span eleven semitones from lowest to highest, while
rdering spans ten semitones. Clearly these are not the smallest ways of
stacking these notes. Either the second or third ordering would be better, since both
span only eight semitones. Now we have to choose between the second and third
orderings. In situations like this, our preference is for the one with the larger intervals
toward the top of the stack, and whose notes thus cluster toward the bottom. The normal form is the ordering that is most packed away from the right side. The third
ordering has only four semitones from its first note to its second-to-last note (G♯–C),
while the second ordering has seven semitones from the first to the second-to-last
(E–B). We thus prefer the third ordering. The normal form of the sonority from
Example 2–3 is [G♯,A,B,C,E]. We will use square brackets to indicate normal forms.

In some ways, the normal form of a pitch-class set is similar to the root position
of a triad. Both are simple, compressed ways of representing sonorities that can occur
in many positions and spacings. There are important differences, however. In traditional tonal theory, the root position of a triad is considered more stable than other
positions, the inversions of the triad being generated from the root position. The normal form, in contrast, has no particular stability or priority. It is just a convenient way
of writing sets so that they can be more easily studied and compared.

Here is the step-by-step procedure for putting a set into normal form:

1. Excluding doublings, write the pitch classes as though they were a scale,
    ascending within an octave. There will be as many different ways of doing this
    as there are pitch classes in the set, since an ordering can begin on any of the
    pitch classes in the set.

2. Choose the ordering that has the smallest interval from first to last (from lowest
    to highest).

3. If there is a tie under Rule 2, choose the ordering that is most clustered away
    from the top. To do so, compare the intervals between the first and second-to-
    last notes. If there is still a tie, compare the intervals between the first and third-
    to-last notes, and so on.

4. If the application of Rule 3 still results in a tie, then choose the ordering begin-
    ning with the pitch class represented by the smallest integer. For example, (A,
    C♯, F), (C♯, F, A), and (F, A, C♯) are in a three-way tie according to Rule 3. So
    we select [C♯, F, A] as the normal form since its first pitch class is 1, which is
    lower than 5 or 9.

Now let us reconsider the sonority from Schoenberg's Orchestral Piece
(Example 2–3), this time using pitch-class integers and following the procedure just
outlined.

1. The five possible orderings are:

$$0\ 4\ 8\ 9\ 11$$
$$4\ 8\ 9\ 11\ 0$$
$$8\ 9\ 11\ 0\ 4$$
$$9\ 11\ 0\ 4\ 8$$
$$11\ 0\ 4\ 8\ 9$$

Notice that each of these orderings is ascending (or clockwise, if you prefer to think of it that way) within a single octave (the first and last elements are less than twelve semitones apart). Having arbitrarily started with the ordering beginning on 0, we just proceed systematically: The second element moves into the first place and the first element goes to the end as we move down the list.

2. We calculate the interval from the first element to the last by subtracting the first from the last:

$$\begin{array}{rll}
\text{First ordering:} & 11 - 0 & = 11 \\
\text{Second ordering:} & 0 - 4 & = 12 - 4 = 8 \\
\text{Third ordering:} & 4 - 8 & = 16 - 8 = 8 \\
\text{Fourth ordering:} & 8 - 9 & = 20 - 9 = 11 \\
\text{Fifth ordering:} & 9 - 11 & = 21 - 11 = 10
\end{array}$$

3. We discover a tie between the second and third orderings.

$$4\ 8\ 9\ 11\ 0$$
$$8\ 9\ 11\ 0\ 4$$

We compare the intervals between their first and second-to-last elements:

$$\begin{array}{rl}
\text{Second ordering:} & 11 - 4 = 7 \\
\text{Third ordering:} & 0 - 8 = 4
\end{array}$$

Since 4 is smaller than 7, we conclude that the third ordering [8,9,11,0,4] is the normal form. There is no need to use Rule 4.

In many cases, rather than following this step-by-step procedure, it will be possible to determine the normal form simply by inspecting the set displayed around a pitch-class clockface. Figure 2–1 displays Schoenberg's set from Example 2–3, and it should be apparent that the normal order is the one that starts on 8.

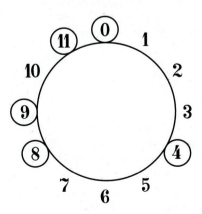

Figure 2–1

Example 2–5 shows the four chords that begin Carl Ruggles's *Lilacs*. Beneath the music, the pitch classes in each chord are identified on a pitch-class clockface. It should be possible, at a glance, to identify the normal forms (which are written beneath the clockfaces).

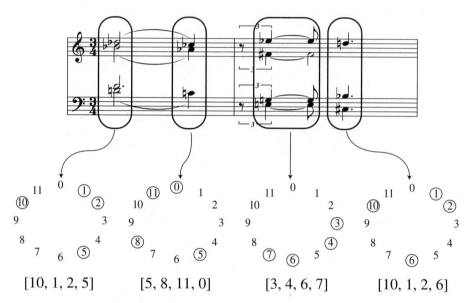

[10, 1, 2, 5]   [5, 8, 11, 0]   [3, 4, 6, 7]   [10, 1, 2, 6]

Example 2–5 Using a pitch-class clockface to determine normal form (Ruggles, *Lilacs,* mm. 1–2).

Or, you might find it easier to play, or imagine playing, the notes on a keyboard, using just one hand and playing them like a scale, ascending within an octave, starting in turn on each note. The arrangement that involves the smallest hand span, and has the biggest gaps toward the top, is the normal form. Whichever method you use, just keep in mind that we are always trying to represent sets in the simplest, most compressed way.

Transposition (T$_n$)

Traditionally, the term *transposition* refers to the transposition of a line of pitches. When, for example, we transpose "My Country, 'Tis of Thee" from C major to G major, we transpose each pitch, in order, by some pitch interval. This operation preserves the ordered pitch intervals in the line (i.e., the contour of the line). Because contour is such a basic musical feature, it is easy to recognize when two lines of pitches are related by transposition.

Things are different when we transpose a line of pitch classes rather than a line of pitches. We will now be adding pitch-class intervals to each pitch class in the line. Example 2–6 contains the main melody that opens the first movement of Schoenberg's String Quartet No. 4 and a transposed statement of the melody from the middle of the movement.

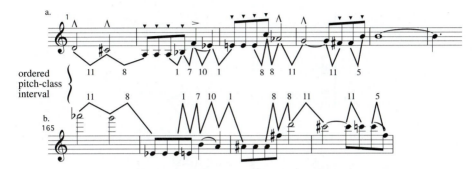

Example 2–6 Two transpositionally related lines of pitch classes (Schoenberg, String Quartet No. 4).

The contours of the two lines are different, so they sound superficially dissimilar. But notice two important features of pitch-class transposition. First, for each pitch class in the first melody, the corresponding member of the second melody lies the same pitch-class interval away—in this case, 6. Second, the ordered pitch-class interval between adjacent elements of the lines is the same in both cases. Both lines have the interval succession 11, 8, 1, 7, etc. That is why, despite their obvious differences, they still sound very similar to one another. (Their shared rhythm helps, too.) The two lines are pitch-class transpositions of one another.

We can describe the same relationship using integer notation. In integer notation, the first melody is: 2, 1, 9, 10, 5, 3, 4, 0, 8, 7, 6, 11. By adding 6 to each integer (mod 12), we produce the transposed version from the middle of the movement (see Figure 2–2).

$$
\begin{array}{rrrrrrrrrrrr}
  & 2 & 1 & 9 & 10 & 5 & 3 & 4 & 0 & 8 & 7 & 6 & 11 \\
+ & 6 & 6 & 6 & 6 & 6 & 6 & 6 & 6 & 6 & 6 & 6 & 6 \\
\hline
= & 8 & 7 & 3 & 4 & 11 & 9 & 10 & 6 & 2 & 1 & 0 & 5
\end{array}
$$

2 1 9 10 5 3 4 0 8 7 6 11 (melody beginning in measure 1)
+ 6 6 6 6 6 6 6 6 6 6 6 6
= 8 7 3 4 11 9 10 6 2 1 0 5 (melody beginning in measure 165)

Figure 2–2

The second line is a pitch-class transposition, at pitch-class interval 6, of the first line. We will represent the operation of pitch-class transposition as T_n, where T stands for transposition and n is the interval of transposition (also known as the "transposition number"). Thus, the second line is related to the first at T_6.

Now we must consider the possibility of transposing not a line but a *set* of pitch classes. A set is a collection with no specified order or contour. As a result, transposition of a set preserves neither order nor contour. The four pitch-class sets circled in Example 2–7 (from Webern's Concerto for Nine Instruments, Op. 24, second movement) despite their obvious dissimilarities, are all transpositionally equivalent.

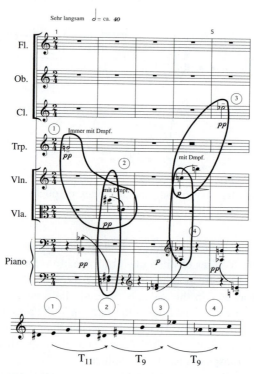

Example 2–7 Transpositionally equivalent pitch-class sets (Webern, Concerto for Nine Instruments, Op. 24).

Beneath the score in Example 2–7, each of the sets is given in normal form—that makes it easy to compare them and to see their transpositional equivalence. To get from Set #1 to Set #2, each pitch class in Set #1 moves down one pitch-class semitone onto a corresponding pitch class in Set #2. To illustrate this, an arrow is drawn from Set #1 to Set #2 and labeled T_{11}. Similarly, Set #2 moves to Set #3 by T_9, and Set #3 moves to Set #4 also by T_9. This will be our usual way of identifying the T_n that connects two sets: we draw an arrow from the first set to the second, and label the arrow with the appropriate T_n.

Because they are transpositionally equivalent, the four sets in Example 2–7 contain the same unordered pitch-class intervals; each of them contains a 1, a 3, a 4, and no others. That gives them a similar sound. Transposition of a set of pitch classes changes many things, but it preserves interval-class content. Along with inversion (to be discussed in the next section), transposition is the only operation that does so and, as a result, it is an important compositional means of creating a deeper unity beneath a varied musical surface.

Now let's look more closely at two melodic fragments from Example 2–7 (see Example 2–8).

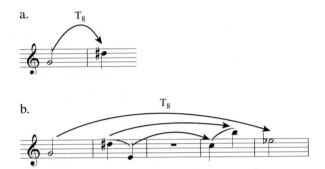

Example 2–8 Transposition within and between two melodic fragments (Webern, Concerto for Nine Instruments, Op. 24).

The first melodic interval is ip+8, and we can imagine the G and D♯ as related by T_8. The very same T_8 is the transposition that leads from the first three-note melodic fragment to the second. Each note in the first fragment moves up eight semitones to a corresponding note in the second fragment. In integer notation, 7 (G) plus 8 is 3 (E♭); 3 (D♯) plus 8 is 11 (B); and 4 (E) plus 8 is 0 (C). The same musical gesture that connects the first note with the second thus also connects the first fragment with the second. In Example 2–8, the arrows indicate the *mappings* brought about by transposition. In moving from the first fragment to the second, T_8 maps G onto E♭, D♯ onto B, and E onto C.

Now we need to discuss more specifically how to transpose a pitch-class set and how to recognize whether two pitch-class sets are related by transposition. To transpose a set, simply add a single pitch-class interval to each member of the set. For example, to transpose [5,7,8,11] by pitch-class interval 8, simply add 8 to each element in the set to create a new set: [1,3,4,7]. (See Figure 2–3.)

$$
\begin{array}{rrrr}
5 & 7 & 8 & 11 \\
+8 & 8 & 8 & 8 \\
\hline
= 1 & 3 & 4 & 7
\end{array}
$$

Figure 2–3

More simply, [1,3,4,7] = T_8 [5,7,8,11]. We read this equation either "[1,3,4,7] is T_8 of [5,7,8,11]" or "T_8 maps [5,7,8,11] onto [1,3,4,7]." By *mapping,* we mean transforming one object into another by applying some operation. Here, applying T_8 to 5 transforms it into, or maps it onto, 1; T_8 maps 7 onto 3; and so on. If the first set was in normal form, the transposition of it will be also (with a small number of exceptions related to Rule 4 for determining normal form).

If two sets are related by transposition at interval n, there will be, for each element in the first set, a corresponding element in the second set that lies n semitones away. In our example above, for each element in the first set, [5,7,8,11], there is a corresponding element in the second set, [1,3,4,7], eight semitones away. Discovering this one-to-one correspondence is easiest when the two sets are both in normal form. The first element in one set corresponds to the first element in the other set, the second to the second, and so on. Furthermore, transpositionally related pitch-class sets in normal form have the same succession of intervals from left to right. Both [1,3,4,7] and [5,7,8,11] have the interval succession 2–1–3 (see Figure 2–4).

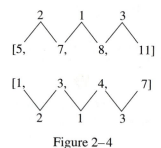

Figure 2–4

Say you are looking at the passage from Stravinsky's *Agon,* shown in Example 2–9, and you suspect there may be some relationship between the two circled sets (beyond the shared pitch classes B♭ and B). First put each in normal form. Both have the interval succession 1–2–1, so we know they are related by transposition. Now compare the corresponding elements. Each member of the second set lies three semitones higher than the corresponding member of the first set. To put it another way, each element in Set 2 minus the corresponding element of Set 1 equals 3 (see Figure 2–5). To put it most simply: Set 2 = T_3 (Set 1). T_3 also is the relationship between the two highest notes in the solo violin, from B♭ in m. 427 to the sustained D♭ in mm. 427–428.

We can represent these transpositional relationships using a combination of *nodes* (circles that contain some musical element, such as a note or a set) and *arrows* (to show the operation that connects the nodes). (See Figure 2–6.) The same operation that moves the music from note to note also moves it from set to set. As a result, while the contents of the nodes in Figures 2–6a and 2–6b are different, the two *networks* are the same. We will make frequent use of networks of this kind to represent musical motion in post-tonal music.

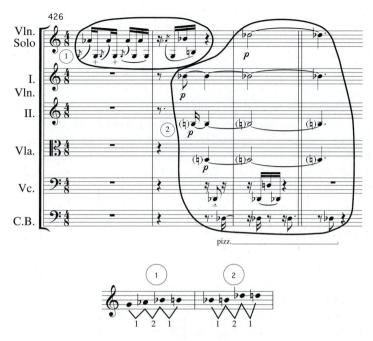

Example 2–9   Transpositionally equivalent pitch-class sets (Stravinsky, *Agon*).

$$
\begin{array}{lrrrr}
\text{Set 2:} & 10, & 11, & 1, & 2 \\
\text{Set 1:} & -\ 7, & 8, & 10, & 11 \\
\hline
= & 3 & 3 & 3 & 3
\end{array}
$$

Figure 2–5

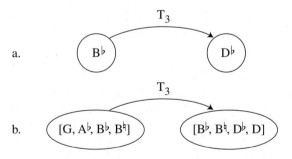

Figure 2–6

We have seen that if we transpose Set 1 at T_3, we map it onto Set 2. Conversely, we would need to transpose Set 2 at T_9 to map it onto Set 1. That is, each element in Set 1 minus the corresponding element of Set 2 equals 9 (see Figure 2–7). To put this relationship most simply: Set 1 = T_9 (Set 2).

$$
\begin{array}{lrrrr}
\text{Set 1:} & 7, & 8, & 10, & 11 \\
\text{Set 2:} & -10, & 11, & 1, & 2 \\
\hline
= & 9 & 9 & 9 & 9
\end{array}
$$

Figure 2–7

If a and b are corresponding elements in two sets related by T_n, then n equals either $a - b$ or $b - a$, depending upon which set you use as your frame of reference. Notice that these two intervals of transposition ($a - b$ and $b - a$) add up to 12. (Try to figure out why this should be so.) The two sets in Example 2–9 are different in many ways, but they are transpositionally equivalent. Post-tonal music makes extensive use of this kind of underlying equivalence.

Inversion (T_nI)

Like transposition, inversion is an operation traditionally applied to lines of pitches. In inverting a line of pitches, order is preserved and contour is reversed—each ascending pitch interval is replaced by a descending one, and vice versa.

Inverting a line of pitch classes is similar in some ways. By convention, when we invert a pitch class we invert it around 0. Pitch class 3, for example, which lies 3 above 0, inverts into -3, 3 below 0. In other words, the inversion of 3 is $0 - 3 = -3 = 9$. Figure 2–8 summarizes the possibilities.

pitch class (n)	*inversion (12 – n)*
0	0
1	11
2	10
3	9
4	8
5	7
6	6
7	5
8	4
9	3
10	2
11	1

Figure 2–8

In fact, inversion is a compound operation: it involves both inversion and trans-position. We will express this compound operation as T_nI, where "I" means "invert" and "T_n" means "Transpose by some interval n." By convention, we will always invert first and then transpose. In Figure 2–8, we inverted and transposed at T_0. Thus, for example, $T_0I(3) = 9$. That is, we invert the 3—that gives us 9. Then we add the transposition number 0 to it, which again gives us 9. We also could transpose by intervals other than 0. For example, $T_5I(3) = 2$. To verify this, we first invert the 3, which gives us 9. Then, to transpose, we add the interval 5, which gives us 2. Remember, always invert first and then transpose. (Sometimes in the theoretical literature the expression I_n is used instead of T_nI, but the meaning remains the same: first invert around 0, as in Figure 2–8, then transpose by interval n.)

Example 2–10 shows two melodies from the beginning of Schoenberg's String Quartet No. 4. These lines of pitch classes are related by inversion.

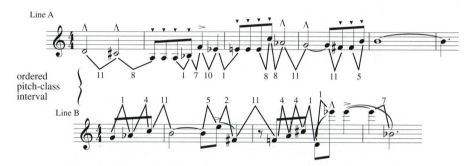

Example 2–10   Two inversionally related lines of pitch classes (Schoenberg, String Quartet No. 4).

Each pitch class in Line B is related by T_9I to the corresponding pitch class in Line A. The first pitch class in Line A corresponds to the first pitch class in Line B, the second to the second, and so on. Let's take one example to verify this. The second note in Line A is C♯, or 1. To perform the operation T_9I on 1, we first invert the 1—that gives us 11. Then, $T_9(11) = 8$. The corresponding note in Line B is, in fact, 8 (A♭). Now let's perform the same operation, T_9I, on the 8 (A♭). Invert the 8—that gives us 4. Then transpose by 9—that gives us 1. So, just as $T_9I(1) = 8$, so $T_9I(8) = 1$. That's because T_nI is its own *inverse,* the operation that undoes the effect of an operation. If you invert something (a note, a line, or a set) by some T_nI and want to get back to where you started, just perform the same T_nI again. By contrast, if you transpose something at T_n, you will need to perform the complementary transposition, T_{12-n}, to get back where you started. For example, to reverse the effect of T_3I, perform T_3I again, but to reverse the effect of T_3, perform T_9.

As with transposition, inversion of a line of pitch classes preserves the ordered pitch-class intervals, only now each interval is reversed in direction. In Line A, the succession of ordered pitch-class intervals is 11–8–1–7, etc. In Line B it is 1–4–11–5, etc. This can probably be seen more clearly using pitch-class integers (see Figure 2–9).

Now we come to the inversion of a *set* of pitch classes. Example 2–11 shows a familiar passage, the opening of Schoenberg's Piano Piece, Op. 11, No. 1. Three sets,

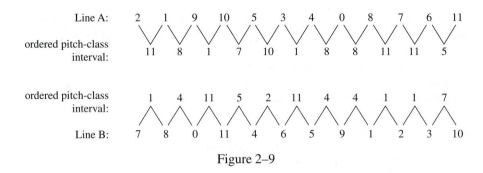

Figure 2–9

each involving a combination of soprano and alto notes, are circled and given in normal form beneath the music.

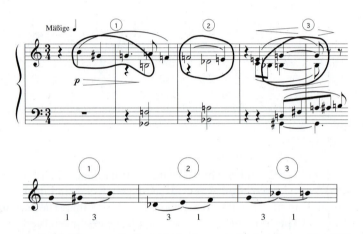

Example 2–11   Three equivalent pitch-class sets (Schoenberg, Piano Piece, Op. 11, No. 1).

Compare the first two sets. Set 2 has the same intervals reading from the top down as Set 1 does reading from the bottom up. Sets that can be written in this way, as mirror images of each other, are related by inversion. Now compare Sets 1 and 3. Again, they are written as mirror images of each other, and thus are related by inversion. Sets related by inversion have the same interval-class content; all three sets in Example 2–9 contain a 1, a 3, a 4, and no other intervals.

Figure 2–10 summarizes the relationships among these sets and uses arrows to indicate the relevant mappings. When sets related by inversion are written as mirror images of each other, the first note of one maps onto the last note of the other, the second onto the second-to-last, and so on. In comparing Set 1 and Set 3, for example, G maps onto B, G♯ onto B♭, and B onto G. The sets are related by T_nI, and to figure out the correct value of n, we take any note in one set and try to map it onto the corre-

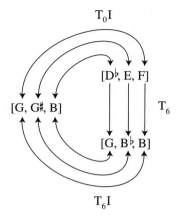

Figure 2–10

sponding note in the other. If we invert G, for example, we get F, and must transpose it at T_6 to map it onto B. Similarly, G♯ and B invert to E and C♯ and must be transposed at T_6 to map them onto B♭ and G. T_6I thus maps Set 1 onto Set 3. It also maps Set 3 onto Set 1—that's why the arrows point in both directions. By the same logic, Sets 1 and 2 are related at T_0I. Sets 2 and 3, both related by T_nI to Set 1, are related to each other by transposition, at T_6.

To invert a set, simply invert each member of the set in turn. For example, to apply the operation T_5I to the set [1,3,4,7], just apply T_5I to each integer in turn. Remembering to invert before we transpose, we get $((12 - 1) + 5, (12 - 3) + 5, (12 - 4) + 5, (12 - 7) + 5) = (4,2,1,10)$. Notice that if we write this new set in reverse order, [10,1,2,4], it will be in normal form. Generally when you invert a set in normal form, the result will be the normal form of the new set written backwards. There are many exceptions to this rule, however, so beware! When in doubt, use the step-by-step procedure outlined earlier in this chapter.

Index Number (sum)

The concept of *index number* offers a simpler way of inverting sets and of telling if two sets are inversionally related. The first two sets from Example 2–11, written using integer notation, are [7,8,11] and [1,4,5]. Remember that when we compared transpositionally related sets, we subtracted corresponding elements in each set and called that difference the transposition number. When comparing inversionally related sets, we will *add* corresponding elements and call that *sum* an index number. When two sets are related by transposition and are written so that they have the same intervals reading from left to right (that will always be true when they are written in normal form), the first note in one set corresponds to the first note in the other, the second to the second, and so on. When two sets are related by inversion and are written so that they are intervallic mirror images of each other (that will usually, but not always, be true when they are written in normal form), the first note in one set will correspond to the last note in the other, the second to the second-to-last, and so on. In comparing Set 1 and Set 2 from Example 2–11, the sum of the corresponding notes is 0 in each case (see Figure 2–11).

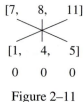

Figure 2–11

The sets are thus related at T_0I; 0 is the index number.

Figure 2–12 shows the first and third sets from Example 2–11: [7,8,11] and [7,10,11].

Figure 2–12

Again, the corresponding elements have a fixed sum, in this case 6. These two sets are related at T_6I. Each set is T_6I of the other. Any two sets in which the corresponding elements all have the same sum are related by inversion, and that sum is the index number.

Let us put this relationship in more general terms. If $T_nI(a) = b$, then $n = a + b$. In other words, inversionally related elements will sum to the index number. To find the index number for two elements, simply add them together. Conversely, to perform the operation T_nI on some pitch class, simply subtract it from n, since if $n = a + b$ then $a = n - b$. To perform the operation T_4I on [11,1,2,6], for example, subtract each element in turn from 4: $(4 - 11, 4 - 1, 4 - 2, 4 - 6) = (5,3,2,10)$, or [10,2,3,5] in normal form.

It may seem strange that addition plays such an important role in talking about T_nI. The idea of *subtracting* two notes, of figuring out the difference between them, makes clear musical sense. But what can it mean, say, to *add* an E to an F? Why is it that the sum of E and F is precisely the value of n that maps E onto F and F onto E under T_nI? To understand why, imagine the E and F on a clockface (Figure 2–13).

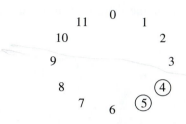

Figure 2–13

The E is at +4. If we invert it, we send it over to −4 (see Figure 2–14).

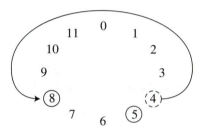

Figure 2–14

Now to get the inverted E to map onto the F we have to transpose it 4 (which gets us back to 0) plus 5 (which gets us to F). (See Figure 2–15.)

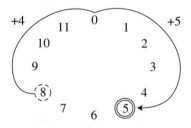

Figure 2–15

So T_9I maps E onto F. By the same logic, if we invert F, it goes from +5 to −5. Now to get it to map onto E, it has to be transposed at n = 9. So T_9I maps F onto E and E onto F.

Inversion (I_y^x)

There is another way of talking about inversion: I_y^x, where x and y are pitch classes that invert onto each other; they may be any pitch classes and they may be the same pitch class. Let's take I_B^G as an example—that's the inversion that maps G and B onto each other (see Figure 2–16).

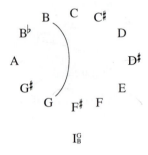

$$I_B^G$$

Figure 2–16

That same inversion also maps C onto F♯, C♯ onto F, D onto E, and D♯ and A onto themselves (see Figure 2–17).

$$I_A^A = I_{G♯}^{B♭} = I_G^B = I_{F♯}^C = I_F^{C♯} = I_E^D = I_{D♯}^{D♯}$$

Figure 2–17

By specifying any one mapped pair, we are simultaneously specifying all of the others. The inversion described in Figure 2–17 could thus be called I_A^A, $I_{G♯}^{B♭}$, I_G^B, $I_{F♯}^C$, $I_F^{C♯}$, I_E^D, or $I_{D♯}^{D♯}$, and it would not matter which of the notes was written on top or on bottom. All of these labels are equally valid—which one we choose depends on the specific musical context.

Look back at Example 2–11 and at Sets 1 and 3. They are related by the inversion that maps the G and B onto each other, so a musically appropriate label in this case would be I_B^G. $I_{B♭}^{G♯}$ would also be appropriate, because the same inversion that exchanges G and B also sends G♯ onto B♭. There are five other possible labels (as in Figure 2–17) but none seems musically relevant in this particular instance. One advantage of I_y^x over T_nI is that it does not emphasize inversion around C as 0, which may not have anything to do with the musical context.

In Example 2–12, the first line from Luciano Berio's *Sequenza for Solo Flute,* the highest six notes (excluding the grace notes) can be understood as two three-note

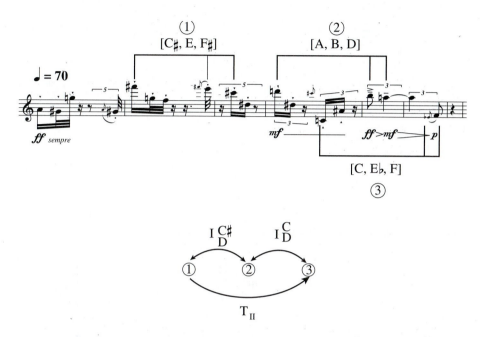

Example 2–12 Three equivalent pitch-class sets (Berio, *Sequenza for Solo Flute*).

sets related by inversion, and the lowest three notes (including the grace note) can be understood as related to one of these by inversion and the other by transposition. The first and second sets are related by inversion at $I_D^{C\sharp}$, a label that emphasizes the notes where they overlap registrally. The labels I_E^B and $I_A^{F\sharp}$, would also have been accurate, and all three labels are equivalent to T_3I (or I_3). The second and third sets are related by inversion at I_D^C, a label that emphasizes the notes at the registral extremes. The labels $I_{E\flat}^B$ and I_A^F would also have been accurate, and all three labels are equivalent to T_2I (or I_2). The first and third sets are related by transposition—the inversion of an inversion is always a transposition.

There are twelve possible inversions, each of which brings about a unique set of mappings (see Figure 2–18). For each inversion, the mappings are indicated with curved lines on the pitch-class clockface and the possible labels, in the form I_y^x, are listed beneath. It is easy to translate from the I_y^x model to the T_nI model of inversion, because $x + y = n$. To find the relevant index number, just add together any pair of mapped notes. The index numbers for each of the twelve inversions are given above the clockfaces in Figure 2–18.

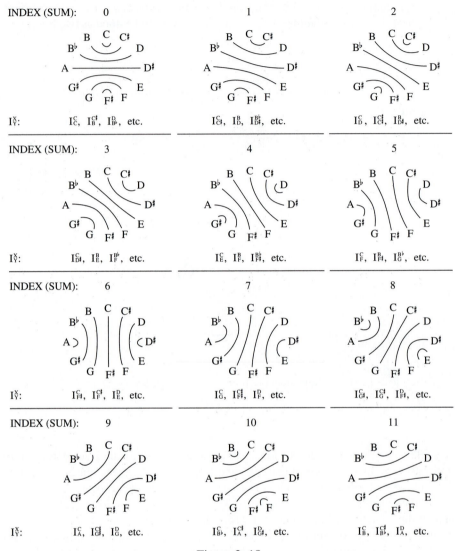

Figure 2–18

Set Class

Consider the collection of pitch-class sets in normal form shown in Figure 2–19. The first column begins with an arbitrarily chosen set, which is then transposed to each of the other eleven transposition levels. Thus, each of the twelve sets is related to the remaining eleven by transposition. The second column begins with an inversion of the set, then again transposes it systematically. In the second column as in the first,

[2,5,6]	[6,7,10]
[3,6,7]	[7,8,11]
[4,7,8]	[8,9,0]
[5,8,9]	[9,10,1]
[6,9,10]	[10,11,2]
[7,10,11]	[11,0,3]
[8,11,0]	[0,1,4]
[9,0,1]	[1,2,5]
[10,1,2]	[2,3,6]
[11,2,3]	[3,4,7]
[0,3,4]	[4,5,8]
[1,4,5]	[5,6,9]

Figure 2–19

each pitch-class set is related by transposition to the other eleven. The sets within each column are sometimes referred to as defining a *Tn-type*. A Tn-type is a class of sets that are all related to each other by transposition. Normally, a Tn-type contains twelve different sets. The twelve minor triads, for example, comprise a single Tn-type as do the twelve dominant-seventh chords.

Now consider all twenty-four of these sets together. Each of the twenty-four is related to all of the others by either transposition or inversion. They form a single, closely related family of sets. A family like this is called a *set class* (also referred to as a *Tn/TnI-type* or a *Tn/I set class*). [1,2,5], [5,6,9], [6,9,10], and twenty-one other pitch-class sets are all members of a single set class.

Normally, a set class will contain twenty-four members, like the one we just discussed. Some, however, have fewer than twenty-four distinct members. Consider the familiar diminished-seventh chord. If we write it out beginning in turn on each of the twelve pitch classes and then invert it and do the same, we quickly notice a good deal of duplication. If we eliminate all the duplicates, we find that this particular set class contains only three distinct members. Few sets are as redundant as this one (although one set, the whole-tone scale, is even more so). Most set classes contain twenty-four members; the rest have between two and twenty-four.

Set-class membership is an important part of post-tonal musical structure. There are literally thousands of pitch-class sets, but a much smaller number of set classes. Every pitch-class set belongs to a single set class. The sets in a set class are all related to each other by either T_n or T_nI. As a result, they all have the same interval-class content. By moving from set to set within a single set class, a composer can create a sense of coherent, directed musical movement.

The passage in Example 2–13 consists of a series of trichords in both hands of the piano part. Within the right-hand part, the trichords are all related by transposition; the same is true within the left-hand part. Each of the parts thus presents six trichords that belong to a distinct Tn-type. At the same time, each trichord in the right

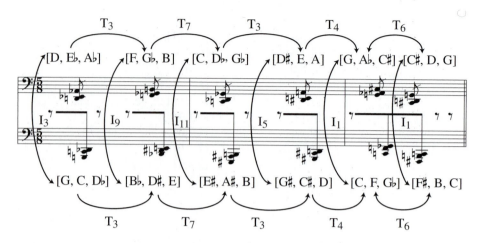

Example 2–13 Twelve trichords belonging to a single set class (Crumb, "Gargoyles," from *Makrokosmos,* Vol. 2, No. 8).

hand is related to each trichord in the left hand by inversion. As a result, all twelve trichords in the passage belong to the same set class (Tn/TnI-type).

Examples 2–14a and 2–14b contain passages that also involve motion from set to set, via transposition or inversion, within a single set class. In both cases, we can understand the music in terms of four equivalent sets, related in pairs by I_1, I_7, or T_6—the network in Example 2–14c applies to each, although the set class is different. Both passages thus draw on the unifying potential of set-class membership, and in strikingly similar ways.

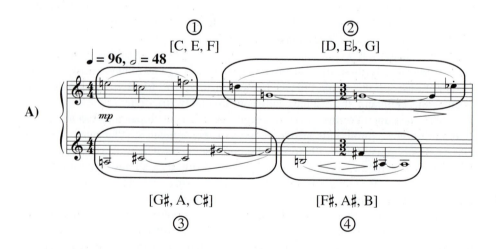

(continued)

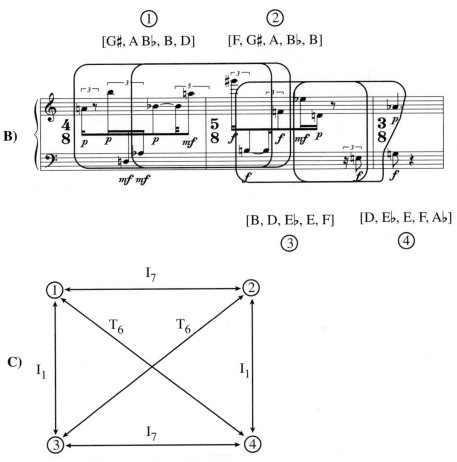

Example 2–14 Four sets belonging to the same set class: A) Wuorinen, *Twelve Short Pieces,* No. 3; B) Stockhausen, *Klavierstück* III; C) network analysis of both passages.

Let's look yet again at the opening section of Schoenberg's Piano Piece, Op. 11, No. 1, to see how a progression involving members of the same set class can create one taut strand in the larger compositional fabric (see Example 2–15). In the first three measures, a single continuous melody descends from its high point on B. In measures 4–8, the melody is reduced to a two-note fragment that reaches up to G three times. In measures 9–11, the opening melody returns in a varied form with a high point of G♯. These three notes, B–G–G♯, are separated in time but associated as contour high points. These are the same pitch classes as the first three notes in the piece and the sustained notes in measures 4–5.

Each note in this large-scale statement is also part of at least one small-scale statement of a member of the same set class. The B in measure 1 is part of the collection B–G♯–G. In measures 4–5, the G is not only part of the sustained chord (G–G♯–B) but also part of the registral grouping G–B♭–B. In measure 10, the G♯ is

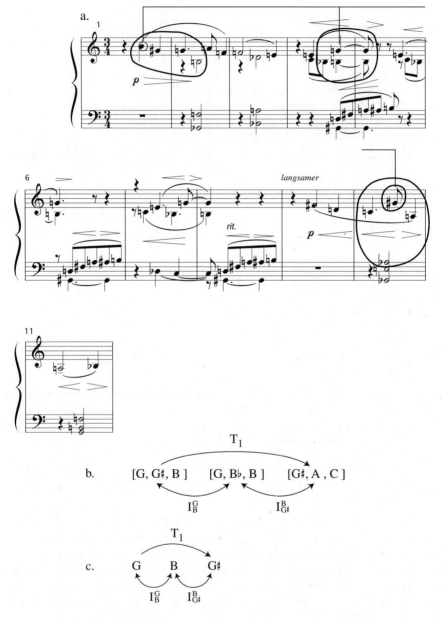

Example 2–15 Progression among members of the same set class.

part of the collection C–G♯–A. These three sets are circled in Example 2–15a and written in normal form in Example 2–15b. The operations that lead from set to set are identified. Example 2–15c shows that the same operations that lead from set to set also can be understood to lead from note to note within the first set. In that sense, relationships embodied in the opening three-note motive are composed-out as that motive is transposed and inverted over the course of the passage.

There are many occurrences of other members of the same set class in this passage, including the chord in measure 3 [A,B♭,D♭], the highest three notes in measure 3 [D♭,E,F], the mid-range notes in measure 4 [B♭,B,D] and the inner notes in the five-note figure in the tenor in measures 4–5 [F♯,A,A♯]. Indeed, the passage is virtually saturated with occurrences of members of this set class. It occurs as a melodic fragment, as a chord, and as a combination of melody and chord. It is articulated by register and, over a large span, by contour. An entire network of musical associations radiates out from the opening three-note melodic figure. Some of the later statements have the same pitch content, some the same pitch-class content. Some are related by transposition, some by inversion. All are members of the same set class. As in tonal music, but with even greater intensity, an initial musical idea grows and develops as the music proceeds. The mere presence of many members of a single set class guarantees a certain kind of sonic unity. But we often will be more interested in the ways in which the music moves from set to set within a set class than in mere set-class membership.

Prime Form

There are two standard ways of naming set classes. The first was devised by the theorist Allen Forte, who pioneered the theory of pitch-class sets. On his well-known list of set classes, he identifies each with a pair of numbers separated by a dash (e.g., 3–4). The first number tells the number of pitch classes in the set. The second number gives the position of the set on Forte's list. Set class 3–4, for example, is the fourth set on Forte's list of three-note sets. Forte's set names are widely used and appear in Appendix 1.

The second common way of identifying set classes is to look at all of the members of the set class, select the one with the "most normal" of normal forms, and use that to name the set class as a whole. This optimal form, called the *prime form,* begins with 0 and is most packed to the left. Of the members of the set class shown in Figure 2–19, two begin with 0: 034 and 014. Of these, (014) is the most packed to the left and is thus the prime form. Those twenty-four sets are all members of the set class with prime form (014). More familiarly, we say that each of those sets "is a (014)." In this book, prime forms will be written in parentheses with no commas separating the elements. T and E will stand for 10 and 11 in this compact format. A set class will generally be identified by both its Forte name and its prime form, and set class will usually be abbreviated as sc. Thus, the sets in Example 2–13 are all members of sc3–5 (016); the sets in Example 2–14A are members of sc3–4 (015); the sets in Example 2–14B are members of sc5–4 (01236); and the sets in Example 2–15 are members of sc3–3 (014). Often, we will omit the Forte-name, in which case these set classes would be identified as sc(016), sc(015), sc(01236), and sc(014).

To identify the set class to which some pitch-class set belongs, you will have to find the prime form of the set class. That process is usually referred to as "putting a set in prime form." Here is how to do it:

ut the set into normal form. (Let's take [1,5,6,7] as an example.)

ranspose the set so that the first element is 0. (If we transpose [1,5,6,7] by T_{11}, we get [0,4,5,6].)

3. Invert the set and repeat steps 1 and 2. ([1,5,6,7] inverts to [11,7,6,5]. The normal form of that set is [5,6,7,11]. If that set is transposed at T_7, we get [0,1,2,6].)

4. Compare the results of step 2 and step 3; whichever is more packed to the left is the prime form. ([0,1,2,6] is more packed to the left than [0,4,5,6], so (0126) is the prime form of the set class of which [1,5,6,7], our example, is a member.)

As with normal form, it will often be possible to determine the prime form just by inspecting a set displayed around a pitch-class clockface. Find the widest gap between the pitch classes. Assign zero to the note at the end of the gap and read off a possible prime form clockwise. Then assign zero to the note at the beginning of the gap and read off another possible prime form counterclockwise. (If there are two gaps of the same size, choose the one that has another relatively big gap right next to it.) Whichever of these potential prime forms has fewer big integers is the true prime form. Figure 2–20 illustrates with the four sets we used in Example 2–5 to determine normal form. It is basically a matter of visualization, and it will get easier with practice.

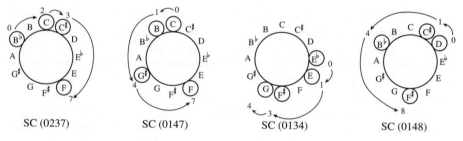

Figure 2–20

In Appendix 1, you will find a list of set classes showing the prime form of each. If you think you have put a set in prime form but you can't find it on the list, you have done something wrong. Notice, in Appendix 1, how few prime forms (set classes) there are. With our twelve pitch classes, it is possible to construct 220 different trichords (three-member sets). However, these different trichords can be grouped into just twelve different trichordal set classes. Similarly, there are only twenty-nine tetrachord classes (four-member sets), thirty-eight pentachord classes (five-member sets), and fifty hexachord classes (six-member sets). We will defer discussion of sets with more than six elements until later.

The list of set classes in Appendix 1 is constructed so as to make a great deal of useful information readily available. Any sonority of between three and nine elements is a member of one of the set classes listed here. In the first column, you will see a list of prime forms, arranged in ascending order. The second column gives

Forte's name for each set class. The third column contains the interval-class vector for the set class. (This is the interval-class vector for every member of the set class, since interval content is not changed by transposition or inversion.) In the fourth column are two numbers separated by a comma; these numbers measure the transpositional and inversional symmetry of the set class—we will discuss these concepts later. Across from each trichord, tetrachord, and pentachord, and some of the hexachords, is another set with all of its relevant information in the reverse order. We will discuss these larger sets later.

Segmentation and Analysis

In the post-tonal music discussed in this book, coherence is often created by relationships among sets within a set class. It is possible to hear pathways through the music as one or more sets are transposed and inverted in purposeful, directed ways. Often, we find that there is not one single best way to hear our way through a piece; rather, our hearings often need to be multiple, as the different paths intersect, diverge, or run parallel to each other. To use a different metaphor, post-tonal music is often like a rich and varied fabric, comprised of many different strands. As we try to comprehend the music, it is our task to tease out the strands for inspection, and then to see how they combine to create the larger fabric.

One of our main analytical tasks, then, is to find the principal sets and show how they are transposed and inverted. But how do you know which sets are the important ones? The answer is that you cannot know in advance. You have to enter the world of the piece—listening, playing, and singing—until you get a sense of which musical ideas are fundamental and recurring. In the process, you will find yourself moving around a familiar kind of conceptual circle. You can't know what the main ideas are until you see them recur; but you can't find recurrences until you know what the main ideas are. The only practical solution is to poke around in the piece, proposing and testing hypotheses as you go. In the process, you will be considering many different *segmentations* of the music, that is, ways of carving it up into meaningful musical groupings.

When you have identified what you think may be a significant musical idea, then look carefully, thoroughly, and imaginatively for its transposed or inverted recurrences. Here are some places to look (this list is not exhaustive!):

1. In a melodic line, consider all of the melodic segments. For example, if the melody is six notes long, then notes 1–2–3, 2–3–4, 3–4–5, and 4–5–6 are all viable three-note groupings. Some of these groupings may span across rests or phrasing boundaries, and that is okay. A rich interaction between phrase structure and set-class structure is a familiar feature of post-tonal music.

2. Harmonically, don't restrict yourself just to chords where all of the notes are attacked at the same time. Rather, consider all of the *simultaneities,* that is, the notes sounding simultaneously at any particular point. Move through the music like a cursor across a page, considering all of the notes sounding at each moment.

3.   Notes can be associated by register. In a melody or a phrase, consider the highest (or lowest) notes, or the high points (or low points) of successive phrases.

4.   Notes can be associated rhythmically in a variety of ways. Consider as a possible group the notes heard on successive downbeats, or the notes heard at the beginning of a recurring rhythmic figure, or the notes that are given the longest durations.

5.   Notes can be associated timbrally in a variety of ways. Consider as a possible group notes that are produced in some distinctive way, for example, by a single instrument in an ensemble, or by a certain kind of articulation (e.g., staccato, pizzicato).

In all of your musical segmentations, strive for a balance between imaginative seeking and musical common sense. On the one hand, do not restrict yourself to the obvious groupings (although these are often a good place to start). Interesting relationships may not be apparent the first, or second, or third time through, and you need to be thorough and persistent in your investigations. On the other hand, you have to stay within the boundaries of what can be meaningfully heard. You can't pluck notes out in some random way, just because they form a set that you are interested in. Rather, the notes you group together must be associated with each other in some musical way. They have to share some distinctive quality (for example, of proximity, or highness, or lowness, or loudness, or longness) that groups them together and distinguishes them from the other notes around them. If, after some repeated, good-faith effort to hear a certain musical grouping, you cannot make it palpably real for yourself, then abandon it and go on to the next thing. The goal is to describe the richest possible network of musical relationships, to let our musical minds and musical ears lead each other along the many enjoyable pathways through this music.

In analyzing post-tonal music, you should feel free to draw on the full range of concepts developed in Chapters 1 and 2 of this book, from the most concrete to the most abstract (see Figure 2–21).

Pitch   ➜ Pitch-class
Pitch intervals   ➜ Ordered pitch-class intervals   ➜ Interval classes
Pitch-class set   ➜ Tn-type   ➜ Set class (Tn/TnI-type)

Figure 2–21

In the process, you may discover how hard it is to find explanations for every single note in a piece or even a short passage. One familiar feature of this music is its resistance to single, all-encompassing explanations. Instead of trying to find a single source for all of the music, try to forge meaningful networks of relationship, teasing out particularly striking strands in the musical fabric, and following a few interesting musical paths. That is an attainable and satisfying goal for musical analysis and musical hearing.

BIBLIOGRAPHY

Many of the basic concepts of post-tonal theory have their origins in the writing and teaching of Milton Babbitt. On normal form, see "Set Structure as a Compositional Determinant" (1961), reprinted in *The Collected Essays of Milton Babbitt,* ed. Stepen Peles, Stephen Dembski, Andrew Mead, and Joseph Straus (Princeton: Princeton University Press, 2003), pp. 86–198. On index number, see "Twelve-Tone Rhythmic Structure and the Electronic Medium" (1962) and "Contemporary Music Composition and Music Theory as Contemporary Intellectual History" (1971), both reprinted in *The Collected Essays of Milton Babbitt,* pp. 109–140 and 270–307. It would be difficult to overestimate Babbitt's influence on post-tonal theory.

Allen Forte *(The Structure of Atonal Music)* and John Rahn *(Basic Atonal Theory)* present slightly different criteria for normal form and for prime form, but these result in only a small number of discrepancies, affecting the following set classes: 5–20, 6–29, 6–31, 7–18, 7–20, and 8–26. This book adopts Rahn's formulation.

The I_y^x model of inversion is David Lewin's. See his *Generalized Musical Intervals and Transformations* (New Haven: Yale University Press, 1987), pp. 50–56.

Schoenberg's Piano Piece, Op. 11, No. 1, has been widely analyzed. George Perle discusses its intensive use of set class 3–3 (014) (which he calls a "basic cell") in *Serial Composition and Atonality.* See also Allen Forte, "The Magical Kaleidoscope: Schoenberg's First Atonal Masterwork, Opus 11, No. 1," *Journal of the Arnold Schoenberg Institute* 5 (1981), pp. 127–68; and Gary Wittlich, "Intervallic Set Structure in Schoenberg's Op. 11, No. 1," *Perspectives of New Music* 13 (1974), pp. 41–55. Ethan Haimo uses the work as a starting point for a critique of pitch-class set theory in "Atonality, Analysis, and the Intentional Fallacy," *Music Theory Spectrum* 18/2 (1996), pp. 167–99. See also a refined network analysis by David Lewin in "Some Aspects of Voice Leading Between Pcsets," *Journal of Music Theory* 42/1 (1998), pp. 15–72.

The problems of segmentation and musical grouping are discussed in Christopher Hasty, "Segmentation and Process in Post-Tonal Music," *Music Theory Spectrum* 3 (1981), pp. 54–73 and Dora Hanninen, "Orientations, Criteria, Segments: A General Theory of Segmentation for Music Analysis," *Journal of Music Theory* 45/2 (2001), pp. 345–434.

Exercises

THEORY

I. Normal Form: The normal form of a pitch-class set is its most compact representation.

    1. Put the following collections into normal form on a musical staff.

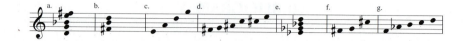

2.   Put the following collections into normal form using integers. Write your answer within square brackets.

   a. 11, 5, 7, 2
   b. 0, 10, 5
   c. 7, 6, 9, 1
   d. 4, 7, 2, 7, 11
   e. the C-major scale
   f. E♭, C, B, B♭, E, G
   g. 9, 11, 2, 5, 9, 8, 1, 2

II.   Transposition: Transposition (T$_n$) involves adding some transposition interval (n) to each member of a pitch-class set. Two pitch-class sets are related by T$_n$ if, for each element in the first set, there is a corresponding element in the second set n semitones away.

   1.   Transpose the following pitch-class sets as indicated. The sets are given in normal form; be sure your answer is in normal form. Write your answer on a musical staff.

   2.   Transpose the following pitch-class sets as indicated. Write your answers in normal form using integer notation.

      a. T$_3$ [8,0,3]
      b. T$_9$ [1,4,7,10]
      c. T$_6$ [5,7,9,11,2]
      d. T$_7$ [9,11,1,2,4,6]

   3.   Are the following pairs of pitch-class sets related by transposition? If so, what is the interval of transposition? All the sets are given in normal form.

      a. [8,9,11,0,4] [4,5,7,8,0]
      b. [7,9,1] [1,5,7]
      c. [7,8,10,1,4] [1,2,4,7,10]
      d. [1,2,5,9] [11,0,3,7]

III.   Inversion: Inversion (T$_n$I) involves inverting each member of a pitch-class set (subtracting it from 12), then transposing by some interval n (which may be 0). Two sets are related by inversion if they can be written so that the interval succession of one is the reverse of the interval succession of the other.

1.   Invert the following pitch-class sets as indicated. Put your answer in normal form and write it on a musical staff.

2.   Invert the following pitch-class sets as indicated. Use integer notation and put your answer in normal form.
      a. T_9I [9,10,0,2]
      b. T_0I [1,2,5]
      c. T_3I [1,2,4,7,10]
      d. $T_{10}I$ [10,11,0,3,4,7]
      e. T_6I [4,7,10,0]
      f. T_4I (the C-major scale)

3.   Are the following pairs of pitch-class sets related by inversion? If so, what is value of n in T_nI? All sets are given in normal form.
      a. [2,4,5,7] [8,10,11,1]
      b. [4,6,9] [4,7,9]
      c. [1,2,6,8] [9,11,2,3]
      d. [4,5,6,8,10,1] [6,8,10,11,0,3]
      e. [8,9,0,4] [8,11,0,4]

IV.   Index Number: In sets related by inversion (T_nI), the corresponding elements sum to n. When the sets are in normal form, the first element of one usually corresponds to the last element of the other, the second element of one corresponds to the second-to-last element of the other, and so on.

1.   For each of the following pairs of inversionally related sets, figure out the index number. Sets are given in normal form.
      a. [5,9,11] [7,9,1]
      b. [4,5,8,11] [10,1,4,5]
      c. [4,5,8,0] [9,0,1,5]
      d. [1,3,6,9] [10,1,4,6]

2.   Using your knowledge of index numbers, invert each of the following sets as indicated. Put your answer in normal form.
      a. T_3I [1,3,5,8]
      b. T_9I [10,1,3,6]
      c. T_0I [1,2,4,6,9]
      d. T_4I [4,5,6,7]

V.   Inversion: Inversion (I_y^x) involves mapping each note in a pitch-class set onto a corresponding note by performing whatever inversion maps x onto y.

1. Invert the following pitch-class set as indicated. Put your answer in normal form and write it on a musical staff.

I^G_B $\quad\quad$ $I^{F\sharp}_G$ $\quad\quad$ I^F_F $\quad\quad$ I^B_C $\quad\quad$ $I^E_{G\sharp}$

2. Invert the following pitch-class sets as indicated. Put your answer in normal form.
    a. $I^{A\flat}_{B\flat}$ [G, A♭, B♭, B]
    b. $I^{A\flat}_A$ [B, C, D, F, F♯]
    c. I^D_D [B, C, D, E, F, G]
    d. $I^{C\sharp}_{C\sharp}$ [F♯, G♯, B, C♯]
    e. $I^D_{A\flat}$ [C♯, D♯, G, A]

3. Using the I^x_y notation, give at least two labels for the operation that connects the following pairs of inversionally related sets.
    a. [G, G♯, B] [G, B♭, B]
    b. [C♯, D, F, G] [G, A, C, C♯]

    c. [A♭, A, D♭, E♭] [A, B, D♯, E]
    d. [D, F, A] [F, A, C]
    e. [G♯, A, A♯, B, C, D] [C♯, D♯, E, F, F♯, G]

VI. Prime Form: The prime form is the way of writing a set that is most compact and most packed to the left, and begins on 0.

1. Put each of the following pitch-class sets in prime form. All sets are given in normal form.
    a. [10,3,4]
    b. [7,8,11,0,1,3]
    c. [G,B,D]
    d. [2,5,8,10]
    e. [4,6,9,10,1]
    f. [C♯,D,G,A♭]

2. Are the following pitch-class sets in prime form? If not, put them in prime form.
    a. (0,1,7)
    b. (0,2,8)
    c. (0,2,6,9)
    d. (0,1,4,5,8,9)

VII. The List of Set Classes (Appendix 1)

1. Name all the tetrachords that contain two tritones.
2. What is the largest number of interval class 4s contained by a tetrachord? Which tetrachords contain that many?

3. Which trichord(s) contain both a semitone and a tritone?
4. Which tetrachords contain one occurrence of each interval class? (Notice that they have different prime forms.)
5. How many trichords are there? How many nonachords (nine-note sets)? Why are these numbers the same?
6. Which hexachords have no occurrences of some interval? of more than one interval?
7. Which hexachord(s) have the maximum (six) occurrences of some interval? Which have five occurrences of some interval?
8. Are there any sets that contain only one kind of interval?

ANALYSIS

I. Crawford, Piano Prelude No. 9, mm. 1–9. (*Hint:* Begin by considering the upper and lower parts separately, but consider also the harmonies formed between them.)

II. Webern, *Concerto for Nine Instruments,* Op. 24, second movement, mm. 1–11. (*Hint:* Begin by considering the first three melody notes (G–D♯–E) as a basic motive and relate it to transpositionally equivalent repetitions of it. Then consider the three notes in measure 1 (G–B♭–B) as a basic motive, and relate it to its transposed repetitions. Finally, combine those two transpositional paths into a single comprehensive view.)

III. Stravinsky, *Agon,* mm. 418 (with pick-up)–429. (*Hint:* Begin with the cadential chord, [B♭, B, D♭, D] and show how it relates to the music that precedes it.)

IV. Webern, Movements for String Quartet, Op. 5, No. 2, beginning through the downbeat of m. 4. (*Hint:* Begin by treating the first three notes in the viola, G–B–C♯, as a basic motivic unit. Look for transposed and inverted repetitions.)

V. Babbitt, *Semi-Simple Variations,* Theme, mm. 1–6. (*Hint:* Imagine the passage as consisting of four registral lines, a soprano that begins on B♭, an alto that begins on D, a tenor that begins on A, and a bass that begins on C♯. Each line consists of six different notes. Analyze the lines separately [with particular attention to their trichords] and in relation to each other.)

EAR-TRAINING AND MUSICIANSHIP

I. Crawford, Piano Prelude No. 9, mm. 1–9. Pianists: play the entire passage. Nonpianists: play the treble parts only. It's mostly a duet—use one hand for each line.

II. Webern, *Concerto for Nine Instruments,* Op. 24, second movement, mm. 1–11. The passage (and, indeed, the entire movement) is divided into a melody, shared by eight melodic instruments, and a piano accompaniment. Learn to play melody and accompaniment separately, then together. Learn to sing the melody, using pitch-class integers in the place of solfège syllables (you will have to transpose all or part of the melody into a comfortable register).

III. Stravinsky, *Agon,* mm. 418 (with pick-up)–429. Play this passage accurately and in tempo at the piano (the tempo is Adagio, ♪ = 112).

IV. Webern, *Movements for String Quartet,* Op. 5, No. 2, beginning through the downbeat of m. 4. Sing the viola melody using pitch-class integers while playing the accompanying chords on the piano.

V. Babbitt, *Semi-Simple Variations,* Theme, mm. 1–6. Write out each of the registral lines as six consecutive whole notes, then learn to sing each one smoothly and accurately.

VI. Learn to identify the twelve different trichordal set-classes when they are played by your instructor. It may be easier if you learn them in the following order, adding each new one as the previous ones are mastered:

    1. 3–1 (012): chromatic trichord
    2. 3–9 (027): stack of perfect fourths or fifths
    3. 3–11 (037): major or minor triad
    4. 3–3 (014): major and minor third combined
    5. 3–7 (025): diatonic trichord
    6. 3–12 (048): augmented triad
    7. 3–5 (016): semitone and tritone
    8. 3–8 (026): whole-tone and tritone
    9. 3–10 (036): diminished triad
  10. 3–2 (013): nearly chromatic
  11. 3–6 (024): two whole-tones
  12. 3–4 (015): semitone and perfect fourth

COMPOSITION

I. Take the first measure or two of one of the compositions discussed in the Analysis section, and, without looking ahead, continue and conclude your own brief composition. Then compare your composition with the published prototype.

II. Write a short piece for your instrument in which the main sense of direction is provided by the purposeful, directed successive transposition of a pitch-class set of your choice.

Analysis 2

Schoenberg, *Book of the Hanging Gardens,*
Op. 15, No. 11
Bartók, String Quartet No. 4, first movement

Schoenberg wrote his *Book of the Hanging Gardens,* Op. 15, in 1908. The song cycle contains fifteen musical settings of poems by Stefan George. The "hanging gardens" described in the poems are those of ancient Babylon, one of the wonders of the ancient world. The gardens appear in George's poems as a kind of magical, ambiguous background for disturbing and inconclusive erotic verse. We will concentrate on the eleventh song in the cycle, but you should be familiar with the others as well. The music for the first thirteen measures of the song, the focus of our discussion, can be found in Example A2–1.

(*continued*)

Example A2–1 Schoenberg, *Book of the Hanging Gardens,* Op. 15, No. 11 (mm. 1–13).

Analysis 2

Example A2–1 (*continued*)

Als wir hinter dem beblümten Tore	When we, behind the flowering gate,
Endlich nur das eigne Hauchen spürten	At last felt only our own breathing,
Warden uns erdachte Seligkeiten?	Was our bliss only imagined?
Ich erinnere . . .	I remember . . .

Learn to sing the melodic line and to play the piano part (neither is difficult). Better yet, learn to sing the melodic line while accompanying yourself.

Let's begin by concentrating on the opening melodic gesture in the right hand of the piano part (see Example A2–2).

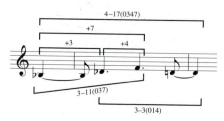

Example A2–2 The opening melodic gesture and its components.

Analysis 2

The four-note gesture is a member of set class 4–17 (0347). It is easy to visualize this melody as a triad with both major and minor thirds, although, as we will see, it occurs later in the song in a variety of guises. The gesture also contains three smaller musical ideas that will become important later: the rising minor triad with which it begins (set class 3–11 (037)), the ascending interval of seven semitones spanned by that triad and divided into a +3 followed by a +4, and the final three notes of the gesture (set class 3–3 (014)). This last set class also is formed by the lowest three notes of the melody, B♭–D♭–D. Sing or play the figure and listen until you can hear all of these musical ideas. Then let us see how this melodic gesture and its components get developed in the subsequent music.

In measure 13, at the end of the passage we are considering, the same gesture comes back at the original transposition level in the piano, and almost simultaneously at T_2 in the voice. These direct references to the opening are particularly appropriate to the text, since the singer at this moment is saying, "Ich erinnere" ("I remember"). The music conveys a sense of memory by recalling musical events heard earlier.

The vocal line beginning in measure 8 also contains echoes, slightly more concealed, of the same melodic gesture (see Example A2–3).

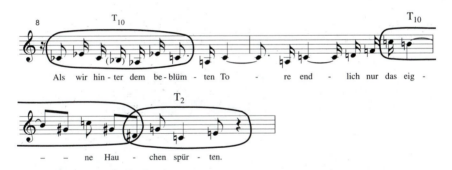

Example A2–3 Some statements of 4–17 (0347) in the vocal line.

The singer begins with a varied statement of the gesture at T_{10}. (The B♭ is an added passing note.) Shortly thereafter, it repeats T_{10} (again in a varied order), and the phrase concludes with T_2. At that moment (the end of measure 10), chords are heard again in the piano, closing off the phrase. Melodically, the voice has used forms of 4–17 (0347) at both two semitones above (T_2) and two semitones below (T_{10}) the original form. These two transposition levels, one a little higher and one a little lower than the original one, give a sense of "not-quite-right"ness to the music that perhaps reflects the uncertainty in the upcoming text: "Was our bliss only imagined?" The singer would like to get back to the form that begins on B♭, but she hasn't quite gotten there yet. Sing the vocal line again, and listen in it for these slightly off-center echoes of the opening melodic gesture. That gesture is developed in an even more concealed

Analysis 2

way in the piano part in measures 3 and 4. The right-hand part in those measures contains two new forms of 4–17 (0347), at T_3 and T_7 (see Example A2–4).

Example A2–4 Statements of 4–17 (0347) in the piano introduction.

Play the piano part in those measures and listen for the resemblances to the opening gesture. Notice how the intervals from that opening gesture are rearranged within the chords. In the T_7 version, for example, notice that the melody, C–A–G♯, is the same set class as the last three notes in the opening gesture: 3–3 (014).

Now let us see if we can assemble the five forms of 4–17 (0347) identified so far into a purposeful transpositional path (see Example A2–5).

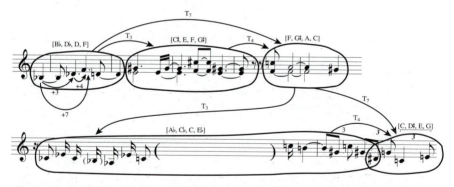

Example A2–5 The initial melodic idea, composed-out through the transpositions of the initial pitch-class set, [B♭, D♭, D, F].

The first three statements, all in the right-hand part in the piano introduction, describe a transpositional path that ascends first three and then four semitones, precisely reflecting the intervals of the first three notes of the song, B♭–D♭–F. The third piano statement leads directly to the entrance of the voice in the same register, three semitones higher, and the voice then transposes an additional four semitones higher, stating again the intervals of the opening melodic fragment. Taken together, then, the

Analysis 2

piano and voice describe two successive statements, over a large musical span, of the melodic intervals of the opening.

This kind of expanded repetition is typical of Schoenberg's music. Frequently, the large-scale succession of events mirrors the small-scale succession of intervals. It also raises an important aspect of musical analysis using pitch-class sets. It is never enough just to identify set classes or just to point out that two collections are members of the same set class. We will always want to know more—why the sets occur at those particular levels of transposition or inversion, and why they occur in the order they do. In this song by Schoenberg, the occurrences of 4–17 (0347) are transposed and ordered so as to reproduce, over a large span, the intervallic succession of the opening melodic gesture.

An even larger-scale statement of 4–17 (0347) at its T_0 transposition [B♭,D♭,D,F] occurs in the bass over the first thirteen measures. Starting in measure 2, the bass sustains an F. In measure 3 it moves down to D and back. In measure 4 it moves to D♭ and essentially remains there through measure 10, embellished by a brief C in measure 5 and a brief C♭ in measure 6, and respelled as C♯ beginning in measure 8. In measure 10, the main bass notes so far—D, F, and D♭—are restated in shorter rhythmic values. Only one additional note is needed to duplicate the pitch-class content of the opening melodic gesture. The missing note, B♭, comes in right at the end of measure 12, both completing a large-scale statement of the melodic gesture and initiating a small-scale statement of it (see Example A2–6).

Example A2–6 A large-scale bass statement of T_0 of 4–17 (0347) culminates in a restatement of the initial melodic gesture.

The opening melodic gesture thus permeates the subsequent music. It is developed in a variety of ways, some obvious and some concealed, some melodic and some harmonic, some small-scale and some large-scale. Play the passage again and listen for this network of developments and relationships. They overlap and interpenetrate each other, but try to hear them simultaneously.

Lots of other things are going on that we have not had a chance to discuss. Let's consider just one of these, the descending bass figure in the first measure. Like the opening melodic gesture, this bass figure influences the subsequent music in interesting ways (see Example A2–7).

Analysis 2

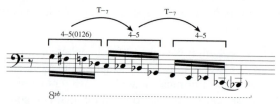

Example A2–7 Occurrences of 4–5 (0126) in the opening bass figure—
a pattern of descending 7s.

The figure begins with G–F♯–F–D♭, then transposes that set down seven semitones twice in succession. The descending 7s subtly recall the ascending 7, B♭–F, that takes place simultaneously in the melodic gesture in the right hand. If the descent shown here were to continue one note further, it would reach B♭; instead, it stops short on C♭, one semitone higher. In a number of different ways, the music seems to strive toward B♭. This feeling of "not-quite-B♭" is one we have remarked on already.

The opening bass figure is even more saturated with occurrences of 4–5 (0126) than we have noted. Two additional forms, beginning on F and B♭, overlap the three already discussed (see Example A2–8).

Example A2–8 Overlapping statements of 4–5 (0126) in the opening bass figure.

Each of the five statements is related by inversion to the ones before and after it. More specifically, each statement inverts around its last two notes to produce the next. This inversional flipping produces an extraordinary motivic saturation even as it propels the music forward.

The first of the two additional forms, F–D♭–C–C♭, is recalled in interesting ways in measures 3–6 (see Example A2–9).

The chord in measure 4 verticalizes that set; meanwhile, the same pitch classes are stated, slowly and melodically, in the bass. In terms of the large-scale statement of 4–17 (0347) discussed above, the C and C♭ in measures 5 and 6 are notes that embellish a more important D♭. But those embellishing tones themselves have an important local role to play in composing out this form of 4–5 (0126). Like set class 4–17, set class 4–5 is developed in this music through transposition and inversion, through melodic and harmonic presentation, and through statement over shorter and longer musical spans.

Analysis 2

Example A2–9 Three different presentations of a single pitch-class set, [B,C,D♭,F], a member of set class 4–5 (0126).

A note about analytical method. When two sets are related by some operation, sometimes the analysis labels the sets (leaving you to infer the operation) and sometimes it labels the operation (leaving you to infer the identity of the sets). Analyses often take the form of graphs that contain nodes (circled notes or sets) and arrows (the operations that connect the nodes). Sometimes we focus on the contents of the nodes, and sometimes on the nature and direction of the arrows. Both are perfectly reasonable things to do and you should select whichever seems most revealing and pertinent in a particular musical context.

You have probably noticed that our explanations sometimes have a way of overlapping one another. Consider, for example, the melody note C in measure 4. We have described it in at least three different ways. It is part of a vertical statement of 4–5 (0126), as shown in Example A2.9; it is also part of a statement of 4–17 (0347) in the right hand and a melodic statement of 3–3 (014). But these interpretations do not contradict each other. The C can function in lots of different ways, depending on how one looks at it. Even better, it can function in lots of different ways simultaneously. A single tone can be, at one and the same time, part of a chord, part of a registral grouping, and part of a melodic line. The richness of associations in this music is one of its most attractive qualities.

Other networks of motivic association operate in this song, interwoven with the ones we have discussed. For example, the chord in measure 2 is a form of set class 4–18 (0147). The same set class returns in measure 8 (F♯, A, C, C♯) and again at the end of the song. It also is developed elsewhere in the song. As another example, the first four notes heard in the song—B♭, G, F♯, and F—make up set class 4–4 (0125). The same set, transposed at T_7, that familiar interval of transposition, occurs as a chord in measure 3 and also is developed elsewhere in the song. The fabric of the song is built up from the interweaving of its motivic threads.

Bartók's String Quartet No. 4 is superficially a very different kind of piece from Schoenberg's *Book of the Hanging Gardens.* It has much more overt repetition, particularly of small melodic fragments. It has a sharper, more propulsive rhythmic profile. Yet underlying these differences, both works share a pitch organization based on the manipulation and interaction of pitch-class sets. Listen to a recording of the quartet, concentrating particularly on the first movement. The music for measures 1–13 is given in Example A2–10.

Analysis 2

Example A2–10 Bartók, String Quartet No. 4, first movement (mm. 1–13).

Analysis 2

Let's begin our analytical examination by looking closely at the music in measures 5–7 (see Example A2–11).

Example A2–11   Expansion from 4–1 (0123) to 4–21 (0246).

Begin by playing this passage on the piano. Something striking happens on the second eighth-note of measure 6, where the chord [C,C♯,D,D♯] expands to [B♭,C,D,E]. The first chord is a member of set class 4–1 (0123) and the second is a member of set class 4–21 (0246). These two set classes, and the idea of expanding or contracting from one to the other, are basic to the way this music goes.

Play each of the parts in turn, starting in measure 5, up through the moment of that expansion. The cello enters on E♭ and descends five semitones to its goal, B♭, taking eleven eighth-notes to do so. Then the viola enters, one semitone higher. It descends a shorter distance, four semitones from E to C, and takes a shorter time, nine eighth-notes, to do so. The second violin descends even more rapidly from F to D (three semitones), while the first violin enters last and covers its allotted span, two semitones from F♯ to E, the most rapidly of all. The passage thus contains a registral and rhythmic accelerando as both the intervallic and durational distances get shorter and shorter. Play that much of the passage and listen for the sense of propulsion toward the goal [B♭,C,D,E].

Now play the rest of the passage in Example A2–11. In measure 6, each note of the second chord, [B♭,C,D,E], is embellished with neighbor notes. The lower instruments have upper neighbor notes, while the higher instruments have lower neighbors. This gives a sense of contracting from 4–21 (0246) toward 4–1 (0123), although the instruments never move at exactly the same time. On the downbeat of measure 7, we find ourselves still on [B♭,C,D,E]. At that moment, the cello states the main melodic motive of the movement. That motive is another member of set class 4–1. The last time we heard that set class was back at the end of measure 5; there, 4–1 was presented as a chord, with C as the lowest note. If we designate that as T_0, then the melody in measure 7 is T_{10}. The idea of moving downward by two semitones—and, more specifically, from C to B♭—is one we will return to. This passage ends with a sforzando statement of [B♭,C,D,E]. Partly because it is stated loudly by all four instruments and then followed by a silence, that chord sounds like a cadential arrival.

The music from the pickup to measure 5 through the first eighth-note of measure 6 fills the chromatic space between C and F♯. Starting on the second eighth-note of measure 6, where 4–1 (0123) expands to 4–21 (0246), the chromatic space between B♭ and E is similarly saturated (see Example A2.12).

Example A2–12 Shift from C–F♯ to B♭–E.

The music in measures 1–13 involves a shift from a focus on C–F♯ to a focus on B♭–E, a shift that takes place precisely on the second eighth-note of measure 6. Play the passage in measures 5–7 once again, and listen for this downward shift.

The opening measures of the piece use set classes 4–1 (0123) and 4–21 (0246) to focus on C–F♯. Let's look closely at the first two measures (see Example A2–13).

Example A2–13 Melodic and harmonic statements of set class 4–21 (0246) and an embellishing statement of 4–1 (0123).

Analysis 2

Play just the first three beats of the first measure. The registral extremes there are the C in the cello and the F♯ in the first violin. At the moment when those extremes are heard (beat 3), the second violin has an E. This seems like an incomplete statement of set class 4–21 (0246). Let's designate that form, [C,D,E,F♯], as T_0. Now play the first violin part through the third eighth-note of measure 2. That melody seems to "compose out" the same set, tracing a descent from F♯ to C by way of E and D. Embedded within that melodic statement of 4–21 is an embellishing statement of 4–1: the first four notes in the first violin are [D♯,E,F,F♯]. Both sets lie within the tritone from C to F♯.

If the beginning of the piece focuses on the tritone C–F♯ and on forms of set classes 4–1 (0123) and 4–21 (0246) that lie within that span, the ending of the first section of the piece shifts to the tritone B♭–E and to forms of 4–1 and 4–21 lying within that span. Look, for example, at a passage beginning in the middle of measure 10 (see Example A2–14).

Example A2–14   The contraction of 4–21 (0246) into 4–1 (0123) and its reexpansion back into 4–21.

The passage consists of six chords, marked A–F on the example. At a glance, it is clear that chords A and C are identical, as are chords D and F. Now play the chords slowly and you will become aware of a deeper similarity. Because the voices cross, chords A, C, D, and F are all identical in pitch content ([B♭,C,D,E]) and all are thus members of set class 4–21 (0246). Similarly, chords B and E have the same pitch content, [C,C♯,D,E♭], and are both members of set class 4–1 (0123). Notice how the voice crossing works. From measure 10 to measure 11, the first violin and cello exchange parts, as do the second violin and viola. The sets are turned instrumentally upside-down without changing their identity. As in measures 5–7, the basic idea of this passage seems to be the contraction of 4–21 into 4–1 and its reexpansion back to 4–21. The expansion to 4–21 has the force of an arrival.

From the beginning of the movement, then, there is a constant interaction of 4–1 (0123) and 4–21 (0246), even as the musical orientation shifts from C–F♯ to B♭–E. This shift is confirmed in the cadence that closes off the passage (see Example A2–15).

Analysis 2

Example A2–15 The final cadence—the merging of set classes 4–1 (0123) and 4–21 (0246) within the tritone B♭–E.

There each voice enters in turn, outlining the T_{10} form of 4–21 [B♭,C,D,E]. When the cello finally brings in its B♭, the other voices crash back in. Now the entire space between B♭ and E has been filled in. The chromatic tetrachord 4–1 (0123) and the whole-tone tetrachord 4–21 (0246) are merged in this final sonority. The two principal set classes of the passage thus are developed, progress from one to the other, define a large-scale shift in pitch location, and ultimately merge into a single cadential sonority.

BIBLIOGRAPHY

The eleventh song from Schoenberg's *Book of the Hanging Gardens* has been analyzed briefly by Tom Demske ("Registral Centers of Balance in Atonal Works by Schoenberg and Webern," *In Theory Only* 9/2–3 (1986), pp. 60–76), and in great and compelling detail by David Lewin ("Toward the Analysis of a Schoenberg Song (Op. 15, No. 11)," *Perspectives of New Music* 12/1–2 (1973–74), pp. 43–86). My own discussion is heavily indebted to the latter.

Bartók's String Quartet No. 4 has been analyzed from many points of view. See Elliott Antokoletz, *The Music of Béla Bartók: A Study of Tonality and Progression in Twentieth-Century Music* (Berkeley and Los Angeles: University of California Press, 1984); Milton Babbitt, "The String Quartets of Bartók" (1949), reprinted in *The Collected Essays of Milton Babbitt,* pp. 1–9; George Perle, "Symmetrical Formations in the String Quartets of Béla Bartók," *Music Review* 16 (1955), pp. 300–312; Roy Travis, "Tonal Coherence in the First Movement of Bartók's Fourth String Quartet," *Music Forum* 2 (1970), pp. 298–371; and Leo Treitler, "Harmonic Procedures in the Fourth Quartet of Béla Bartók," *Journal of Music Theory* 3 (1959), pp. 292–98.

Chapter 3
Some Additional Relationships

Common Tones under Transposition (T_n)

When a pitch-class set is transposed or inverted, its content will change entirely, partially, or not at all. Tones held in common between two different members of the same set class can provide an important musical continuity. Conversely, an absence of common tones may emphasize the contrast between two different members of the same set class.

When you transpose a pitch-class set by interval n, the number of common tones will be equal to the number of times the interval n occurs in the set (with one exception, to be discussed later). If a set contains three occurrences of interval class 2, for example, there will be three common tones at T_2 or T_{10} (see Example 3–1a). The major scale contains six instances of interval class 5, so there will be six common tones when the scale is transposed up or down by five semitones (T_5 or T_7). (See Example 3–1b.)

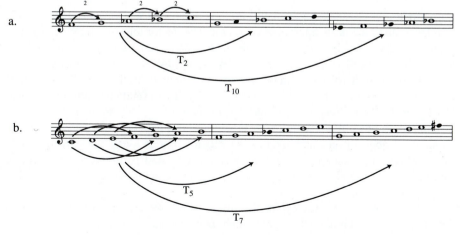

Example 3–1 Common tones under transposition.

To understand why it works this way, concentrate on the mappings involved. When a set is transposed at T_n, each member of the set maps onto a note that lies n semitones higher. If two of the notes in the set were n semitones apart to begin with, transposing by n semitones maps one of the notes onto the other, producing one common tone. That mapping will happen as many times as there are occurrences of interval n in the set. In other words, for every occurrence of a given interval n, there will be one common tone under T_n.

For example, consider the operation T_3 applied to [4,5,7,8], a member of set class 4–3 (0134). There are two occurrences of interval class 3 in the set, between 4 and 7 and between 5 and 8. As a result, when the set is transposed up three semitones, the 4 maps onto the 7 and the 5 maps onto the 8. Similarly, when it is transposed down three semitones (T_9), the 8 maps onto the 5 and the 7 onto the 4 (see Figure 3–1).

$$[4,\ 5,\ 7,\ 8] \xrightarrow{\ \ T_3\ \ } [7,\ 8,\ 10,\ 11] \qquad\qquad [4,\ 5,\ 7,\ 8] \xrightarrow{\ \ T_9\ \ } [1,\ 2,\ 4,\ 5]$$

Figure 3–1

The tritone (interval class 6) is an exception. Because the tritone maps onto itself under transposition at T_6, each occurrence of interval class 6 in a set will create *two* common tones when the set is transposed at T_6. For example, consider [4,9,10], a member of set class 3–5 (016). It contains a single tritone. When the set is transposed at T_6, the 4 maps onto the 10 and the 10 simultaneously maps back onto the 4. As a result, both the 4 and the 10 are held in common at T_6 (see Figure 3–2).

$$[4,\ 9,\ 10] \xrightarrow{\ \ T_6\ \ } [10,\ 3,\ 4]$$

Figure 3–2

To figure out quickly how many common tones a set will have at any transposition level, just look at its interval-class vector. The vector tells you how many times each interval class occurs in any set, which also tells you how many common tones there will be under T_n for any value of n. Set 4–3 (0134), for example, has the vector 212100, and will therefore retain two common tones at T_1 (or T_{11}) and T_3 (or T_9) and a single common tone at T_2 (or T_{10}) and T_4 (or T_8). It will retain no common tones at T_5, T_6, or T_7. These results will hold for all members of the set class. Notice, in Example 3–2, how Stravinsky uses common tones in a passage from *Agon* to create a chain of members of set class 4–3, linked by their common tones. Transposition at T_4 produces one common tone, while transposition at T_{11} and T_3 produces two common tones each. The overall motion, T_6, produces no common tones because the set being transposed contains no i6s.

The interval-class vector for the major scale, set class 7–35 (013568T), is 254361. Notice that it has a different number of occurrences of each interval class. As a result, it will have a different number of common tones at each transpositional level

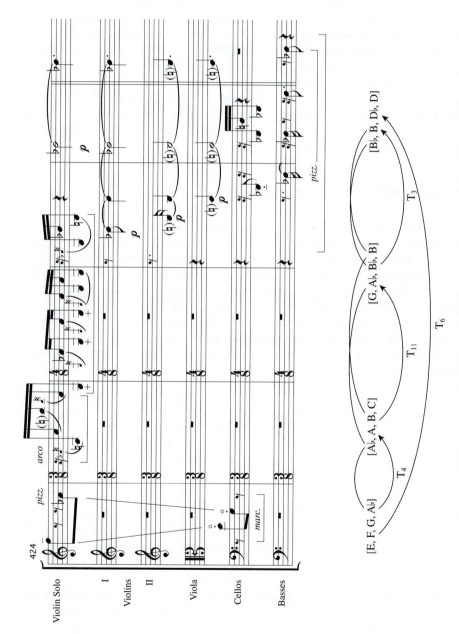

Example 3–2 A chain of members of set class 4–3 (0134) (Stravinsky, *Agon*).

(except at the semitone and the tritone, where it will have two common tones). Because of this property (called "unique multiplicity of interval class"), the major scale (and the natural minor scale, a member of the same set class) can create the hierarchy of closely and distantly related keys that is so essential to tonal music. When the scale is transposed up a perfect fifth (T_7), six of the seven pitch classes are held in common. This is one reason why the tonality of the dominant is considered closely related to that of the tonic. By contrast, when the major scale is transposed down a semitone, only two tones are held in common; VII is therefore considered a relatively remote tonality. For contrast, consider the interval-class vector of the whole-tone scale: 060603. For each transpositional level, there will either be six common tones (that is, a duplication of the original scale) or none. No gradual hierarchy exists here, just a stark either/or.

Transpositional Symmetry

There is a small handful of sets that, like the whole-tone scale, are capable of mapping entirely onto themselves under transposition. Sets with that capacity are said to be *transpositionally symmetrical*. If the interval-class vector contains an entry equal to the number of notes in the set (or half that number in the case of the tritone), then the set has this property. For example, scan the vector entries for the tetrachords in Appendix 1, looking for vector entries of 4 (or 2 in the tritone column). There are three tetrachords that have such entries: 4–9 (0167), 4–25 (0268), and 4–28 (0369). All map onto themselves at T_6, and 4–28 also maps onto itself at T_3 (and T_9).

Transpositional symmetry is a rare property—only twelve set classes have it (these are listed in Figure 3–3).

3–12 (048)	9–12 (01245689T)
4–9 (0167)	8–9 (01236789)
4–25 (0268)	8–25 (0124678T)
4–28 (0369)	8–28 (0134679T)
6–7 (012678)	
6–30 (013679)	
6–20 (014589)	
6–35 (02468T)	

Figure 3–3

Evidently this property has been of importance to composers, because most of these set classes are familiar ones, including the augmented triad (3–12), the French augmented sixth chord (4–25), the diminished seventh chord (4–28), the "Petrushka chord" (6–30), the hexatonic scale (6–20), the whole-tone scale (6–35), and the octatonic scale (8–28).

Looking down the middle column in Appendix 1, the number before the comma measures the degree of transpositional symmetry, that is, the number of transpositional levels at which the set class or set classes on that line of the Appendix will map onto themselves. The number is always at least 1, because every set maps onto itself at T_0, and thus is transpositionally symmetrical in at least that trivial sense. The twelve set classes listed in Figure 3–3 have a degree of transpositional symmetry greater than 1. The set class 3–12 (048), for example, also known as the augmented triad, maps onto itself at three levels: T_0, T_4, and T_8. It thus has a degree of transpositional symmetry of 3.

Common Tones under Inversion (T_nI)

The procedure for figuring out the common tones under inversion (T_nI) is similar to that under transposition (T_n), only now we will be concerned not with intervals (differences) but with index numbers (sums). When discussing common tones under T_n, we considered the intervals formed by each pair of elements in a set. Now, in discussing common tones under T_nI, we need to consider the index numbers (sums) formed by each pair of elements in a set.

Imagine a pair of elements in a set. The sum of those two elements will produce an index number n such that T_nI maps those elements onto each other. For example, consider [1,3,6,9], a member of set class 4–27 (0258). The sums of each pair of elements in this set are shown in Figure 3–4.

[1,3,6,9]
1 + 3 = 4
1 + 6 = 7
1 + 9 = 10   Each of these sums represents
3 + 6 = 9   two common tones.
3 + 9 = 0
6 + 9 = 3

Figure 3–4

Each of these sums is an index number. For each sum, there will be two common tones under T_nI for that value of n. For example, T_7I of [1,3,6,9] is [10,1,4,6]. The 1 maps onto the 6 and the 6 maps onto the 1. This double mapping will occur under T_nI for any value of n that is a sum of elements in the set.

There is an additional factor to consider. Unlike T_n (other than the trivial case of T_0), T_nI can map a pitch class onto itself. Any pitch class will map onto itself under T_nI where n is the sum of that pitch class with itself. In the case of [1,3,6,9], the 9, for example, will map onto itself under T_{9+9}I = T_6I. The sum of each element with itself will produce a value of n such that T_nI will keep that element as a common tone. The sums of each element in [1,3,6,9] with itself are shown in Figure 3–5.

[1,3,6,9]

$1 + 1 = 2$

$3 + 3 = 6$ Each of these sums represents

$6 + 6 = 0$ one common tone.

$9 + 9 = 6$

Figure 3–5

For each of these sums, there will be one common tone under T_nI for that value of n.

We can compile all of these sums for [1,3,6,9] into what we will call an *index vector*, remembering that the sums of different elements will yield two common tones, while the sums of elements with themselves will yield one common tone. For each of the twelve possible values of n, we can list the number of common tones under T_nI (see Figure 3–6).

n =	0	1	2	3	4	5	6	7	8	9	10	11
no. of common tones:	3	0	1	2	2	0	2	2	0	2	2	0

Figure 3–6

The largest number of common tones, three, is retained at T_0I, which maps the 3 and the 9 onto each other and the 6 onto itself. Two common tones are retained at T_3I, T_4I, T_6I, T_7I, T_9I, and $T_{10}I$; one common tone is retained at T_2I. No common tones are retained at T_1I, T_5I, T_8I, or $T_{11}I$, because the sums 1, 5, 8, and 11 cannot be produced by adding members of [1,3,6,9] either to each other or to themselves. The number of common tones under T_nI for every value of n can be read from the vector.

A simpler way to figure out the number of common tones under T_nI is to construct an addition table. Write the set along the vertical and horizontal axes and add as indicated. Such an addition table for [3,4,7,8] is shown in Figure 3–7.

	3	4	7	8
3	6	7	10	11
4	7	8	11	0
7	10	11	2	3
8	11	0	3	4

Figure 3–7

This table neatly performs all of the additions required; it adds each element to each other element twice and adds each element to itself once. As a result, each occurrence of a number inside the table represents a single common tone. The number 11 occurs four times, so there will be four common tones at $T_{11}I$; the number 3 occurs twice, so there will be two common tones at T_3I; and so on. It is easy to rearrange this information in the form of an index vector, or simply to read it directly from the table.

This addition table has another advantage—it shows not only how many tones will be held in common under T_nI, but also which ones. Each index number in the table lies at the intersection of two tones. Those are the tones mapped onto one another by that index number. In the table in Figure 3–7, for example, 10 occurs at the intersection of 3 and 7; 3 and 7 are thus held in common at $T_{10}I$. Similarly, 8 occurs in the table at the intersection of 4 with itself, so 4 will be held in common at T_8I.

Appendix 2 lists index vectors for the prime-form of each set class and for the set related by T_0I to the prime form. Unlike the interval vector, the index vector is not the same for every member of a set class. Fortunately, once you know the index vector for the prime form and for its T_0I, the index vectors for all the remaining members can be deduced easily from the simple rules given in Appendix 2. The interval-class vectors in Appendix 1 and the index vectors in Appendix 2 should enable you to find the number of common tones any pitch-class set will retain under T_n or T_nI for any values of n.

Common tones under T_n and T_nI can be an important source of musical continuity. Example 3–3 contains the first ten measures of the third of Webern's *Movements for String Quartet*, Op. 5, a composition that makes intensive use of set class 3–3 (014).

Six pairs of 3–3s are marked on the score. Look first at the T_n–related pairs. The transposition levels used, 8 and 11, produce one common tone each, as we know from the interval-class vector of 3–3: 101100. And notice the special treatment this common tone receives in each case—it is always retained in exactly the same register. The common pitch class is expressed as a common pitch.

The same thing is true of the T_nI-related pair in measure 3. The index vector for the first set, [8,9,0], is 100012102200; the index vector for the second set, [0,3,4], is 100220121000. You could discover that either by simply doing an addition table for the sets, as discussed earlier, or by looking up the vectors in Appendix 2 (and performing the proper rotations). Both index vectors show that each of these sets holds one common tone at T_0I. Since they are related by T_0I, that means they will share a single pitch class. That common tone is C, which is retained here not only in the same register but in the same instrument. In measure 9, the two T_3I-related forms of 3–3 share two common tones, C and E♭. Notice how Webern arranges these notes to sound together simultaneously. He thus uses common tones under both T_n and T_nI to create smooth, continuous voice leading as the music progresses among the members of set class 3–3 (014).

Inversional Symmetry

Some set classes contain sets that can map entirely onto themselves under inversion. Such set classes are said to be *inversionally symmetrical* and, of the 220 set classes listed in Appendix 1, seventy-nine have this property. The index vector for a set with this property will have an entry equal to the number of notes in the set.

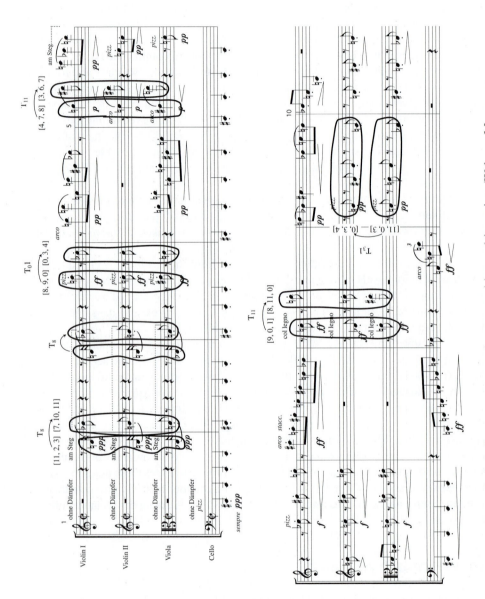

Example 3–3 Common tones under transposition and inversion (Webern, Movements for String Quartet, Op. 5, No. 3).

Sets that are inversionally symmetrical can be written so that the intervals reading from left to right are the same as the intervals reading from right to left. Usually, but not always, this intervallic palindrome will be apparent when the set is written in normal form. Occasionally, a note has to be written twice to capture the modular wraparound (see Figure 3–8).

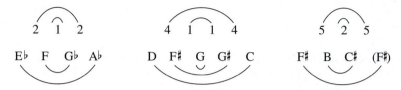

Figure 3–8 Three sets written to display their inversional symmetry.

The sense of inversionally symmetrical sets as their own mirror image is even more apparent when they are written around a pitch-class clockface (see Figure 3–9).

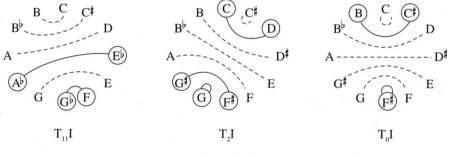

Figure 3–9

In inversionally symmetrical sets, all the notes in the set are mapped either onto other notes in the set or onto themselves under some T_nI. Every note in the set has an inversional partner also in the set.

Schoenberg's Orchestra Piece Op. 16, No. 3 begins with the five note chord displayed around a pitch-class clockface in Example 3–4A (the musical score can be found back in Example 2–3). The symmetry of the chord should be apparent—each note of the chord has an inversional partner also within the chord, and the E balances itself as a center of symmetry. It would be easy to write such a chord so as to realize its symmetry in pitch space: the three chords in Example 3–4B arrange those five pitch classes so that they describe the same pitch intervals reading from bottom to top as they do from top to bottom. These three chords are *pitch symmetrical*—they are symmetrical in register and their pitch intervals form a palindrome. Any symmetrical pitch-class set can be arranged symmetrically in pitch space. But that is not what Schoenberg did. His actual chord, shown in Example 3–4C, is *pitch-class*

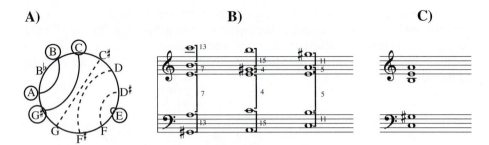

Example 3–4 Inversional symmetry: A) Schoenberg's chord written on a pitch-class clockface; B) three hypothetical pitch symmetrical arrangements; C) Schoenberg's actual arrangement—symmetry of pitch class, not pitch.

symmetrical, but not pitch symmetrical. The inversional symmetry is still there—every note in the chord has its inversional partner also in the chord—but it is felt only in the more abstract pitch-class space, not in the more concrete, immediate pitch space.

The melody by Boulez in Example 3–5 is based entirely on sets that are inversionally symmetrical.

Example 3–5 Inversionally symmetrical sets (Boulez, *Le Marteau sans Maître,* "L'Artisanat furieux," mm. 6–9, vocal part).

Some of these are arranged pitch-symmetrically, but most are not. Compare, for example, the two forms of sc4–3 (0134): [A, B♭, C, C♯] at the beginning of the melody and [C♯, D, E, F] at the end. The first one is asymmetrical in pitch space (the B♭ would have had to be an octave lower to make it pitch symmetrical), while the second is pitch symmetrical—its pitch intervals are the same reading from bottom to top as from top to bottom.

While inversional symmetry is an important compositional resource generally, it can play a particularly decisive role when the symmetry is realized in pitch space. Any member of set class 3–1 (012), for example, is abstractly symmetrical no matter how it is deployed, but its symmetry can be dramatically reinforced by the arrangement of the notes in register. See, for example, how Varèse arranges the set [C, C♯, D] at the beginning of *Hyperprism* (Example 3–6).

Example 3–6 Pitch symmetry (Varèse, *Hyperprism,* mm. 1–12, percussion parts omitted).

C♯ enters in a middle register in the tenor trombone, soon reinforced by horns. At the end of measure 4, D comes in twenty-three semitones below and then, in measure 12, the low D is balanced symmetrically by the high C, 23 semitones above the middle C♯. A vast pitch space is articulated symmetrically, a,nd the symmetry is reinforced by the grace notes in measure 4 (involving the F four semitones above C♯) and the quick embellishment in measure 11 (involving the A four semitones below C♯). In this passage, C♯ is literally the central tone. The role of inversional symmetry in establishing a sense of pitch centricity is a topic to which we will return in Chapter 4.

Like set classes that are transpositionally symmetrical, those that are inversionally symmetrical can be easily identified in Appendix 1. In the middle column, the number after the comma measures the degree of inversional symmetry—it tells the number of inversional levels that map a set onto itself. Many sets cannot map onto themselves under inversion, and thus have a degree of inversional symmetry that is 0. Some sets can map onto themselves at one or more than one inversion levels. The set 3–6 (024), for example, has a degree of symmetry of (1, 1). It maps onto itself at one transpositional level (T_0) and one inversional level (in this case, T_4I). The most symmetrical set of all is the whole-tone scale; it maps onto itself at six transpositional and six inversional levels.

Inversional symmetry is a reasonably common property, but inversional symmetry at more than one level is rare—only the eleven set classes listed in Figure 3–10 have that property.

	Degree of inversional symmetry	
3–12 (048)	3	9–12 (01245689T)
4–9 (0167)	2	8–9 (01236789)
4–25 (0268)	2	8–25 (0124678T)
4–28 (0369)	4	8–28 (0134679T)
6–7 (012678)	2	
6–20 (014589)	3	
6–35 (02468T)	6	

Figure 3–10

It is interesting to compare this list with the list of transpositionally symmetrical sets in Figure 3–3. Virtually all of the set classes that are transpositionally symmetrical are also inversionally symmetrical at more than one level (6–30 is the only exception), and every set class that is inversionally symmetrical at more than one level is also transpositionally symmetrical. And, as noted earlier, set classes with one or both of these properties have often proven attractive to composers, including the augmented triad (3–12), the diminished seventh chord (4–28), and the hexatonic (6–20), whole-tone (6–35), and octatonic (8–28) scales.

The greater the number of operations that map a set onto itself, the smaller the number of distinct sets in the set class. Most set classes have a degree of symmetry of (1,0) and contain twenty-four distinct sets. For all set classes, dividing the number of self-mapping operations into twenty-four will give you the number of sets in the set class. Let's use the prime-form of set 4–9 (0167) as an example to see why this is so. The set-class 4–9 has a degree of symmetry of (2,2). The four operations that map it onto itself are T_0, T_6, T_1I, and T_7I. (This can be figured out by looking at the interval-class and index vectors.) Now consider another member of this set class, [1,2,7,8]. This is simultaneously T_1, T_7, T_2I, and T_8I of [0,1,6,7]. Each member of the set class can be created by four different operations:

[0,1,6,7]	T_0, T_6, T_1I, T_7I
[1,2,7,8]	T_1, T_7, T_2I, T_8I
[2,3,8,9]	T_2, T_8, T_3I, T_9I
[3,4,9,10]	T_3, T_9, T_4I, $T_{10}I$
[4,5,10,11]	T_4, T_{10}, T_5I, $T_{11}I$
[5,6,11,0]	T_5, T_{11}, T_6I, T_0I

But there are only twenty-four possible operations in all—twelve values of n for T_n, and twelve values of n for T_nI. As a result, twenty-four divided by the number of operations that will produce each member of the set class equals the number of distinct members of the set class. In this case, twenty-four divided by four equals six, and set-class 4–9 has only six members.

Z-Relation

Any two sets related by transposition or inversion must have the same interval-class content. The converse, however, is not true. There are several pairs of sets (one pair of tetrachords and octachords, three pairs of pentachords and septachords, and fifteen pairs of hexachords) that have the same interval-class content, but are *not* related to each other by either transposition or inversion and thus are *not* members of the same set class. Sets that have the same interval content but are not transpositions or inversions of each other are called *Z-related sets,* and the relationship between them is the *Z-relation.* (The Z stands for "zygotic," meaning "twinned.")

Sets in the Z-relation will sound similar because they have the same interval-class content, but they won't be as closely related to each other as sets that are members of the same set class. If the members of a set class are like siblings within a tightly knit nuclear family, then Z-related sets are like first cousins.

Composers have been particularly interested in the two "all-interval" tetrachords: 4–Z15 (0146) and 4–Z29 (0137). They are called all-interval tetrachords because, as suggested by their shared interval-class vector, 111111, both tetrachords contain one occurrence of each of the six interval classes. Example 3–7 contains two passages from Elliott Carter's String Quartet No. 2. In the first passage (Example 3–7A), the second violin plays two 3s (E–G and F–A♭) while the viola plays two 6s (C–F♯ and E♭–A)—in this quartet Carter often differentiates instruments in this way by assigning each a distinctive interval. The vertical combination of those intervals produces either 4–Z15 or 4–Z29. In the second passage (Example 3–7B), a form of 4–Z15 is stated melodically in the second violin while the other three instruments combine to create a form of 4–Z29.

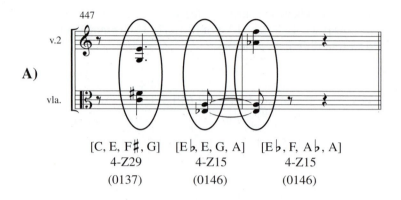

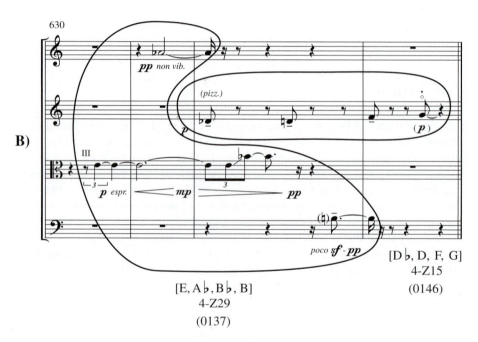

Example 3–7 The Z-relation (Carter, String Quartet No. 2).

In Example 3–8, the familiar beginning of the first of Schoenberg's Piano Pieces, Op. 11, the Z-relation creates a strong connection between the opening six-note melody and the left-hand accompanimental figure that follows.

Any set with a Z in its name has a *Z-correspondent,* another set with a different prime form but the same interval vector. On the set list in Appendix 1, the Z-related hexachords are listed across from one another, but you will have to look through the list for the Z-related sets of other sizes.

Example 3–8 The Z-relation (Schoenberg, Piano Piece, Op. 11, No. 1).

Complement Relation

For any set, the pitch classes it excludes constitute its *complement.* The complement of the set [3,6,7], for example, is [8,9,10,11,0,1,2,4,5]. Any set and its complement, taken together, will contain all twelve pitch classes. For any set containing n elements, its complement will contain 12 – n elements.

There is an important intervallic similarity between a set and its complement. You might think that whatever intervals a set has lots of, its complement will have few of, and vice versa. It turns out, however, that a set and its complement always have a proportional distribution of intervals. For complementary sets, the difference in the number of occurrences of each interval is equal to the difference between the size of the sets (except for the tritone, in which case the former will be half the latter). If a tetrachord has the interval-class vector 021030, its eight-note complement will have the vector 465472. The eight-note set has four more of everything (except for the tritone, of which it has two more). The larger set is like an expanded version of its smaller complement.

Because interval content is not changed by transposition or inversion, this intervallic relationship remains in force even when the sets are transposed or inverted. Thus, even if the sets are not *literally complementary* (i.e., one contains the notes excluded by the other), the intervallic relationship still holds so long as the sets are *abstractly complementary* (i.e., members of complement-related set classes). For example, [0,1,2] and [0,1,2,3,4,5,6,7,8] are not literal complements of each other. In fact, all the members of the first set are contained in the second. However, they are members of complement-related set classes and thus have a similar distribution of intervals. Complement-related sets do not have as much in common as transpositionally or inversionally related sets, but they do have a similar sound because of the similarity of their interval content.

The affinity of complement-related set classes extends beyond their intervallic content. Complement-related set classes always have the same degree of symmetry and thus the same number of sets in the class. If set X is Z-related to set Y, then the complement of X will be Z-related to the complement of Y. There are the same number of trichord- and nonachord-classes (12), of tetrachord- and octachord-classes

(29), and of pentachord- and septachord-classes (38) (hexachords will be discussed later). In each of these ways, sets and set classes resemble their complements.

The complement relation is particularly important in any music in which the twelve pitch classes are circulating relatively freely and in which the aggregate (a collection containing all twelve pitch classes) is an important structural unit. Consider the relatively common situation at the beginning of Schoenberg's String Quartet No. 3, where a melody (here divided between first violin and cello) is accompanied by an ostinato that contains all the pitch classes excluded by the melody (Example 3–9).

Example 3–9 Complementary sets in melody and accompaniment (Schoenberg, String Quartet No. 3).

The melody and the accompaniment have a similar sound because they contain a similar distribution of intervals.

   The final four-note chord of the second of Schoenberg's Little Piano Pieces, Op. 19, is a form of 4–19 (0148), a set prominent throughout that piece and common in much of Schoenberg's music (Example 3–10).

Example 3–10 The complement relation (Schoenberg, Little Piano Piece, Op. 19, No. 2).

The last eight notes of the piece (which, of course, include that final four-note chord) are a form of 8–19 (01245689), the complementary set class. Compare the interval-class vectors of these two sets: the vector for 4–19 is 101310 and the vector for 8–19 is 545752. Both sets are particularly rich in interval class 4. In fact, no four- or eight-note set contains more 4s than these do. And notice how prominently the 4s are featured in the music. Because of the complement relation, the final four-note chord sounds similar to the larger eight-note collection of which it is a part.

   The list of sets in Appendix 1 is arranged to make it easy to see the complement relation. Complementary set classes are always listed right across from one another. If you look up 4–19 (0148) and 8–19 (01245689), you will see that this is so. As a further aid, the names of complementary sets always have the same number following the dash. Thus, 4–19 and 8–19 are complements of each other, as are 3–6 and 9–6, 5-Z12 and 7-Z12, and so on. These features of the list make it very easy to look up large sets. Say you have a nine-note set that you want to find on the list. You could put it in prime-form and look it up, but that would be a time-consuming operation since the set is so big. It is far easier to take the three notes *excluded* by the nine-note set and put them in the prime-form, then look up that trichord on the list—the prime-form of the original nine-note set will be directly across from it.

   You may notice that there are some sets, exclusively hexachords, that have nothing written across from them. Hexachords like that are *self-complementary*—they and their complements are members of the same set class. For a simple example, consider the hexachord [2,3,4,5,6,7]. Its complement is [8,9,10,11,0,1]. But both of these sets are members of set class 6–1 (012345). In other words, self-complementary hexachords are those that can map onto their complements under either T_n or T_nI.

   If a hexachord is not self-complementary, then it must be Z-related to its complement. Remember that, with complementary sets, the difference in the number of occurrences of any interval is equal to the difference in the size of the two sets. But a hexachord is exactly the same size as its complement. As a result, a hexachord always has exactly the same interval content as its complement. If it is also related to its complement by T_n or T_nI, then it is self-complementary. If not, then it is Z-related to its complement. The hexachords on the list are thus either written with nothing across from them or they are written across from their Z-correspondents. This inter-vallic relationship between complementary hexachords is extremely important for twelve-tone music, and we will discuss it further in subsequent chapters.

Subset and Superset Relations

If set X is included in set Y, then X is a subset of Y and Y is a superset of X. A set of n elements will contain 2^n (2 to the nth power) subsets. A five-note set, for example, will contain the following subsets: the null set (a set containing no elements), five one-note sets, ten two-note sets (these are also called intervals), ten three-note sets, five four-note sets, and one five-note set (the original set itself). That makes a total of 2^5 (2 to the 5th power) or thirty-two subsets. The null set, the one-note sets, and the set itself will usually not be of particular interest as subsets. Even so, that still leaves lots of subsets to be considered ($2^n - (n + 2)$), and naturally, the bigger the set the more numerous the subsets.

     In order not to be overwhelmed by the possibilities, there are two things to bear in mind. First, some of the subsets may be members of the same set class. Consider set class 4–25 (0268), for example, which is something of an extreme case. As Figure 3–11 shows, all of its three-note subsets are members of the same set class, 3–8 (026).

The set	Its subsets	Their set-names and prime forms
	[2,6,8]	3–8 (026)
4–25 (0268)	[6,8,0]	3–8 (026)
	[8,0,2]	3–8 (026)
	[0,2,6]	3–8 (026)

Figure 3–11

Most set classes are not as restricted in their subset content as this one, but there is often some redundancy.

     To get a complete picture of the subset content of a set, it may be useful to con-struct an *inclusion lattice,* which lists all of the subsets of a given set as well as the subsets of those subsets. Figure 3–12 contains an inclusion lattice for set-class 6–20

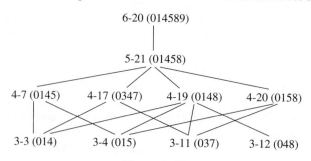

Figure 3–12

(014589), a set class also known as the hexatonic collection (to be discussed in Chapter 4). All six of the five-note subsets of 6–20 are members of set-class 5–21. The five four-note subsets of 5–21 in turn represent four different tetrachord classes, and these contain certain trichord classes as their subsets.

The final six-note chord of Schoenberg's Op. 19, No. 2 (discussed earlier with reference to Example 3–10), is a member of set-class 6–20—see Example 3–11. Schoenberg has arranged the chord so that its highest and lowest four notes represent set-class 4–19 and its highest and lowest three notes are augmented triads (set-class 3–12). Comparing the music in Example 3–11 with the inclusion lattice in Figure 3–12 gives a sense of what Schoenberg did in relation to what he might have done.

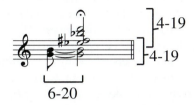

Example 3–11 Set-class 6-20 (014589) arranged to project two forms of set-class 4-19 (0148) as registral subsets (Schoenberg, *Little Piano Piece,* Op. 19, No. 2).

That brings us to the second important limitation on the otherwise vast world of subsets and supersets: only a small number will be musically significant in any specific musical context. Like any six-note set, the final sonority of Schoenberg's Little Piano Piece contains many subsets, but only a small number of those can be heard as meaningful musical groupings, identified by shared register or articulation. For example, it makes no musical sense to combine the G in the middle register with the top three notes—F♯, B♭, D—even though that combination creates another form of set class 4–19 (0148). Those four notes simply don't belong together musically. With the same final six-note sonority, Schoenberg could have grouped G, F♯, B♭, and D together, but chose not to. Similarly, he could have revoiced the sonority to emphasize subsets that were members of set classes other than 4–19, but again he chose not to. The subsets of a set are a kind of abstract musical potential; the composer chooses which to emphasize and which to repress.

As with the complement relation, the subset/superset relation can be either literal or abstract. Set X is a literal subset of Set Y if all of the notes of X are contained in Y. Set X is the abstract subset of Set Y if any transposed or inverted form of X is contained in Y, that is, if any member the set class that contains X is found among the subsets of Y. [E, F, G] is the literal subset of [C♯, D, E, F, G]. The T_5 transposition of [E, F, G], [A, B♭, C], is not a literal subset of [C♯, D, E, F, G]. But the set-class that contains it, 3–2 (013), can be found among the literal subsets of [C♯, D, E, F, G]— both [C♯, D, E] and [E, F, G] represent it. So [A, B♭, C] is an abstract, not a literal, subset of [C♯, D, E, F, G]. In the same abstract sense, we would say that set-class 3–2 is a subset of set-class 5–10.

In both the literal and abstract senses, these "inclusion" relations are not as strong as many of the relationships discussed earlier, like the Z-relation or the complement relation, but can still be musically interesting. Smaller collections can frequently be heard combining into larger ones and larger collections dividing into smaller ones.

Transpositional Combination

The process of combining smaller sets to form larger ones and dividing larger sets into smaller ones is particularly interesting when the smaller sets are related by inversion or transposition. We have already discussed inversional symmetry. Any time you combine two sets related by inversion, you get a set that is inversionally symmetrical. Conversely, any inversionally symmetrical set can be divided into at least one pair of inversionally related subsets. *Transpositional combination* (TC) is the combination of a set with one or more transpositions of itself to create a larger set. The larger set, which can then be divided into two or more subsets related by transposition, is said to have the TC property, and sets with this property have often proven of interest to composers.

In Example 3–12, from Stravinsky's *Symphony of Psalms,* the bass part (cellos and contrabasses) begins with ip3, F–A♭.

Example 3–12 Transpositional combination (Stravinsky, *Symphony of Psalms,* first movement).

Another ip3, E–G, follows immediately a semitone lower. That combination of two 3s a semitone apart is written 3*1, where the asterisk stands for "transposed by." One also could think of the figure as two semitones (E–F and G–A♭) related at T_3, or 1*3. Either way, that combination of 1 and 3 produces a form of sc4–3 (0134). The same combination produces a different member of the same set class, [B♭, B, C♯, D] in the alto voice (oboes and english horn). These two tetrachords, created by transpositional combination, are themselves combined at T_6 to create an eight-note set. We can summarize the process as: (3*1) * 6. In other words, a 3 is transposed by 1, and the resulting tetrachord is transposed at T_6. The passage can thus be built up from its smallest components through transpositional combination.

Contour Relations

Throughout this book thus far we have focused on pitches, pitch classes, and their intervals. We have explored ways that lines and sets of pitches and pitch classes can move through and be related in pitch-space and pitch-class space. And the relationships have been, in some cases, quite abstract. As listeners, we may sometimes find it easier to attend to the general shapes of music, its motions up and down, higher and lower. These are aspects of musical *contour*. To make sense of musical contour, we do not need to know the exact notes and intervals; we only need to know which notes are higher and which are lower.

Compare three four-note fragments from a melody from Crawford's String Quartet (see Example 3–13).

Example 3–13 A recurring contour-segment (CSEG) (Crawford, String Quartet, first movement, mm. 6–7).

The fragments are intervallically distinct, and represent three different set classes. But their contours are the same. Each begins on its second-highest note, continues with its lowest and its second-lowest notes, and concludes on its highest note. In Example 3–13, that contour is represented as a string of numbers enclosed within angle-brackets: <2013>. The notes in each fragment are assigned a number based on their relative position in the fragment. 0 is assigned to the lowest note, 1 to the next-lowest, and so on. The highest note will always have a numerical value that is 1 less than the number of different notes in the fragment. The numbers are then arranged, in order, to describe the musical contour. <2013> is a *contour segment*, or *CSEG*, and this intervallically varied melody is unified, in part, by three presentations of that single CSEG.

At the end of the movement, the second violin has a varied version of the same melody (see Example 3–14).

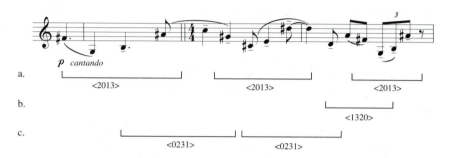

Example 3–14 Members of a CSEG-class (Crawford, String Quartet, first movement, mm. 72–75).

The notes are different, but the same CSEG, <2013> is represented three times (Example 3–14a). The CSEG created by the four notes beginning on D is <1320> (Example 3–14b). <2013> and <1320> are related by inversion. The highest note in one is replaced by the lowest note in the other, the second-highest by the second-lowest, and so on. They are mirror images of each other. And just as when we compare two lines of pitch classes, the numbers in the corresponding order positions always add up to the same sum, in this case 3. One additional CSEG, <0231>, occurs twice (Example 3–14c). <0231> and <1320> are retrograde-related—each is the same as the other written backwards. Similarly, <0231> and <2013> are related by retrograde-inversion—each is the inverted and backwards version of the other.

Like pitch-class sets, CSEGs can be gathered into CSEG-classes. CSEGs related by inversion, retrograde, or retrograde-inversion belong to the same CSEG-class. The three CSEGs of Example 3–14, and one more that is not shown, <3102>, are the four members of a single CSEG-class. Crawford's violin melody seems to be interested in the reshaping of this basic shape. Of the four members of this CSEG-class, we select the one that begins on the lowest note to act as prime form. Crawford's melodic fragments all belong to the CSEG-class with prime-form <0231>.

The CSEG-classes for CSEGs of three and four notes are listed in Figure 3–13 (the CSEG-classes proliferate rapidly after that). Approaching contour in this way permits us to discuss musical shapes and gestures with clarity, but without having to rely on more difficult discriminations of pitches, pitch-classes, and their intervals. Contour can be particularly revealing, however, when studied in relationship to pitch and pitch class. There, it becomes possible to discuss similarities of shape in the presentation of different set classes and, conversely, the divergent shapes given to members of the same set class.

Contour can also be useful in talking about musical elements other than pitch. In Example 3–15, a measure from a piano piece by Stockhausen, the right-hand melody (D7–C♯6–C5–G5) and its dynamics (fff–ff–pp–p) can both be understood as expressing CSEG <3201>. Just as the pitches move from highest to second-highest

Name	Prime-form
3–1	<012>
3–2	<021>
4–1	<0123>
4–2	<0132>
4–3	<0213>
4–4	<0231>
4–5	<0312>
4–6	<0321>
4–7	<1032>
4–8	<1302>

Figure 3–13

to lowest to second-lowest, the dynamics move from loudest to second-loudest to softest to second-softest. The pitch contour and the dynamic contour are the same.

Example 3–15 Same contour, CSEG <3201>, expressed in both pitch and dynamics (Stockhausen, *Klavierstück* II, m. 14).

Contour can be particularly valuable as a way of talking about music that is indefinite as to pitch, like a lot of experimental music written since 1950. Example 3–16 shows the opening of Morton Feldman's *Projection No. 1 for Solo Cello*. The dotted lines function as barlines, and each measure contains four beats (at a tempo of beat = 72). Each square or rectangle indicates a musical event, and the duration of the event is shown by the length of the rectangles, which last for between one and five beats in this passage. There are three different timbres indicated (diamond = harmonics; P = pizzicato; A = arco) and, within each timbre, relative pitch is indicated by the vertical position of the square or rectangle. The first three pizzicato notes, for example, fall in a middle register, a low register, and then a high register—they thus describe CSEG <102>. Now consider the temporal distance between the pizzicato notes: four beats from the first note to the second; one beat from the second to the third; and eight beats from the third to the fourth. That durational contour also can be described by CSEG <102>: a medium duration followed by a short duration and then a long duration. Similar kinds of patterning can be found elsewhere in the piece, structuring the pitches and the durations both independently and in relation to each other.

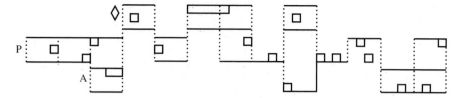

Example 3–16 Same contour, CSEG <102> expressed by both pitch and duration (Feldman, *Projection No. 1 for Solo Cello*).

A complete piece by John Cage is shown in Example 3–17. The piece consists of four events, indicated by dots, and these occur at the times indicated below the graphics—the first two events occur between thirty-six and sixty seconds after the beginning of the piece and the third and fourth events occur between 1:24 and 1:36. The first two events are to be played in some way that does not involve the piano (that is the meaning of the letter A, for "auxiliary sounds") while the last two events are to be played in the interior of a piano (I stands for "interior"). Beyond that, each of the four events is characterized by four qualities: (1) duration, measured by proximity to the dotted line labeled D; (2) dynamics, measured by position between the solid lines marked soft and loud; (3) pitch, measured by distance from the dotted line labeled F, which indicates the lowest frequencies; and (4) timbre, measured by distance from the line marked T, which indicates the fewest possible overtones. Within each of those four domains, the four events of the piece describe a particular contour:

Durations: <1230>   Dynamics: <1302>   Pitch: <3201>   Timbre <2031>

All are different, which may suggest the structural heterogeneity of this work, its resistance to analytical coherence. By contrast, the dynamic and timbre contours are inversions of each other, that is, the louder the note the least rich in overtones, and the richer in overtones the softer. That may suggest some degree of coordination among the dimensions. Either way, contour provides a useful vantage point for apprehending the piece.

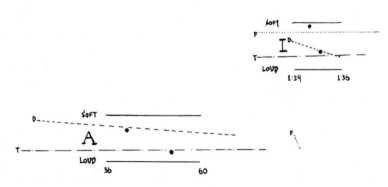

Example 3–17 Contours of duration, dynamics, pitch, and timbre (Cage, *For Paul Taylor and Anita Dencks*).

Composing-Out

To organize the larger musical spans and draw together notes that may be separated in time, composers of post-tonal music sometimes enlarge the motives of the musical surface and project them over significant musical distances. This musical procedure is sometimes called *composing-out*—we would say that a motive from the musical surface is *composed-out* at a deeper level of structure (other related terms are "enlargement," "concealed repetition," "motivic parallelism," "nesting," and "self-similarity").

Example 3–18 shows the first four vocal phrases of a song by Webern. The melody begins with four notes: D–D♭–E♭–G♭. The same notes, in the same order, are composed-out as the first notes of the four vocal phrases (Example 3–18A). A somewhat more subtle kind of composing-out involves the last four notes of the first phrase: F–A♭–E–B♭ (Example 3–18B). These return, reordered and transposed at T_6, in the last notes of the four vocal phrases. The boundary notes at the beginning and ends of phrases thus compose-out the notes and intervals of the musical surface.

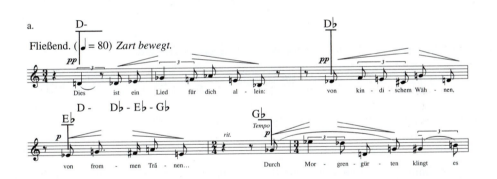

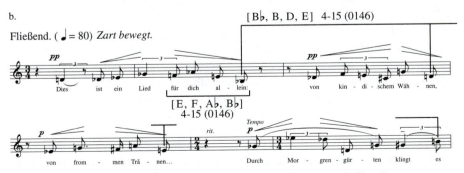

Example 3–18 Composing-out (Webern, Song, Op. 3, No. 1).

In the aria from Thea Musgrave's *Mary Queen of Scots* shown in Example 3–19, the accompaniment consists of a single chord, E♭–A–D, which is transposed downward and then back up to its starting point. The same three notes, although in different order and registral arrangement, are also stated as the long notes within the vocal line. Two additional statements of the same set class—3–5 (016)—may be found within the vocal line, and these are indicated in Example 3–19. In this way, the notes of a harmony are composed-out melodically over the span of an entire phrase.

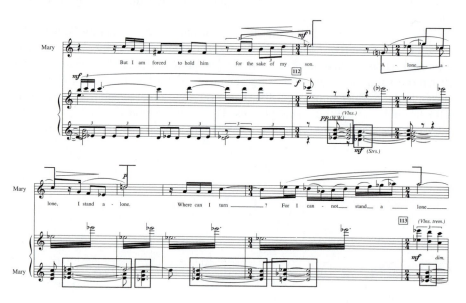

Example 3–19 Composing-out (Musgrave, *Mary, Queen of Scots,* excerpt from Act III).

Example 3–20 reproduces the first section of the first of Schoenberg's Piano Pieces, Op. 11, a passage we have already looked at several times. We noted previously the extent to which set class 3–3 (014) pervades the musical surface. Example 3–20 shows two large-scale statements of the same set class, one in the upper voice and one in the bass. As we observed in Chapter 2, the three melodic high points, B–G–G♯, constitute a large-scale statement of set class 3–3. These three pitches, widely separated in time, are associated by their shared register and contour position. Furthermore, these are the same three pitches with which the piece began.

A similar thing happens in the bass. The left-hand part begins with two chords (measures 2–3); the bass notes are G♭ and B♭. After contrasting material, two more chords are heard at the end of the section (measures 10–11); the bass notes now are G♭ and G. That final G completes a large-scale statement of another form of set class 3–3. These three pitches, G♭–B♭–G, are associated by their shared register and articu-

Example 3–20 Large-scale statements, in soprano and bass, of set class 3–3 (014) (Schoenberg, Piano Piece, Op. 11, No. 1).

lation. Like the large-scale melodic statement, this large-scale bass statement draws together and unifies this section of music.

Linear projections of this kind may extend over very large spans of music, including entire pieces. Stravinsky's ballet *Les Noces (The Wedding)* begins with the melody in Example 3–21a, which consists of [B, D, E] (the grace note F♯ is excluded). At the beginning of the third scene of the ballet, that set is transposed two semitones higher and repeated with extraordinary insistence (Example 3–21b). The ballet concludes with a protracted coda that consists of slow, obsessive repetitions of still another transposition of the original fragment, now five semitones below the original: [G♯, B, C♯] (Example 3–21c). The large-scale progression, one that spans the entire ballet, thus composes-out the intervallic shape of the original motive (Example 3–21d). Here is composing-out over a truly monumental span!

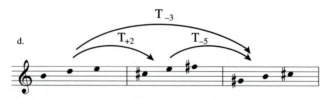

Example 3–21 Composing-out (Stravinsky, *Les Noces*).

Voice Leading

One useful way of describing the voice leading of post-tonal music involves attending to the pitch-class counterpoint created by transposition and inversion. As we have seen, transposition and inversion involve mapping notes from one set to the next. Those mappings can be understood to comprise post-tonal voices, which move through the musical texture.

In Example 3–22, from a song by Webern, the boxed chords are all members of set-class 3–5 (016).

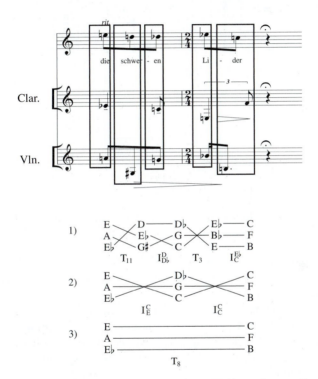

Example 3–22 Transformational voice leading (Webern, Songs, Op. 14, "Die Sonne," mm. 23–24).

The horizontal and diagonal lines trace the pitch-class mappings induced by the specified operations. Three voices move through the progression. One begins on E and moves down to the bottom of the third chord before returning to its original position in the highest register. The middle and lowest voices also move through the chords and return to their original position at the end. The second level of the analysis simplifies the five-chord progression into two inversional moves, each of which exchanges the vocal part with the lowest sounding part. Finally, the third level describes the progression as the transposition at T_8 (actually a pitch transposition down four semitones) of the first chord onto the last chord. At each level, the harmonies are bound together by the motions of the voices.

The passage in Example 3–23, from Webern's Movements for String Quartet, Op. 5, No. 3, consists of groups of two or three chords, all members of set-class 3–3 (014), interspersed with canonic interjections.

Example 3–23 Transformational voice leading (Webern, Movements for String Quartet, Op. 5, No. 3, mm. 1–8).

The instrumentation and registration of the chords reflects their voice leading to a remarkable degree, exclusively so in the first violin, and one with one brief voice crossing in the second violin and viola.

The second level of the analysis isolates one chord from each group of chords: the first chord from the first group and the last chord in each group thereafter. The intervals of transposition—T_1, T_3, and T_4—are the same as the intervals contained within set-class 3–3 (014), which is the chord being transposed. The voice leading thus follows a motivic path.

Another movement from the same piece also involves a progression of chords in the upper three instruments (see Example 3–24). These six chords represent three different set classes: the first and second chords are related by transposition, as are the third, fourth, and fifth chords. The analytical problem is to connect the second chord to the third and the fifth chord to the sixth. In a situation like this, it may be useful to imagine that the chords are almost-but-not-quite related by transposition (or inversion). In the progression from the second chord to the third, we can describe the relationship as a quasi-T_2 or a *fuzzy*-T_2: three of the voices deviate from T_2, but they do so as little as possible, by only a semitone each (Example 3–24a). In moving from the fifth chord to the sixth, the deviation from an actual transposition is even smaller—only one voice is off, and it's off by only one semitone. Transpositions (or

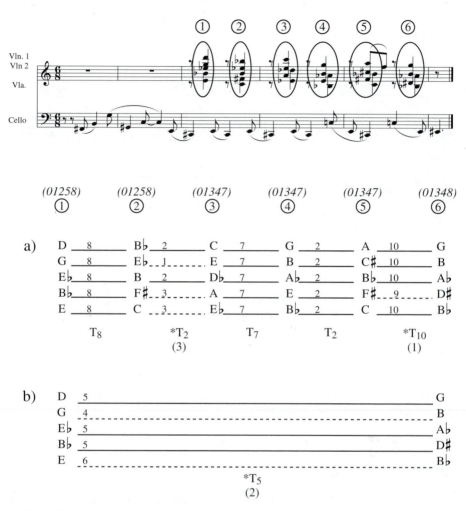

Example 3–24 Transformational voice leading, with fuzzy transposition (Webern, Movements for String Quartet, Op. 5, No. 5).

inversions) that are a bit off are designated with an asterisk and the amount of the deviation, known as the *offset,* is indicated in parentheses. In the voice leading, actual mappings are shown with a solid line, fuzzy mappings with a dotted line.

In this passage, the individual transpositional moves combine to create a single, larger transpositional move: from the first chord to the last is a fuzzy-transposition at $*T_5$, with an extremely small offset of only two semitones (Example 3–24b). The progression as a whole, embracing members of three different set classes, can thus be heard as a single, unified gesture, with clear, parallel voice leading.

Of course, the voice leading does not have to be parallel. In the passage shown in Example 3–25, there are five chords representing four different set classes. The fuzzy transpositions and inversions that connect the chords produce a voice leading in which the voices cross.

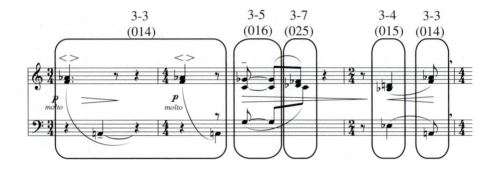

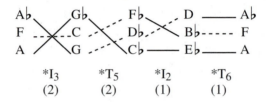

Example 3–25 Transformational voice leading, with fuzzy transposition and inversion (Sessions, Piano Sonata, first movement).

Atonal Pitch Space

In discussing voice leading, we were talking about actual sets of pitch classes and the ways in which individual notes in one set move onto individual notes in another. It is also possible to talk more abstractly about the voice leading between and among set classes. Given a set belonging to one set class, we might ask how much semitonal adjustment would be necessary to turn it into a member of a different set class.

As an example, take the trichord [G, A, B], a member of sc(024). Let's see what happens if we adjust each of its notes, in turn, either up or down by semitone. We would get six different trichords representing three different set classes:

$$
\begin{array}{l}
[\text{G}\sharp, \text{A}, \text{B}] = (013) \\
[\text{F}\sharp, \text{A}, \text{B}] = (025) \\
[\text{G}, \text{A}\flat, \text{B}] = (014) \\
[\text{G}, \text{B}\flat, \text{B}] = (014) \\
[\text{G}, \text{A}, \text{B}\flat] = (013) \\
[\text{G}, \text{A}, \text{C}] = (025)
\end{array}
$$

In general terms, we can say that sc(024) is offset by a distance of only one voice-leading semitone from sc(013), sc(014), and sc(025). If we applied the same procedure to all of the trichord-classes, we would end up with a map like the one in Example 3–26.

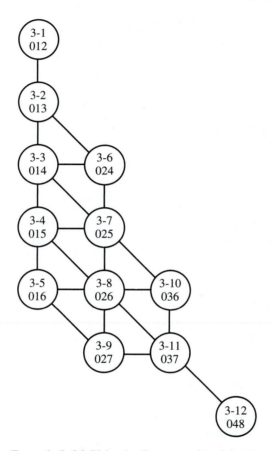

Example 3–26 Voice-leading space for trichords.

In this *voice-leading space,* the trichords are shown in relative proximity to each other. The closer two trichords are on the map, the less semitonal distance there is between them. Each line on the map represents one semitone of offset (that is, one semitone of voice-leading adjustment or voice-leading distance), and the distances accumulate in a consistent way. From (012), one semitone of offset will take you to (013), two semitones of offset will take you to (014) or (024), three semitones of offset will take you to (015) or (025), and so on, up to the maximum of six semitones of offset between (012) and (048).

As the size of the sets increases, it becomes harder to represent the space on a two-dimensional page. But the trichordal map in Example 3–26 suggests the possibility of understanding a passage of music as a journey through a voice leading space defined by semitonal offset—sometimes the moves will be to nearby destinations, involving only a small amount of adjustment; other times the music may make large harmonic leaps.

BIBLIOGRAPHY

Common tones under transposition and inversion are discussed in Forte, *The Structure of Atonal Music,* pp. 29–46, and Rahn, *Basic Atonal Theory,* pp. 97–115. Robert Morris has demonstrated the use of addition tables to discuss common tones under inversion in his review of Rahn's book in *Music Theory Spectrum* 4 (1982), pp. 138–55, and again in his own *Composition with Pitch Classes.* For a more general discussion of matrices of this kind, see Bo Alphonce, *The Invariance Matrix* (Ph.D. dissertation, Yale University, 1974).

Inversional symmetry has been a central theme in the work of David Lewin. See, for example, his "Inversional Balance as an Organizing Force in Schoenberg's Music and Thought," *Perspectives of New Music* 6/2 (1968), pp. 1–21; "A Label-Free Development for 12-Pitch-Class Systems," *Journal of Music Theory* 21/1 (1977), pp. 29–48; and "Transformational Techniques in Atonal and Other Music Theories," *Perspectives of New Music* 21 (1982–83), pp. 312–71.

The Z-relationship was first described by David Lewin in "The Intervallic Content of a Collection of Notes," *Journal of Music Theory* 4 (1960), pp. 98–101. The use of the label "Z" to refer to this relationship is a coinage of Allen Forte's (see *The Structure of Atonal Music,* pp. 21–24).

The intervallic relationship of complementary sets was first discovered by Milton Babbitt with regard to hexachords. Generalizing this relationship to sets of other sizes was the work of Babbitt and Lewin (see Lewin's "The Intervallic Content of a Collection of Notes"). Babbitt discusses the development of his theorem about hexachords and its subsequent generalization in *Milton Babbitt: Words About Music,* ed. Stephen Dembski and Joseph N. Straus (Madison: University of Wisconsin Press, 1987), pp. 104–6.

Subset and superset relations are discussed in Forte, *The Structure of Atonal Music,* pp. 24–29, and Rahn, *Basic Atonal Theory,* pp. 115–17.

The term "transpositional combination" and its theoretical development are the work of Richard Cohn. See his "Inversional Symmetry and Transpositional Combination in Bartók," *Music Theory Spectrum* 10 (1988), pp. 19–42.

My discussion of contour is based on Robert Morris, *Composition with Pitch Classes* (New Haven: Yale University Press, 1987), pp. 26–33, and "New Directions in the

Theory and Analysis of Musical Contour," *Music Theory Spectrum* 15/2 (1993), pp. 205–28; Michael Friedmann, "A Methodology for the Discussion of Contour: Its Application to Schoenberg's Music," *Journal of Music Theory* 29/2 (1985), pp. 223–48; Elizabeth West Marvin and Paul Laprade, "Relating Musical Contours: Extensions of a Theory for Contour," *Journal of Music Theory* 31/2 (1987), pp. 225–67 (see also in same issue, Michael Friedmann, "A Response: My Contour, Their Contour," pp. 268–74); and Elizabeth West Marvin, "The Perception of Rhythm in Non-Tonal Music: Rhythmic Contours in the Music of Edgard Varese," *Music Theory Spectrum* 13/1 (1991), pp. 61–78.

On composing-out in post-tonal music, see Allen Forte, "New Approaches to the Linear Analysis of Music," *Journal of the American Musicological Society* 41/2 (1988), pp. 315–48, and "Concepts of Linearity in Schoenberg's Atonal Music: A Study of the Opus 15 Song Cycle," *Journal of Music Theory* 36/2 (1992), pp. 285–382; Christopher Hasty, "On the Problem of Succession and Continuity in Twentieth-Century Music," *Music Theory Spectrum* 8 (1986), pp. 58–74; and Joseph N. Straus, "A Principle of Voice Leading in the Music of Stravinsky," *Music Theory Spectrum* 4 (1982), pp. 106–124. For a good general survey of this topic, see Brian Alegant and Donald McLean, "On the Nature of Enlargement," *Journal of Music Theory* 45/1 (2001), pp. 31–72.

Approaches to post-tonal voice leading include two articles by David Lewin: "Transformational Techniques in Atonal and Other Music Theories," *Perspectives of New Music* 21 (1982–83), pp. 312–71 and "Some Ideas about Voice Leading Between Pcsets," *Journal of Music Theory* 42/1 (1998), pp. 15–72, and three articles by Robert Morris: "Compositional Spaces and Other Territories," *Perspectives of New Music* 33/1–2 (1995), pp. 328–58; "Equivalence and Similarity in Pitch and Their Interaction with Pcset Theory," *Journal of Music Theory* 39/2 (1995), pp. 207–44; and "Voice-Leading Spaces," *Music Theory Spectrum* 20/2 (1998), pp. 175–208. See also Shaugn O'Donnell, "Transformational Voice Leading in Atonal Music" (Ph.D. dissertation, City University of New York, 1997); John Roeder, "A Theory of Voice Leading for Atonal Music" (Ph.D. dissertation, Yale University, 1984); "Harmonic Implications of Schoenberg's Observations of Atonal Voice Leading," *Journal of Music Theory* 33/1 (1989), pp. 27–62; "Voice Leading as Transformation," *Musical Transformation and Musical Intuition: Essays in Honor of David Lewin,* ed. Raphael Atlas and Michael Cherlin (Boston: Ovenbird Press, 1995), pp. 41–58; and Henry Klumpenhouwer, "A Generalized Model of Voice-Leading for Atonal Music" (Ph.D. dissertation, Harvard University, 1991). My own views are presented in "Voice Leading in Atonal Music," *Music Theory in Concept and Practice,* ed. James Baker, David Beach, and Jonathan Bernard (Rochester: University of Rochester Press, 1997), pp. 237–74, and "Uniformity, Balance, and Smoothness in Atonal Voice Leading," *Music Theory Spectrum* 25/2 (2003), pp. 305–52.

The term "atonal pitch space" is adapted from Fred Lerdahl, *Tonal Pitch Space* (Oxford: Oxford University Press, 2001), which also contains a discussion of post-tonal voice leading. See also Richard Cohn, "A Tetrahedral Graph of Tetrachordal Voice-Leading Space," *Music Theory Online* 9 (2003).

Exercises

THEORY

I.   Common tones under transposition (T_n): The number of pitch classes held in common when a set is transposed by interval n is equivalent to the number of occurrences of n in the set (except the tritone, where the number of common tones will be equivalent to 2n).

   1.   Using the set list (Appendix 1), find examples of the following:
        a. tetrachords that retain two common tones at T_2
        b. pentachords that retain four common tones at T_4
        c. hexachords that retain two common tones at T_6

   2.   For each of the following sets (given in normal form), determine the number of common tones at T_1, T_4, and T_6. Identify which tones will remain in common.
        a. [3,4,5]
        b. [1,3,7,9]
        c. [2,3,6,7,10,11]
        d. [1,5,7,8]

   3.   Some sets map onto themselves under T_n (are transpositionally symmetrical). Do any of the following sets have that capacity? At what interval(s) of transposition?
        a. [F,G,B,C♯]
        b. [B,C,D♯,G]
        c. [A,B♭,B,E♭,E,F]
        d. [C♯,F,A]

II.   Common tones under inversion (T_nI): The number of common tones under inversion depends on the number of times the sum n results from adding members of the set to each other (or to themselves).

   1.   Construct index vectors for the following sets (given in normal form):
        a. [4,5,7,8,0]
        b. [6,8,9,10,11,1]
        c. [1,3,7,8]
        d. [5,8,11,1]

   2.   For each of these sets, how many common tones will there be at T_2I? T_4I? T_6I? T_9I? Which tones will be held in common?

   3.   To find the index vector for any set, you must identify its relationship to the prime form of its set class, then perform the appropriate rotation on the index vector for the prime form (or T_0I of the prime form) given in Appendix 3. Use the index vectors in Appendix 3 to identify the number

of common tones retained by each of the following sets at T_0I, T_3I, T_4I, and $T_{10}I$.

   a. [4,8,9]
   b. [10,11,2,4]
   c. [0,2,3,6,9]
   d. [3,4,6,9,10,11]

4. Some sets map onto themselves under inversion (are inversionally symmetrical). Do any of the following sets have that capacity? At what indexes of inversion (T_nI)? First, write each set on a pitch-class clockface and inspect it. Then, confirm your impression by constructing an index vector or looking it up in Appendix 3.

   a. [A, B♭, B, C, C♯, D]
   b. [C♯, D, F, F♯, A, B♭]
   c. [G, A♭, D♭, D]
   d. [B, C, D, E, F, G, A]

III. Set-class membership: The number of sets in a set class is equal to 24 divided by the number of operations that will map the set onto itself. (**N.B.** All sets map onto themselves at least at T_0.)

1. Among the tetrachords, which set classes have fewer than 24 members? Which have fewer than twelve members? Among all set classes, which has the fewest members?

2. For each of the following set classes, specify the number of sets in the set class and the number of operations that will map the set onto itself.

   a. 3–6 (024)
   b. 4–9 (0167)
   c. 4–28 (0369)
   d. 6–7 (012678)

IV. Z-relation: Two sets that are not members of the same set class (are not related by transposition or inversion) but that have the same interval vector are Z-related.

1. Identify the Z-correspondent of the following set classes:

   a. 4–Z15 (0146)
   b. 5–Z37 (03458)
   c. 6–Z6 (012567)
   d. 6–Z44 (012569)

2. Identify the two Z-related sets that share each of the following interval vectors:

   a. 222121
   b. 111111
   c. 224322
   d. 433221

V.   Complement relation: For any set, the pitch classes it excludes constitute its complement. Sets that are not literally complementary may still be members of complement-related set classes.

1.   Complement-related set classes have proportionally related interval vectors. For each of the following set classes its interval vector is provided. Figure out the interval vector of the complementary set class without using the set list in Appendix 1.
a.   3–3 (014)   101100
b.   4–18 (0147)   102111
c.   8–27 (0124578T)   456553
d.   7–Z12 (0123479)   444342

2.   To find the prime form of a collection of more than six elements, take the complement of the collection, put it in prime form, and look it up in Appendix 1. The prime form of the original collection will be found directly across from it. Put the following collections in prime form:
a.   0, 1, 3, 4, 5, 6, 9, 10
b.   1, 2, 3, 4, 6, 8, 10, 11
c.   0, 1, 3, 5, 6, 8, 10
d.   0, 1, 2, 4, 5, 6, 7, 9, 11

VI. Subsets: If set class X is included in set class Y, then X is a subset of Y and Y is a superset of X.

1.   For each of the sets below, extract all of its subsets, put them in normal form, and identify the set class to which each belongs.
a.   [0,1,6,7]
b.   [0,1,4,8]
c.   [0,1,3,6,9]
d.   [0,2,4,7,9]

2.   Answer these questions about some familiar large collections:
a.   How many major or minor triads, 3–11 (037) are contained in the octatonic collection, 8–28 (0134679T)?
b.   Of which trichord does the major scale contain the most occurrences? Of which tetrachord?
c.   The three-note subsets of the whole-tone collection, 6–35 (02468T), are members of how many different set classes?

VII. Transpositional Combination: Sets that can be divided into two or more subsets related by transposition have the property of transpositional combination.

1.   Combine each of the sets below with a transposition of itself to create a larger set. By changing the transposition level you can create different

larger sets. How many different larger sets can you create? Give their name and prime-form.

 a. [C, D, F]
 b. [E, F, G, A♭]
 c. [F, A, C]

2. All of the following sets have the TC-property. Divide them into their transpositionally related subsets. (**N.B.** There may be more than one way to do this.)

 a. [B, C, E, G]
 b. [E, F, G, A♭]
 c. [G, A♭, B♭, D♭, D, E]

VIII. Contour: Contours can be described with CSEGs, ordered series of numbers where 0 indicates the lowest note, 1 the next-lowest, and so on. CSEGs can be grouped into CSEG-classes based on the operations of inversion, retrograde, and retrograde-inversion.

1. Write five musical realizations of each of the following CSEGs.

 a. <1032>
 b. <120>
 c. <1010123>

2. Identify the prime form and the remaining members of the CSEG-class for each of the following CSEGs.

 a. <1230>
 b. <3021>
 c. <120>
 d. <2301>

3. For the following melody (from Crawford, *Diaphonic Suite No. 1*, second movement), identify the CSEG and CSEG-class for each bracketed segment:

ANALYSIS

I. Stravinsky, *Agon,* "Bransle Gay," mm. 310–35. (*Hint:* Consider the two complementary hexachords, [B♭, B, C, D, E♭, F] and [C♯, E, F♯, G, A♭, A] as basic units. How are they ordered? Transposed? Inverted?

II. Schoenberg, *Little Piano Piece,* Op. 19, No. 2. (*Hint:* The G–B dyad is central to the piece which, to some extent, is built symmetrically around it. G and B are related to each other at I_B^G, and there are many other sets that also are related to each other at I_B^G.)

III. Crumb, *Vox Balaenae* (Voices of the Whales) "Vocalise." (*Hint:* Imagine [D, E, F, A♭, B♭, B] as a basic idea for the movement. Look for its transpositions and think about the different ways it can be divided into trichords related at T_6.)

EAR-TRAINING AND MUSICIANSHIP

I. Stravinsky, *Agon,* "Bransle Gay," mm. 310–35. Write a piano reduction of, and learn to play, mm. 311–14. When you can play the notes with confidence, add the castanet part by intoning "ta-ta-taah-taah."

II. Schoenberg, *Little Piano Piece,* Op. 19, No. 2. Learn to play the entire piece. In mm. 1–4, sing the right-hand melody using pitch-class integers in the place of solfege syllables while playing the left-hand part on the piano. You will need to omit the right-hand B in measure 2, and transpose the D two octaves lower.

III. Crumb, *Vox Balaenae* (Voices of the Whales) "Vocalise." Sing the vocal part up through the arrival of the climactic B♮ at the end of the third system.

COMPOSITION

I. Take the first measure or two of one of the compositions listed above in the Analysis section and, without looking ahead, continue and conclude your own brief composition. Then compare your composition with the published piece.

II. Many of the relationships discussed in this chapter are abstract, and may seem remote from audible musical realities. Choose one of the topics of this chapter (common tones under transposition and inversion, transpositional and inversional symmetry, transpositional combination, the Z-relation, the complement relation, the subset/superset relation) and write a brief composition that features the relationship and makes it as audible as possible. The composition should be in the style of a four-part chorale.

Analysis 3

Webern, Movements for String Quartet, Op. 5, No. 4
Berg, "Schlafend trägt man mich," from Four Songs, Op. 2

In common-practice tonal music, form is usually articulated by shifts in tonality. In a major-key sonata form, for example, what distinguishes the first theme area from the second theme area in the exposition is primarily its tonality: the first theme occurs in the tonic, the second theme in the dominant. In post-tonal music, formal areas are articulated by other means. Listen to the fourth of Webern's Movements for String Quartet, Op. 5, and think about its form. (The score is available in many anthologies.)

There are many musical signs that measures 7–9 constitute a distinct formal section. Things occur in that passage that don't occur either before or after, like the long sustained notes in the cello and second violin. The repeated figure in the viola also is something unique to this section, as is the set class represented by that figure, 3–12 (048). In these ways, measures 7–9 are set apart from the rest of the piece. If measures 1–6 constitute a single section, measures 7–9 make up a contrasting section. Measures 11–12, as we will see, recall musical ideas from the first section. The result is a kind of ABA form.

This form is further delineated by three statements of a single ascending seven-note figure. It occurs in measure 6, at the end of the A section; in measure 10, at the end of the B section; and in measure 13, at the end of the movement (see Example A3–1).

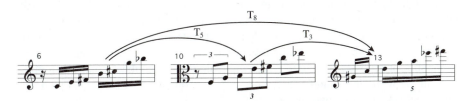

Example A3–1 A recurring seven-note figure that divides the piece into three parts.

These lines are pitch transpositions of one another—the contour is the same in each case. Learn to sing the figure (you will need to transpose it into a comfortable register). Now play all three figures and listen for the transpositional relationships among them.

The seven-note figure is a member of set class 7–19 (0123679) with interval vector 434343. The first and second figures are related at T_5, the second and third at T_3, and, therefore, the first and third at T_8. From our knowledge of common tones under transposition, we would expect there to be four common pitch classes between the first and second forms (T_5), four common pitch classes between the second and third forms (T_3), and three common pitch classes between the first and third forms (T_8). All

Analysis 3

of these common-tone relationships are important, but the link between the first and second forms is particularly central to the way the piece goes (see Example A3–2).

Example A3–2 Common tones link the first two statements of the seven-note figure.

These two statements of the seven-note figure have four pitch classes in common: C, E, F♯, and B. This collection is a member of set class 4–16 (0157). Notice that these common tones occur as a contiguous group in both of the figures. In both cases the E and F♯ occur together, with the B and C changing places before and after. Play these two statements of the seven-note figure again and listen for the common tones.

The musical ideas expressed by the seven-note figures resonate throughout the piece. Let's look closely at the opening measures for some particularly striking echoes. First, play the first-violin tremolos in measures 1–2 (see Example A3–3). That instrument plays the same four notes that are common to the first two statements of the seven-note figure: B, C, E, and F♯. Now play the two tremolo chords in the violins in measures 1–2. The first chord is a member of set class 4–8 (0156); the second chord is a member of set class 4–9 (0167). Moving from the first to the second, the high E moves to F♯, while the B and C exchange places. Compare this motion to the relationship between the first two seven-note figures (look again at Example A3–2).

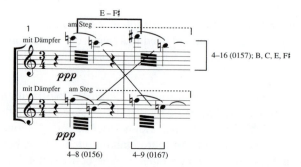

Example A3–3 The E–F♯ motive occurs in the top line, while B and C exchange places.

Analysis 3

As the piece continues, the E–F♯ motive is heard again and again. The highest notes in measures 1–4 move back and forth between E and F♯, as the music expands from 4–8 (0156) to 4–9 (0167) and back again. The same E–F♯ motive is echoed twice in the viola in measures 2 and 3. In the B section, which contrasts in so many ways with the opening material, the E–F♯ motive is stated vertically many times between the sustained note in the cello and the lowest tone in the viola's ostinato (see Example A3–4).

Example A3–4 The E–F♯ motive recurs in the B section, still as part of 4–16 (0157).

This makes a nice link between the A and B sections. The cello is playing a harmonic, so its E sounds two octaves higher than written. It is thus only two semitones below the F♯, further emphasizing their association. The lowest four notes in the passage, [E,F♯,B♭,B], form set class 4–16 (0157). Another member of the same set class, [B,C,E,F♯], was heard back in the A section. These two sets have two notes in common, the crucial E–F♯ motive, creating another nice link between the A and B sections.

Play the following parts on the piano, listening for the recurrence of the E–F♯ motive, its association with B and C, and its place within statements of set class 4–16 (0157): the tremolo chords in measures 1–2; the viola part in measures 2–3; the ascending seven-note figure in measure 6; the lower three parts in measures 7–9; the ascending seven-note figure in measure 10. The common tones between the first two seven-note figures are thus part of an important path through the piece.

Now let's turn to a canon that starts in measure 3 in the first violin, then continues in the second violin and the cello (see Example A3–5).

Learn to sing the four-note canonic subject, F♯–B–F–C. Like the second tremolo chord, it is a member of set class 4–9 (0167); in fact, the canonic subject simply states, in descending order, the notes of that chord. The first and third statements of this melodic figure have the same pitch-class content. The second statement has two tones in common with both of these, namely B and F. These notes come in the middle of the first figure, at either end of the second figure, and back in the middle of the third figure. Play the three figures and listen for this pattern of common tones. At the

Analysis 3

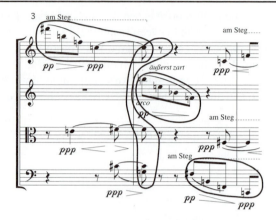

Example A3–5 A three-voice canon, with a member of set class 4–9 (0167) as its subject.

moment the second figure begins, on the downbeat of measure 4, another member of the same set class occurs vertically: [C,C♯,F♯,G]. The passage thus starts on one form of 4–9, moves through two others (one melodic and one harmonic), and then returns to where it started.

There is one more statement of set class 4–9 (0167) in the piece, the pizzicato chord in measure 12 (see Example A3–6).

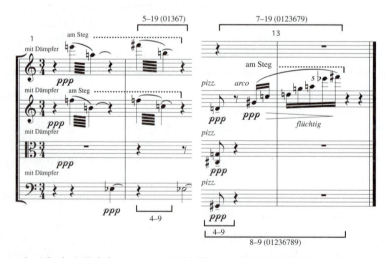

Example A3–6 A link between 4–9 (0167) and 7–19 (0123679) via the complement relation.

This is one of the reasons why the final section of the piece sounds like a modified repeat of the opening section. It also is interesting to note that the last eight pitch classes of the piece (the pizzicato chord in measure 12 together with the final seven-

Analysis 3

note figure) form set class 8–9 (01236789), the complementary set class. Similarly, the tremolo chord in measure 2, together with the E♭ in the cello, forms set class 5–19 (01367), the complement of the seven-note figure. The complement relationship thus links the four-note canonic subject with the thrice-repeated seven-note figure. This link between 4–9 and 7–19, made explicit in the last two measures of the piece, is one of the reasons why these final measures make a satisfying ending.

The five statements of 4–9 (0167) create a coherent musical path, one that culminates and concludes in measure 12 (see Figure A3–1).

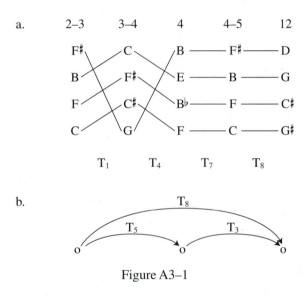

Figure A3–1

Set-class 4–9 is highly symmetrical (four self-mapping operations) and, as a result, members of that set class can be understood to map onto each other in four different ways. The first two forms, [F, F♯, B, C] and [C, C♯, F♯, G] can map onto each other at T_1, T_7, T_0I and T_6I. In Figure A3–1, I have selected T_1, and all of the subsequent labels, because they seem musically most pertinent. For the most part, these five statements of 4–9 are actual pitch transpositions of each other—that's why the voice-leading lines generally run parallel to each other. Only the second statement is registrally reordered. By combining the first two and the last two transpositional moves, it is possible to trace a larger path through the piece. Along that larger path, shown in Figure A3–1b, T_5 and T_3 combine to create a larger T_8. That is precisely the same as the path traversed by the ascending seven-note figure (look back at Example A3–1). Both paths culminate and conclude in the final two measures of the work.

Another canon begins on the last eighth-note of measure 4 between the first violin and cello, overlapping the end of the previous canon (see Example A3–7).

123

Analysis 3

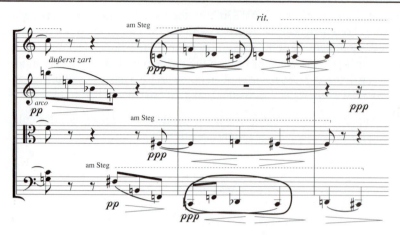

Example A3–7 A second canon, overlapping the first, with set class 3–4 (015) as its head-motive.

The same canon repeats in measure 11, again making the last section sound like a modified repeat of the first section, then breaks off abruptly. The head-motive of this canon forms set class 3–4 (015). Along with set class 3–5 (016), this is the most important trichord in the piece. During the canon, virtually every vertical sonority in the passage is a member of either 3–4 or 3–5. The same musical ideas that make up the melodies are also used to harmonize those melodies (see Example A3–8).

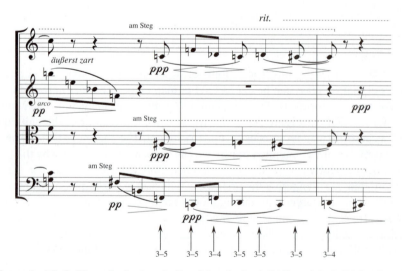

Example A3–8 The principal melodic trichords, 3–4 (015) and 3–5 (016), also occur as simultaneities.

Analysis 3

The trichords 3–4 (015) and 3–5 (016) are subsets of the principal tetrachords of the piece, 4–8 (0156) and 4–9 (0167). 4–8 contains two occurrences of 3–4 and two of 3–5, while all of the trichordal subsets of 4–9 are members of 3–5. The use of these sonorities is so consistent in this piece that they take on the status of quasiconsonances. On the third beat of measure 5, for example, a "dissonant" D in the first violin must "resolve" to C♯ in order to create one of these referential pitch-class sets. Play the passage beginning with the pickup to measure 5 and listen for the integrated use of those trichords as both melodies and harmonies and for the resolution of that D.

Example A3–9 shows the music for the first phrase of a song by Alban Berg.

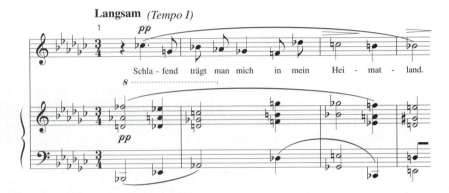

Example A3–9 The first phrase of Berg, "Schlafend trägt man mich," from Four Songs, Op. 2.

The single line of text, from a poem by Alfred Mombert, can be translated as, "Sleeping, I am carried back to my homeland."

This is a relatively early work by Berg, one of his Four Songs, Op. 2, written in 1910. These four songs mark Berg's definitive break with traditional tonality. The song we are discussing here does have a key signature of six flats, which would seem to suggest the key of E♭ minor (or G♭ major), and indeed the song does end with a strong E♭ in the bass. It has been suggested that the key signature, and this final bass note, are a subtle reference to Berg's teacher, Arnold Schoenberg, the first letter of whose last name is the German symbol for E♭ ("Es" in German). Apart from this symbolic reference, however, the key signature seems to have no significance, since every single note in the song has an accidental in front of it. Let us then put aside thoughts of E♭ minor and see how the music is organized.

The piano part in the phrase shown above consists of seven chords. Play them and listen carefully. No two are identical, but they all sound very similar. All are members of the same set class, 4–25 (0268), except for the second, fifth, and seventh chords, which are members of 3–8 (026). The missing note, the note that would make them also members of 4–25, is supplied in the voice part (see Example A3–10).

Analysis 3

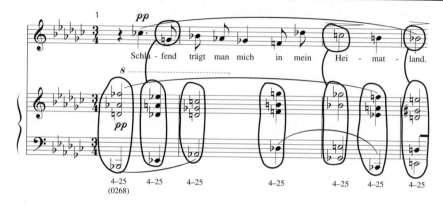

Example A3–10 All seven chords in the piano are members, either complete or incomplete, of set class 4–25 (0268).

Set class 4–25 (0268) has some special properties. It maps onto itself twice under transposition and twice under inversion (you can see this in Appendix 1). As a result it has only six distinct members. Example A3–11 shows the six members of set class 4–25 and the operations that produce each.

Example A3–11 The six distinct forms of set class 4–25 (0268).

With this in mind, we can go back to the music and notice that it cycles through all six forms and, at the end, returns to the form it began on (see Example A3–12).

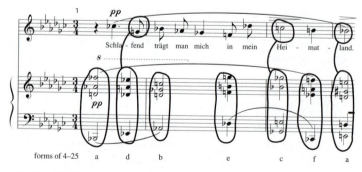

Example A3–12 The passage cycles through the six forms of set class 4–25 (0268) and returns to its starting point.

Analysis 3

This nicely captures the idea expressed in the text of returning to a homeland. Play the passage again and listen for this sense of return. The right hand returns to its starting position (one octave lower), while the left hand is a tritone away (but still part of the collection).

We can further refine our understanding of the progression by considering subsets and supersets. Set class 4–25 (0268) is a subset of the whole-tone collection, set class 6–35 (02468T). There are only two distinct forms of the whole-tone collection, the most symmetrical set of all. Three of the six forms of 4–25 are subsets of one of those forms and the other three are subsets of the other (see Example A3–13).

Example A3–13 Three forms of 4–25 (0268) are subsets of one whole-tone collection; the other three forms of 4–25 are subsets of the other whole-tone collection.

Berg's chord progression thus involves an alternation of whole-tone collections. The first chord comes from the first collection, the second chord from the second collection, the third chord from the first collection, and so on.

So far we have talked only about the chords. Now let's turn our attention to the voice leading, the way the chords are connected to one another. The chords contain only the even interval classes: 2, 4, and 6. (You can inspect the interval vector for 4–25 (0268) and for 6–35 (02468T) to verify this.) Notice that the four voices in the progression move only by odd interval classes: 1, 3, and 5. As a result, each time a voice moves, it must move to a note outside the collection where it started. That is why, as we observed above, each chord in the progression is a subset of a different whole-tone collection from the chords immediately before and after it.

In this progression, the motion from any one chord to the next can be described in four different ways: T_{11}, T_5, and two different inversions (these will vary from chord to chord). None of these operations is consistently reflected in the actual registral lines—the soprano, alto, tenor, and bass of these chords. The bass voice is the most consistent in its movements. It always moves by ordered pitch-class interval 5. It begins on B♭, then cycles through E♭, A♭, D♭, G♭, and C♭, and ends on E, a tritone away from where it began. The upper three voices are not quite so regular until the fourth chord, exactly halfway through the progression, where they begin to descend steadily in semitones. By the fourth chord, all four voices are pitch-class interval three above where they started. At the end of the progression, the upper voices have descended back to their starting point while the bass has ascended an additional three—it is now six above its starting point (see Example A3–14).

Analysis 3

Example A3–14 The voice leading connects two statements of [D,E,A♭,B♭].

The progression as a whole thus involves motion away from an initial sonority and back to it. Play the progression again and listen for the ascending 5s in the bass, the contrasting descending 1s in the upper voices, and the way they come together in the middle and at the end of the progression.

The voice part plays in and out of this underlying framework. Its notes are usually members of the chord or whole-tone collection stated or implied in the piano part. Only one note, the initial C♭, cannot be explained in this way. It really "should be" a B♭ in order to fit into the first chord. The first vocal phrase does come to rest on B♭ on the word "Heimatland" ("homeland"). If B♭ is associated with home, then the initial "wrong note," C♭, suggests being away from home and perhaps of striving toward home. Sing the melody first by itself and then while playing the accompaniment. Listen for the way it weaves in and out of the piano chords, and for that resistant C♭.

Melodically, the singer's part is freer than the lines in the progression, although its last four notes, on "mein Heimatland," move in descending 1s just like the upper three lines in the piano. There also are motivic links between the voice and piano parts. For example, the set class formed by the first three notes in the voice part, 3–3 (014), is echoed at T_5 by the first three notes in the top of the piano part (see Example A3–15).

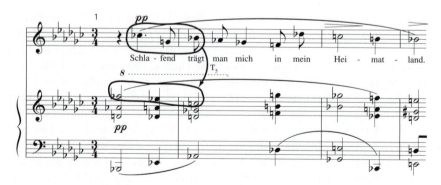

Example A3–15 Two statements of set class 3–3 (014), related at T_5.

Analysis 3

The idea of transposition by +5, of course, is associated with the relentless ascending 5s of the bass part. Furthermore, set class 3–3 (014), particularly with the pitch classes C, E♭, and F♭, occurs in important places elsewhere in the song. The singer sings those very notes in measure 9, and the most heavily stressed notes in the vocal part—the F♭ in measure 9, the E♭ in measure 11, and the C in measure 15—compose out that set over a large span. The contrapuntal complex of the opening—a series of statements of 4–25 (0268) where the bass moves by +5 and the upper parts by –1, with the singer weaving in and out in a motivically associated way—is typical of the song as a whole and, to some extent, of the other songs of Op. 2 as well.

BIBLIOGRAPHY

Webern's Movement for String Quartet, Op. 5, No. 4, has been widely discussed and analyzed. See Charles Burkhart, "The Symmetrical Source of Webern's Opus 5, No. 4," *Music Forum* 5 (1980), pp. 317–34; David Beach, "Pitch Structure and the Analytic Process in Atonal Music: An Introduction to the Theory of Sets," *Music Theory Spectrum* 1 (1979), pp. 7–22; George Perle, *Serial Composition and Atonality,* 6th ed., pp. 16–19; David Lewin, "An Example of Serial Technique in Early Webern," *Theory and Practice* 7/1 (1982), pp. 40–43; Allen Forte, "A Theory of Set Complexes for Music," *Journal of Music Theory* 8/2 (1964), pp. 173–77; Hubert S. Howe Jr., "Some Combinational Properties of Pitch Structures," *Perspectives of New Music* 4/1 (1965), pp. 57–59; Allen Forte, "Aspects of Rhythm in Webern's Atonal Music," *Music Theory Spectrum* 2 (1980), pp. 90–109; and Benjamin Boretz, "Meta-Variations, Part IV: Analytic Fallout (I)," *Perspectives of New Music* 11/1 (1972), pp. 217–23.

On Berg's song, see George Perle, "Berg's Master Array of the Interval Cycles," *Musical Quarterly* 63/1 (1977), pp. 1–30; Craig Ayrey, "Berg's 'Scheideweg': Analytical Issues in Op. 2/ii," *Music Analysis* 1/2 (1982), pp. 189–202; Douglas Jarman, "Alban Berg: The Origins of a Method," *Music Analysis* 6/3 (1987), pp. 273–88; and Dave Headlam, *The Music of Alban Berg* (New Haven: Yale University Press, 1997).

Chapter 4
Centricity, Referential Collections, and Triadic Post-Tonality

Tonality

Traditional common-practice tonality, the musical language of Western classical music from roughly the time of Bach to roughly the time of Brahms, is defined by six characteristics:

1. Key. A particular note is defined as the tonic (as in "the key of C♯" or "the key of A") with the remaining notes defined in relation to it.
2. Key relations. Pieces modulate through a succession of keys, with the keynotes often related by perfect fifth, or by major or minor thirds. Pieces end in the key in which they begin.
3. Diatonic scales. The principal scales are the major and minor scales.
4. Triads. The basic harmonic structure is a major or minor triad. Seventh chords play a secondary role.
5. Functional harmony. Harmonies generally have the function of a tonic (arrival point), dominant (leading to tonic), or predominant (leading to dominant).
6. Voice leading. The voice leading follows certain traditional norms, including the avoidance of parallel perfect consonances and the resolution of intervals defined as dissonant to those defined as consonant.

In common-practice tonality, these six attributes interact in a variety of mutually reinforcing ways. It is perfectly possible, however, for music to have only a few or even just one of these attributes without having all of them. Music like that has a clear connection to common-practice tonality without actually being tonal, strictly speaking.

Of these six attributes, the first four characterize a significant body of post-tonal music, although often in nontraditional ways. Post-tonal music has various ways of creating a sense of focus on a particular note or harmony—among the most important of these is inversional symmetry. Post-tonal music has various ways of creating a sense of large-scale harmonic motion, often following the path of an interval cycle. Post-tonal music often makes use of diatonic scales, and a number of other common scales as well, including octatonic, hexatonic, and whole-tone scales. Post-tonal music frequently uses triads, although they are commonly combined in nontraditional ways. The last two attributes, however, play negligible roles. Functional harmony—harmonies with a tonic, dominant, or predominant function—remain important in a variety of popular musics, but not, generally speaking, in music of the Western art tradition. As a result, Roman numerals and function symbols will not be of much use in the analyzing the repertoire discussed in this book. Traditional voice leading, with its avoidance of parallel perfect consonances and its normative resolutions of dissonances to consonances, has largely been abandoned by both the art and popular traditions.

Centricity

All tonal music is centric, focused on specific pitch classes or triads, but not all centric music is tonal. Even without the resources of tonality, music can be organized around referential centers. A great deal of post-tonal music focuses on specific pitches, pitch classes, or pitch-class sets as a way of shaping and organizing the music. In the absence of functional harmony and traditional voice leading, composers use a variety of contextual means of reinforcement. In the most general sense, notes that are stated frequently, sustained at length, placed in a registral extreme, played loudly, and rhythmically or metrically stressed tend to have priority over notes that don't have those attributes.

For a simple example, consider the opening of the third of Webern's Movements for String Quartet, Op. 5 (see Example 4–1). A C♯ pedal runs through the passage. By brute repetition, the C♯ is established as an important pitch center in the passage. We inevitably hear the other events in the passage in relation to it. The C♯ receives special treatment throughout the piece and is the last note of the piece, played in octaves, triple-forte, by all four instruments. Though the piece is by no stretch of the imagination in C♯ major or C♯ minor, the C♯ certainly has a centric function. In principle, a pitch-class set, or even a set class, can also act as a referential center if it is sufficiently reinforced.

In post-tonal music, a sense of key or pitch-class center is often present only fleetingly. Consider, for one last time, the opening of Schoenberg's Piano Piece, Op. 11, No. 1 (look back at Example 2–15). It has a lyrical melody, complete with expressive appoggiaturas, and a chordal accompaniment. It has a traditional feel, and was written in 1908, in the earliest stages of Schoenberg's interest in writing music without a key signature. But a tonal hearing and a tonal analysis are virtually impossible to sustain. There exist published analyses of the passage, by three respected authorities, in three different keys. One says it's in E; one says it's in F♯, and one says it's in G. In a sense, they are all right, and there are other possible keys to be heard here as well. But no key shapes the structure in any deep or reliable way. Rather, tonality operates in this piece like a ghost, haunting the structure with its presence, but impossible to pin down in any satisfactory way. A complete account of the work, and others like it, will have to take into account the ghostly remnants of traditional tonality, but for a thorough analytical account and a richly satisfactory understanding, our traditional tonal analysis simply won't be of much use.

Example 4–1 C♯ as pitch center (Webern, Movements for String Quartet, Op. 5, No. 3).

Discussing pitch centricity in post-tonal music is more complicated than identifying the tonic of a tonal piece. In post-tonal music, we can talk about an entire spectrum of centric effects. At one extreme, represented by much twelve-tone music, there is little or no sense of centricity. Even so, of course, the pitch classes are not treated identically, and it is important to be sensitive to any kind of special treatment accorded to pitch classes or pitch-class sets. At the other extreme, many post-tonal pieces are deeply preoccupied by questions of centricity.

Inversional Axis

Centricity in post-tonal music can be established by various kinds of direct emphasis and reinforcement: centric pitches are usually stated longer, louder, more often, and higher (or lower) than noncentric pitches. In addition, centricity in post-tonal music can be based on inversional symmetry. An inversionally symmetrical set has an *axis of symmetry,* a midpoint around which all of the notes balance. An axis of symmetry may function as a pitch or pitch-class center.

In the beginning of the passage from Sofia Gubaidulina's String Trio shown in Example 4–2a, all three instruments establish the pitch B4 as a central tone.

(continued)

Example 4–2 Inversional symmetry (Gubaidulina, String Trio, first movement).

b.

Example 4–2 Continued

As new notes are added, they are usually balanced around that central note (Example 4–2b): A♯, one or thirteen semitones below is balanced by C, one or thirteen semitones above; A3 is balanced by C♯6; G♯3 is balanced by D6; and G3 is balanced by D♯6. The only exceptions to the pattern are that F4 is balanced against F♯5 instead of F5 and that the last two low notes, F♯3 and F3, lack partners. Otherwise, B5 is the axis of symmetry and literally the central tone in the passage.

In some passages, notes radiate outward from a central tone in an *expanding wedge*. In the ninth of Ligeti's Ten Pieces for Wind Quintet, the three instruments (the horn and bassoon are tacet) are in canon (Example 4–3a). The shared canonic line begins on E♭ and then radiates outward (Examples 4–3b).

a.

*Throughout the piece the attacks are "level". That is, attack without special accentuation, sustain the tone ff. break off suddenly to breathe (without diminuendo), re-enter "level" just as suddenly, etc. Always take a good breath (breathing can be clearly audible).

Example 4–3 Expanding wedge (Ligeti, Ten Pieces for Wind Quintet, No. 9).

Example 4–3 Continued

A *contracting wedge,* where everything converges on the axis note, can have strong cadential force, as at the end of the first movement of Bartók's String Quartet No. 5 (Example 4–4a). The lines begin on E in four different octaves, and then converge on the cadential B♭ (Example 4–4b).

Example 4–4 Contracting wedge (Bartók, String Quartet No. 5, first movement).

Something similar happens in the fifth movement of the same string quartet, but now the symmetry is realized in pitch-class space rather than in pitch space (Example 4–5a). The passage begins with the dyad C–D♭ and expands in a symmetrical wedge. When the wedge reaches F♯–G, both notes are doubled at the octave. Finally, the original dyad C–D♭ returns, but in a different octave from its first statement. Because of octave displacements, it is easier to grasp the inversional symmetry with a pitch-class clockface (Example 4–5b). On such a clockface, the axis of

Example 4–5 Inversional axis (Bartók, String Quartet No. 5, fifth movement).

symmetry consists of two notes (or two pairs of notes) a tritone apart—these are the *poles* of the axis.

Bartók makes similar use of an inversional axis in pitch-class space in his Bagatelle, Op. 6, No. 2 (see Example 4–6a). The piece begins with repeated A♭s and B♭s in the right hand to which an expanding melodic wedge is added in the left hand: B and G (a semitone above and below the repeated figure); C and G♭ (two semitones above and below); D♭ and F (three semitones above and below); D and F♭ (four semitones above and below); and finally E♭, a pitch-class that can be understood to be five semitones both above and below. The only one of the twelve pitch classes that has not been heard is A, which lies right in the middle of the repeated figure, a kind of silent

a.

b.

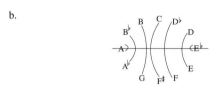

c.

Example 4–6 Inversional Axis (Bartók, Bagatelle, Op. 6, No. 2).

center around which everything balances (see Example 4–6b). A is the pitch axis, but A–E♭ is the pitch-class axis. The E♭ does not play much of a centric role in this opening phrase, but later in the piece the opening music returns transposed at T_6 (Example 4–6c). At that point, the pitch-class axis is still A–E♭, but now it is the E♭ that is particularly emphasized.

There are twelve axes of inversion, and these can be identified by either the sum of the balancing pairs of notes or by the axis notes themselves (see Figure 4–1). For each sum n, the inversional axis will pass through n/2 and n/2 + 6. For example, if the sum of the balanced notes is 8, the inversional axis will be 4–10. If the sum is odd, the axis will pass between two pairs of notes. For example, if the sum of the balanced notes is 7, the inversional axis passes between 3 and 4 and between 9 and 10. We will write that axis as 1/2–7/8.

The twelve inversional axes have the potential to function like the twelve major/minor keys of traditional tonality, including the possibility that music might "modulate" from one axis to another. The beginning of Bartók's *Sonata for Two Pianos and Percussion,* shown in Example 4–7a, features a seven-note chromatic motive that is symmetrical around its first note. The first statement (in measure 2, repeated an octave higher in measure 3) is symmetrical around F♯ while the second

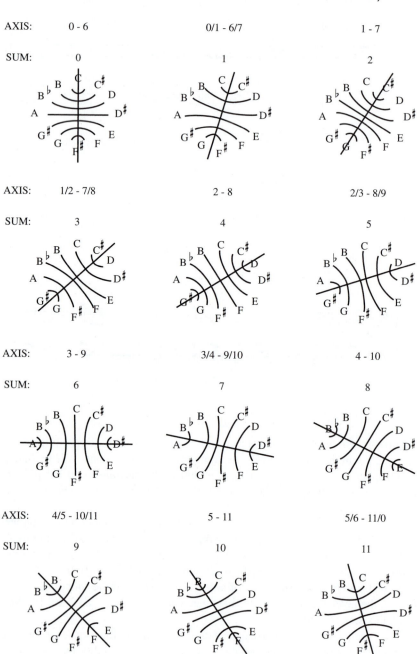

Figure 4–1

Example 4–7 Shifting axes of inversion (Bartók, Sonata for Two Pianos and Percussion, first movement, percussion parts omitted).

statement (measure 5) is symmetrical around C. These share the same axis of symmetry: 0–6 (sum 0). The two overlapped entries of the motive in measure 8–9 are symmetrical on G and then D♭. These share a different axis of symmetry: 1–7 (sum 2). The passage has shifted its centricity from one axis to another (Example 4–7b).

The Diatonic Collection

Composers of post-tonal music often use certain large sets as sources of pitch material. By drawing all or most of the smaller sets from a single large referential set, composers can unify entire sections of music. By changing the large referential set, the composer can create a sense of large-scale movement from one harmonic area to another. Many large collections are available, but four in particular have attracted extensive compositional and theoretical attention: the diatonic, octatonic, hexatonic, and whole-tone collections. Each of these collections has remarkable structural properties and harmonic resources and each is associated with a distinctive sound world.

The *diatonic collection* is any transposition of the seven "white notes" of the piano. It is set class 7–35 (013568T). This collection is, of course, the basic referential source for all of Western tonal music. A typical tonal piece begins within one diatonic collection, moves through other transposed diatonic collections, then ends where it began. All the major scales, (natural) minor scales, and church modes are diatonic collections. Diatonic collections also are common in twentieth-century music. Large stretches of music by Stravinsky and others can be referred to one or more diatonic collections. In post-tonal music, however, the diatonic collection is used without the functional harmony and traditional voice leading of tonal music.

Example 4–8 illustrates nonfunctional, static diatonicism in Stravinsky's *Petrushka.* Although the centricity of the passage is clear (on G for the first eight measures, then shifting to A), it is not traditionally tonal—just try analyzing it with Roman numerals! It does, however, use only diatonic collections. These collections define distinct harmonic areas. In the first eight measures, only the "white notes" are used. In measure 9, F♮ is replaced by F♯, resulting in a different diatonic collection, a transposition of the first. With the change in collection, we have a sense of large-scale shift from one area to another. The change coincides with a change in centricity, creating a clear musical articulation.

The opening of *Petrushka* moves from G-Mixolydian (G–A–B–C–D–E–F–G) to A-Dorian (A–B–C–D–E–F♯–G–A). There are seven possible orderings of the diatonic collection: Ionian (equivalent to the white notes from C to C), Dorian (from D to D), Phrygian (E–E), Lydian (F–F), Mixolydian (G–G), Aeolian (A–A), and Locrian (B–B). Each of these orderings can begin on any of the twelve pitch classes. In analyzing post-tonal diatonic music, we will usually want to know both the centric tone and the scalar ordering.

In some cases, a centric tone can be difficult to determine or musically irrelevant. Then, it may be necessary to refer to the diatonic collections in some more neutral way, without reference either to centric tone or ordering, by simply stating the number of accidentals needed to write the collection. In this terminology, the twelve diatonic collections are: 0-sharp, 1-sharp, 2-sharp, 3-sharp, 4-sharp, 5-sharp, 6-sharp or 6-flat, 5-flat, 4-flat, 3-flat, 2-flat, and 1-flat. For example, C-Lydian, G-Ionian, E-Aeolian, and F♯-Locrian, among seven different scalar orderings, all represent the 1-sharp collection. Conversely, the 2-flat collection, for example, might be represented by B♭-Ionian, C-Dorian, D-Phrygian, etc. There are twelve different diatonic

Example 4–8 Two diatonic collections (Stravinsky, *Petrushka,* Russian Dance).

collections, each of which can be ordered in seven different ways (Figure 4–2 summarizes the possibilities).

The diatonic collection provides a strong link to earlier music, but it acts in a new way, as primarily a referential source collection from which surface motives are drawn. In tonal music, the diatonic collection is usually divided up (partitioned) vertically into triads. In post-tonal diatonic music, triads are used but other harmonies also occur. For example, 4–23 (0257) and 3–9 (027) are diatonic subsets that occur in tonal music only infrequently and as dissonant by-products of voice leading. In Stravinsky's diatonic music, however, they are particularly common. Example 4–9 shows a diatonic passage from the beginning of Stravinsky's opera *The Rake's Progress.*

As we observed back in Chapter 1 (Example 1–12), on virtually every beat in this passage one finds either A–B–E or A–D–E, two forms of set class 3–9 (027).

Collection name	Possible orderings (scales)
0-sharp (or 0-flat)	C-Ionian, D-Dorian, E-Phrygian, F-Lydian, G-Mixolydian, A-Aeolian, B-Locrian
1-sharp	C-Lydian, D-Mixolydian, E-Aeolian, F♯-Locrian, G-Ionian, A-Dorian, B-Phrygian
2-sharp	C♯-Locrian, D-Ionian, E-Dorian, F♯-Phrygian, G-Lydian, A-Mixolydian, B-Aeolian
3-sharp	C♯-Phrygian, D-Lydian, E-Mixolydian, F♯-Aeolian, G♯-Locrian, A-Ionian, B-Dorian
4-sharp	C♯-Aeolian, D♯-Locrian, E-Ionian, F♯-Dorian, G♯-Phrygian, A-Lydian, B-Mixolydian
5-sharp	C♯-Dorian, D♯-Phrygian, E-Lydian, F♯-Mixolydian, G♯-Aeolian, A♯-Locrian, B-Ionian
6-sharp (or 6-flat)	C♯-Mixolydian, D♯-Aeolian, E♯-Locrian, F♯-Ionian, G♯-Dorian, A♯-Phrygian, B-Lydian
5-flat	C-Locrian, D♭-Ionian, E♭-Dorian, F-Phrygian, G♭-Lydian, A♭-Mixolydian, B♭-Aeolian
4-flat	C-Phrygian, D♭-Lydian, E♭-Mixolydian, F-Aeolian, G-Locrian, A♭-Ionian, B♭-Dorian
3-flat	C-Aeolian, D-Locrian, E♭-Ionian, F-Dorian, G-Phrygian, A♭-Lydian, B♭-Mixolydian
2-flat	C-Dorian, D-Phrygian, E♭-Lydian, F-Mixolydian, G-Aeolian, A-Locrian, B♭-Ionian
1-flat	C-Mixolydian, D-Aeolian, E-Locrian, F-Ionian, G-Dorian, A-Phrygian, B♭-Lydian

Figure 4–2

Example 4–9 Static, nontriadic diatonic music (Stravinsky, *The Rake's Progress*).

Together, they form set class 4–23 (0257), a favorite of Stravinsky's. The passage is clearly centered on A and on the perfect fifth A–E. But Stravinsky fills in that fifth not with the traditional third, but with seconds and fourths, creating the sonorities most characteristic of his own music. The music is diatonic, but it is neither triadic nor tonal. Rather, the collection acts as a kind of harmonic field from which smaller musical shapes are drawn.

A significant amount of music that is often described as "minimalist" makes use of the diatonic collection as Stravinsky does, in nontraditional and harmonically nonfunctional ways. Example 4–10a shows the basic pattern from Steve Reich's *Piano Phase,* composed in 1967. It consists of five notes of the two-sharp collection, [B, C♯, D, E, F♯], although scalar order is hard to specify (E–Dorian? B–Aeolian?). The collection is presented as an interlocking of two figures, a three-note pattern (E–B–D) and a two-note pattern (F♯–C♯). A rhythmic sense of three-against-two is thus built in.

Example 4–10 A diatonic collection (Reich, *Piano Phase*).

Piano Phase is written for two pianists. The first player just repeats the pattern of Example 4–10a throughout the entire piece. The second player enters in unison and then, after a while, gradually increases the tempo until the second part has moved one-sixteenth note ahead. At this point, the second part locks back into the tempo of the first and together they play the music shown in Example 4–10b—a canon at the distance of one sixteenth-note. After a while, the second part moves ahead again until it locks back in two sixteenth-notes ahead, as in Example 4–10c—a canon at the distance of two sixteenth-notes. The entire piece involves moving in and out of phase in this manner until, after twelve stages, the original unison is restored.

From a collectional point of view, the piece is incredibly static—only five diatonic pitch classes are used throughout. But there is also remarkable variety produced by the gradual rhythmic shifts. For example, it is interesting to compare the harmonic dyads in Examples 4–10b and 4–10c. In Example 4–10b, a note from one of the two original figures (E–B–D and F♯–C♯) always sounds with a note from the other, and the intervals that result are often dissonant. In Example 4–10c, a note from one of the two original figures always sounds with a note from the same figure, and the intervals that result are generally consonant. This alternation of relatively consonant and relatively dissonant stages persists throughout the piece. The underlying five-note diatonic collection never changes, but its internal relationships are always shifting, always caught up in a dynamic process of change.

The Octatonic Collection

The *octatonic collection* has been another post-tonal favorite, particularly in the music of Bartók and Stravinsky. This collection, 8–28 (0134679T), has many distinctive features. First, it is highly symmetrical, both transpositionally and inversionally. It maps onto itself at four levels of transposition and four levels of inversion. As a result, it has only three distinct forms (just like its complement, the diminished-seventh chord). Figure 4–3 shows the three octatonic collections. The three octatonic

$$\text{OCT}_{0,1} \quad [0,1,3,4,6,7,9,10]$$
$$\text{OCT}_{1,2} \quad [1,2,4,5,7,8,10,11]$$
$$\text{OCT}_{2,3} \quad [2,3,5,6,8,9,11,0]$$

Figure 4–3

collections are identified by the numerically lowest pitch-class semitone that uniquely defines them. So $\text{OCT}_{0,1}$ is the octatonic collection that contains C and C♯, $\text{OCT}_{1,2}$ contains C♯ and D; and $\text{OCT}_{2,3}$ contains D and E♭.

Each octatonic collection contains two of the diminished-seventh chords and excludes the third (see Figure 4–4). When written out as a scale, the octatonic collection consists of alternating 1s and 2s (unlike the diatonic scale, where 2s predominate and the 1s are asymmetrically placed). It can be written in only two different ways, either beginning with a 1 and alternating 1–2–1–2–1–2–1 or beginning with a 2 and alternating 2–1–2–1–2–1–2.

Its subset structure is comparably restricted and redundant. Like the octatonic collection itself, many of its subsets are inversionally and/or transpositionally symmetrical. Each subset can be transposed at T_0, T_3, T_6, and T_9 without introducing any notes foreign to the collection. Conversely, it is possible to generate the octatonic collection by successively transposing any of its subsets at T_0, T_3, T_6, and T_9. If you take a major triad, for example, and combine it with its transpositions at T_3, T_6, and T_9, you create an octatonic collection. The partial list of subsets of $\text{OCT}_{0,1}$ in Figure 4–5

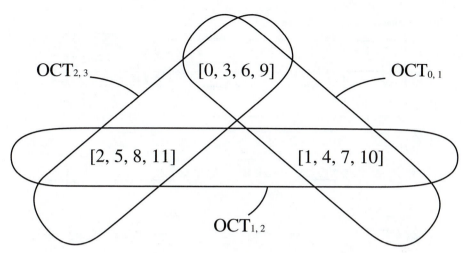

OCT$_{2,3}$ [0, 3, 6, 9]   OCT$_{0,1}$

[2, 5, 8, 11]   [1, 4, 7, 10]

OCT$_{1,2}$

Figure 4–4

Set class	Members
3–2 (013)	[C, C♯, D♯], [D♯, E, F♯], [F♯, G, A], [A, A♯, C] Also, in inversion, [C♯, D♯, E], [E, F♯, G], [G, A, A♯], [A♯, C, C♯]
3–11 (037) (major or minor triad)	[C, D♯, G], [D♯, F♯, A♯], [F♯, A, C♯], [A, C, E] Also, in inversion, [C, E, G], [D♯, G, A♯], [F♯, A♯, C♯], [A, C♯, E]
4–3 (0134)	[C, C♯, D♯, E], [D♯, E, F♯, G], [F♯, G, A, A♯], [A, A♯, C, C♯]
4–10 (0235) (minor or dorian tetrachord)	[C♯, D♯, E, F♯], [E, F♯, G, A], [G, A, A♯, C], [A♯, C, C♯, D♯]
4–26 (0358) (minor seventh chord)	[C, D♯, G, A♯], [D♯, F♯, A♯, C♯], [F♯, A, C♯, E], [A, C, E, G]
4–27 (0258) (dominant or half-diminished seventh chord)	[C, E, G, A♯], [D♯, G, A♯, C♯], [F♯, A♯, C♯, E], [A, C♯, E, G] Also, in inversion, [C, D♯, F♯, A♯], [D♯, F♯, A, C♯], [F♯, A, C, E], [A, C, D♯, G]
4–28 (0369) (diminished seventh chord)	[C, D♯, F♯, A], [C♯, E, G, A♯]

Figure 4–5

shows that the octatonic collection contains many familiar formations, and that these always occur multiple times.

Example 4–11 contains brief octatonic passages by Bartók, Stravinsky, and Messiaen. The Bartók begins by combining one form of 4–10 (0235) in the left

Example 4–11 Three octatonic passages (Bartók, *Mikrokosmos,* No. 101, "Diminished Fifth"; Stravinsky, *Petrushka,* Second Tableau; Messiaen, *Quartet for the End of Time,* third movement, "Abime des Oiseaux").

hand with its tritone transposition in the right hand. The result is the complete $OCT_{2,3}$. In measure 12, the larger collection shifts to an incomplete $OCT_{0,1}$, now created by tritone-related forms of 3–7 (025). In measure 19, the music shifts back to $OCT_{2,3}$. The large-scale harmonic organization of the passage, and of the rest of the work, is determined by the motion among the octatonic collections. The passage by Stravinsky combines two major triads a tritone apart to create an incomplete $OCT_{0,1}$. The passage by Messiaen does not parse quite so easily, although it too is concerned with transposing its constituent subsets, such as 3–2 (013) by T_3 and T_6. In post-tonal music, and even in earlier music, octatonic collections frequently emerge as by-products of transpositional schemes involving minor thirds and tritones.

The Whole-Tone Collection

In addition to the diatonic and octatonic collections, the whole-tone collection, set class 6–35 (02468T), also occurs frequently in post-tonal music. The whole-tone collection has the highest possible degree of symmetry, both transpositional and inversional, and its set class contains only two distinct members. We can refer to them as WT_0 (the whole-tone collection that contains pitch-class C) and WT_1 (the whole-tone collection that contains pitch-class C♯). They also are sometimes called the "even" or "odd" collections, because all of the pitch-class integers in WT_0 are even (0, 2, 4, 6, 8, 10), while those in WT_1 are odd (1, 3, 5, 7, 9, 11).

The intervallic and subset structures of the whole-tone collection are predictably restricted and redundant. It contains only even intervals: interval-classes 2, 4, and 6. It contains only three different trichord-classes, 3–6 (024), 3–8 (026), and 3–12 (048), three different tetrachord-classes, 4–21 (0246), 4–24 (0248), and 4–25 (0268), and a single pentachord-class, 5–33 (02468). Figure 4–6 presents this information in the form of an *inclusion lattice*—set classes are connected to those they either contain or are contained within, with the whole-tone collection itself written at the top.

Example 4–12 shows two passages that are based on a single whole-tone collection: WT_0. The Debussy features descending whole-tone scales in parallel 4s. The bass B♭ in measures 5–7 asserts itself as a centric tone. The Cowell is from a wild piece called "The Banshee" that is played on the strings of the piano. According to the composer's performance instructions, A "indicates a sweep with the flesh of the finger from the lowest string up to the note given" and B tells the performer to "sweep lengthwise along the string of the note given with the flesh of the finger." At the top of each glissando, the goal note belongs to WT_0, and these descend through the entire whole-tone scale.

Both passages in Example 4–13 involve contrast between the two whole-tone collections. In the Bartók, a melody from one of the whole-tone collections is paired with an accompaniment from the other. In the Crumb, a vocalise from one of the whole-tone collections gives way to a final distant echo from the other.

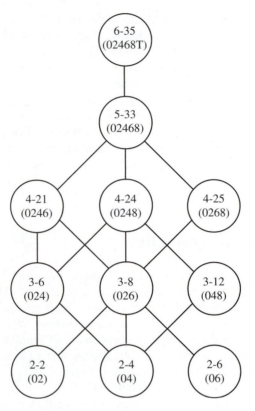

Figure 4–6

Example 4–12 A whole-tone collection (Debussy, "Voiles"; Cowell, "The Banshee").

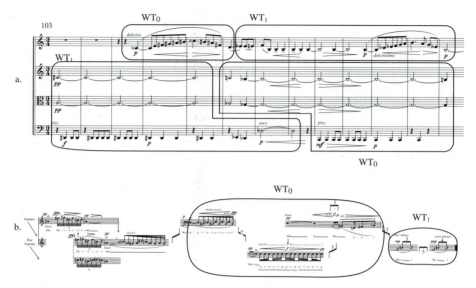

Example 4–13 Two whole-tone collections (Bartók, String Quartet No. 1, first movement; Crumb, *Ancient Voices of Children*).

The Hexatonic Collection

Like the octatonic and whole-tone collections, the hexatonic collection, set-class 6–20 (014589), occurs frequently in post-tonal music and has many striking properties. It is both transpositionally and inversionally symmetrical at three different levels. As a result, there are only four distinct members of this set class, identified by the numerically lowest pitch-class semitone that uniquely defines them (see Figure 4–7).

$$HEX_{0,1} \quad [0, 1, 4, 5, 8, 9]$$
$$HEX_{1,2} \quad [1, 2, 5, 6, 9, 10]$$
$$HEX_{2,3} \quad [2, 3, 6, 7, 10, 11]$$
$$HEX_{3,4} \quad [3, 4, 7, 8, 11, 0]$$

Figure 4–7

When written out as a scale, the hexatonic collection alternates 1s and 3s (compare the octatonic scales, which alternate 1s and 2s). The hexatonic collection can be thought of as a combination of two augmented triads related by semitone—each hexatonic collection contains two of the four augmented triads and excludes the other two (see Figure 4–8).

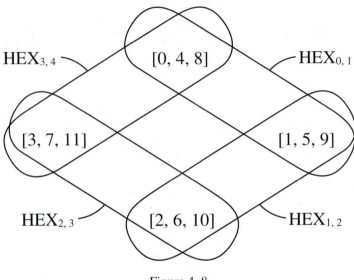

Figure 4–8

Because of its internal symmetries and redundancies, the hexatonic collection has a limited subset structure—see the inclusion lattice provided in the previous chapter as Figure 3–11. Among its subsets are some familiar formations, like the major seventh chord, the major or minor triad, and the augmented triad. As a result, it is possible to write music that is hexatonic, but nonetheless has a somewhat traditional feel.

Example 4–14 shows three hexatonic passages. Schoenberg's six-note chord represents $HEX_{2,3}$—its highest three and lowest three notes are both augmented triads. In the Bartók, the upper three parts arpeggiate an augmented triad, F–A–C♯, up into the stratosphere. Far below, the cello plays a melody that centers on an A-minor triad, A–C–E. Together, melody and accompaniment project $HEX_{0,1}$. In the Babbitt, first violin and viola play only $HEX_{0,1}$ while second violin and cello play only the complementary $HEX_{2,3}$. Both of these hexatonic collections are arranged to feature combinations of i3 and i4.

Collectional Interaction

The four collections discussed thus far (diatonic, octatonic, whole-tone, and hexatonic) often occur in productive interaction with each other. Music may shift from one to another and musical passages can be understood in terms of the interpenetration of one by another. The diatonic and octatonic collections make a particularly effective pair because, despite their obvious structural differences, they share many subsets. The octatonic collection is rich in triads—it contains four major triads and four minor triads. It also contains other diatonic harmonies, including the scale-

Example 4–14 Hexatonic collections (Schoenberg, *Little Piano Piece,* Op. 19, No. 2; Bartók, String Quartet No. 2, first movement; Babbitt, String Quartet No. 2).

segment 4-10 (0235) and minor, half-diminished, and dominant seventh chords. All of these harmonies can create points of intersection in music that uses both diatonic and octatonic collections.

The beginning of Stravinsky's *Symphony of Psalms* makes extensive use of $OCT_{1,2}$ beginning on E: E–F–G–A♭–B♭–B–C♯–D. Set class 4–3 (0134), featured in this ordering, was described by Stravinsky as the basic idea for the entire work. He referred to that set class as "two minor thirds joined by a major third." The famous opening chord, known as the "Psalms chord," is immediately followed by music drawn from the octatonic collection that contains it (see Example 4–15).

Example 4–15 The "Psalms chord" heard as a subset of an octatonic collection on E.

At rehearsal no. 2, the chord is stated again (for the fourth time). Now, however, the chord is followed by music drawn from a *diatonic* collection (E-Phrygian) that contains it (see Example 4–16).

Example 4–16 The "Psalms chord" heard as a subset of E-Phrygian.

The chord is an element common to $OCT_{1,2}$ on E and to E-Phrygian. It links the contrasting types of music in this movement. The large-scale harmonic organization of the movement involves contrasting octatonic and diatonic sections, with important interactions and links between the two.

Because of the extreme symmetry of the octatonic collection, it often produces a centric conflict. Consider, for example, the position of triads within the collection. If it is ordered to begin with a semitone, major and minor triads can be constructed on the first, third, fifth, and seventh degrees of the scale (see Example 4–17).

Example 4–17 The triadic resources of the octatonic collection.

Because the triad can be used to reinforce pitch classes, this symmetrical disposition frequently results in a static polarity of competing centers. Sometimes tritone-related pitch classes are poised against one another, competing for priority. Sometimes, as in the first movement of the *Symphony of Psalms,* the competing centers are pitch-class interval 3 apart. In that movement, E and G compete for centric priority. Their competition can be heard even in the first chord. That chord has E in the bass, but G is the note that is most heavily doubled. A tension between E and G continues throughout the movement, with G winning out in the end. This kind of centric polarity is typical of octatonic music, and the polarity is reinforced here by the nature of the octatonic-diatonic interaction.

It also is possible for one octatonic collection to interact with another, or for one diatonic collection to interact with another. When diatonic collections interact, composers often use collections that share six common tones. In the passage in Example 4–18, Stravinsky combines A-Aeolian with F-Ionian. The F and A compete

Example 4–18 A combination of A-Aeolian and F-Ionian (Stravinsky, Serenade in A).

as centers, as do the F-major and A-minor triads. Look at the sonority formed on the downbeat of each of the first five measures. It has A in the outer voices, but F is always present in an inner voice. The triad is F major, but the A is the most prominent tone. On the last beat of measure 5, the right hand arrives on an A-minor triad, but beneath it the bass insists on F. That sonority combines triads on A and F just as the passage as a whole combines diatonic collections on A and F.

   Large collections may interact and interpenetrate over the course of a passage or a piece. In analyzing post-tonal music, one must be sensitive not only to the motivic interplay of the surface, but to the larger referential collections that lurk beneath the surface.

Interval Cycles

We can gain a useful perspective on the diatonic, octatonic, whole-tone, and hexatonic collections, and on other important collections, by concentrating on the intervals that can generate them. Figure 4–9 shows what happens if we start on any pitch class and move repeatedly by any interval, thus creating an *interval cycle.*

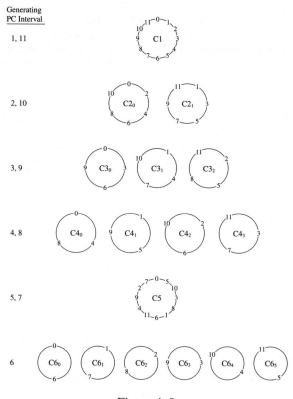

Figure 4–9

If we move by i1 or i11, we get the cycle of semitones, or C1. Moving around the cycle clockwise involves motion by i1; moving counterclockwise involves motion by i11. Either way, the cycle takes us through all twelve pitch classes before returning to its starting point. As a result, there is only one C1-cycle. There are two C2-cycles, however, one moving through the even pitch classes and one through the odd pitch classes. There are three C3-cycles, corresponding to the three diminished-seventh chords, and four C4-cycles, corresponding to the four augmented triads. The C5-cycle is the familiar "circle of fourths or fifths." As with C1, there is only one C5-cycle, because C5 takes us through all twelve tones before returning to its starting point. There are six C6-cycles, each corresponding to one of the six tritones.

Many important collections have their origins in the interval cycles. The chromatic scale corresponds to C1. The two whole-tone collections correspond to the two C2-cycles. The octatonic collection results from a combination of any two of the three C3-cycles. The hexatonic collection results from combining either of the even C4-cycles (C4$_0$ or C4$_2$) with either of the odd C4-cycles (C4$_1$ or C4$_3$). (Combining two even or two odd C4-cycles produces a whole-tone collection.) The diatonic collection corresponds to any contiguous seven-note segment of C5 (and the pentatonic collection corresponds to any five-note segment of C5). The C6-cycles can be combined in various ways to produce whole-tone collections or octatonic collections. From this cyclic point of view, we can imagine the four referential collections studied in this chapter as creating a distinctive sound world from generation by a single interval: the whole-tone from i2, the octatonic from i3, the hexatonic from i4, and the diatonic from i5.

A *cyclic set* is one that consists of an entire cycle or a segment of a cycle. A diatonic collection is a cyclic set because it consists of a seven-note segment of C5. Other, smaller cyclic sets also play a prominent role in post-tonal music. Bartók's String Quartet No. 3, for example, begins with a four-note segment of C1 (C♯–D–D♯–E) and ends with a four-note segment of C5 (C♯–G♯–D♯–A♯) (see Example 4–19). That both sets are in a sense generated from C♯ is no coincidence—Bartók himself thought of this quartet as "in C♯."

In the phrase from an Ives song shown in Example 4–20, the melody consists of five-note segments of the two C2-cycles (accidentals affect only the notes they immediately precede). The accompanying chords, in contrast, are generally five-note segments of C5, and they are arranged registrally to reveal their cyclic origins.

The interval cycles can also be used to guide large-scale motions in post-tonal music. In the fourth movement of Bartók's String Quartet No. 6, the music is headed for a cadence on a C-minor triad in measure 13 (see Example 4–21). That cadential goal is approached in the cello by a descending 1-cycle (E–E♭–D–D♭–C) and in the first violin by an ascending 2-cycle (A–B–C♯–E♭). The 3-cycle, although not part of this cadential progression, shapes the main theme of the movement (and of the quartet as a whole).

The 3-cycle also shapes the opening section of Varèse's *Density 21.5* for solo flute (Example 4–22). For the first ten measures, the principal melodic boundary tones are those of C3$_1$, C♯–E–G–B♭, and the melody gradually rises an octave from C♯4 to D♭5. The arrival on D5 in measure 11, marked *fff,* signals a shift of harmonic orientation.

Example 4–19 Cyclic sets (Bartók, String Quartet No. 3, first six and last four measures).

Example 4–20 Cyclic sets (Ives, "The Cage," from *114 Songs*).

Example 4–21 Interval cycles (Bartók, String Quartet No. 6, fourth movement).

Example 4–22 An interval cycle (Varèse, *Density 21.5*).

Triadic Post-Tonality

Familiar major and minor triads are basic harmonies in several different post-tonal styles of composition, including neoclassicism, neotonality, and minimalism. In many cases, we find extended progressions of triads that are not constrained by the norms of traditional tonality. In particular, the triads do not relate to each other functionally, as predominants, dominants, or tonics. Such music is triadic, but still distinctively post-tonal.

There are two principal types of triadic progression in post-tonal music. The first is *motivic:* the triads are projected along certain well-defined pathways. One such motivic pathway involves the interval cycles. In Example 4–23, the opening of Crumb's *Makrokosmos,* all twelve minor triads are arranged to follow the 1-cycle.

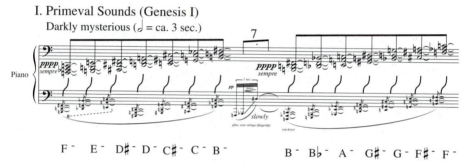

Example 4–23 Minor triads projected through complete 1-cycle (Crumb, *Makrokosmos*).

The roots of the triads in the right-hand part descend by semitone through an entire octave (the roots are given in capital letters with a + or – symbol to indicate triad quality). At the same time, the actual notes gradually ascend from the depths, with each note moving upward to the nearest available position in the next chord. Each right-hand triad is preceded by a grace-note triad a tritone lower in the left hand. These left-hand triads also trace a 1-cycle, in parallel tritones with the right hand.

A different kind of motivic patterning is evident in Example 4–24, the end of an orchestral song by Britten. Here, the triads are all major, and they are arranged symmetrically around D-major. C♯+ and E♭+ surround D+ symmetrically and always wedge toward it. The C+ at the cadence balances the E+ in measure 30. The key signature and the final chord both suggest that D+ is the tonic, but its tonicity is created by inversional symmetry, not by traditional harmonic functions.

A third kind of motivic pathway is illustrated in Example 4–25, from a string quartet by Shostakovich. At the end of the passage, we hear a progression of four minor triads: G–, A♭–, B♭–, and D–. The triads are preceded by a twelve-note melody in the cello. The final notes of that melody (D, E♭, and F) come back as the highest notes of the triads. In that sense, the triads simply harmonize, in a parallel and nonfunctional way, a previous melody. There is an additional, more subtle motivic link

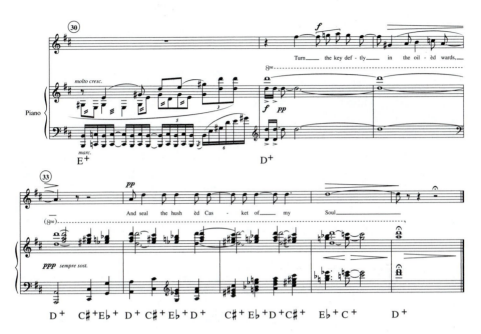

Example 4–24 Symmetrical arrangement of major triads around D (Britten, Serenade for Tenor, Horn, and Strings, Op. 31, "Sonnet").

between the melody and the triads. A member of sc(0137) is embedded in the melody, and the succession of triadic roots describes another member of the same set class. So both the soprano melody and the root progression follow a motivic path.

The second principal kind of harmonic succession in post-tonal music involves *triadic transformations* that connect triads of different quality (major goes to minor and vice versa). Triadic transformations are defined by two qualities: *voice-leading parsimony* and *contextual inversion*. Voice-leading parsimony means that the triads are connected in the smoothest possible way, with the voices moving as little as possible. The most parsimonious voice leading involves two voices motionless (there are two common tones) and the voice that does move does so by only one semitone. Slightly less parsimonious voice leading might involve two voices motionless and one moving by two semitones, or one voice motionless and two voices moving by one semitone each. Contextual inversion means that to get from one triad to the next, you invert around one or two of the notes in the first triad—remember that a major triad and a minor triad can always be understood as related by pitch-class inversion.

Figure 4–10 illustrates four triadic transformations. The first is called P, and it relates a major and minor triad that contain the same perfect fifth and share the same root, like C$^+$ and C$^-$. When C-major moves to C-minor (or vice versa), E moves to E♭ (or vice versa)—a single voice moving by semitone. These two triads are related by the inversion that maps C and G onto each other. The second transformation is called L,

Example 4–25 Motivic progression of triads (Shostakovich, String Quartet No. 12, second movement).

and it relates a major and minor triad that contain the same minor third—the third of the major triad becomes the root of the minor triad (and vice versa). In moving between C⁺ and E⁻, for example, you invert around their shared minor third, and that produces parsimonious voice leading, with C moving a semitone to B. The third transformation is called R, and it relates a major and minor triad that contain the

Triadic Transformations

Name	Description	Contextual Inversion	Parsimonious Voice Leading	Example
P (Parallel)	Major and minor triad share the same root	Invert around the shared perfect fifth	One voice moves by 1 semitone	
L (Leading-tone)	The third of a major triad becomes the root of a minor triad	Invert around the shared minor third	One voice moves by 1 semitone	
R (Relative)	The root of a major triad becomes the third of a minor triad.	Invert around the shared major third	One voice moves by 2 semitones	
SLIDE	Major and minor triad share the same root	Invert around the note that is the third of both triads	Two voices move by 1 semitone	

Figure 4–10

same major third. Inverting around that shared major third will cause one voice to move by two semitones. Moving from C^+ to A^-, for example, involves the inversion that exchanges C and E and moves G to A.

These three transformations are widely used in post-tonal music (and in late-nineteenth-century chromatic music as well) Their theoretical description originates with the theorist Hugo Riemann and has been elaborated in contemporary neo-Riemannian theory. To these, we add one additional transformation that Lewin calls SLIDE. This transformation relates a major and minor triad that share the same third, like C^+ and $C\sharp^-$. This transformation involves contextual inversion around a single note (rather than a pair of notes) and it causes two voices to move, although they each move only by semitone.

These transformations can occur independently, or they can be combined into larger progressions. Figure 4–11 illustrates one important abstract possibility. If we start with C^+ and move by P and L in alternation, we create a cycle of six triads: major and minor triads built on C, E, and A♭. Each move around the cycle involves changing a single note by one semitone, so the voice leading as we move around the cycle is as parsimonious as possible. Each triad differs from the adjacent triads by only a single semitone. The cycle as a whole involves only six different pitch classes, and these correspond to one of the hexatonic collections, $HEX_{3,4}$. The triads that lie opposite each other on the cycle (like C^+ and $G\sharp^-$) are known as *hexatonic poles*—they have no notes in common and together they exhaust the hexatonic collection. The four *hexatonic systems,* or *LP-cycles,* are illustrated in Figure 4–11.

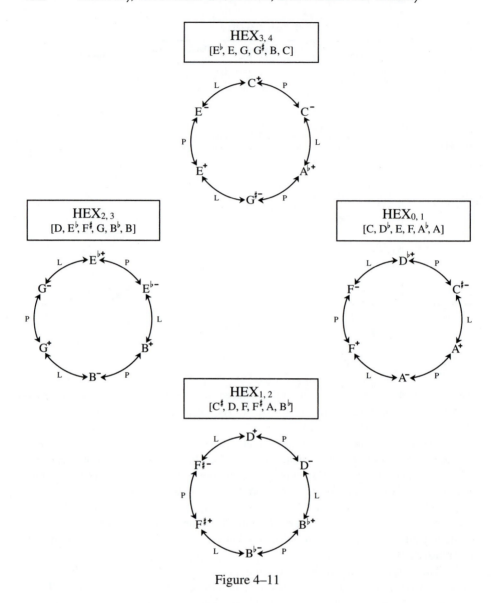

Figure 4–11

A different cycle, a *PLR-cycle,* is illustrated in Figure 4–12. This cycle consists of the six triads (three major and three minor) that all share a single pitch class, in this case pitch-class C. Each triad in the cycle differs from its neighbors by only one or two semitones. Two of the triads lying opposite each other are related by SLIDE.

John Adams, whose music is often triadic, uses SLIDE to connect two triads in *Harmonium* (see Example 4–26). E♭-major and E-minor share G as their third, and

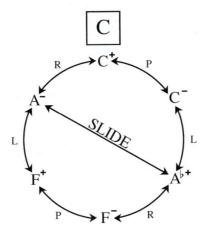

Figure 4–12

that shared note, along with the smooth motions in the other voices, binds together these tonally distant chords.

In his opera *Nixon in China,* Adams uses L to connect triads (see Example 4–27). All four chords in the two L-progressions are drawn from the same hexatonic system, HEX$_{2,3}$.

In another minimalist opera, Glass's *Einstein on the Beach,* triads are often related by contextual inversion and parsimonious voice leading. In the progression shown in Example 4–28, one that occurs with some frequency in the opera, the first three chords belong to the same hexatonic system—the first two are related by L and the second and third by a combination of P-followed-by-L. The first and third chords are hexatonic poles. From the A-major chord, the progression concludes in tonally normal fashion: IV–V–I. But even here there is a sense of inversional symmetry— just as the A$^+$ is approached by triads whose roots are four semitones above and below it, the cadential E$^+$ is approached by triads whose roots are five semitones above and below it.

Shostakovich's music could hardly be described as minimalist in any sense, but it also uses progressions of triads shaped by contextual inversion and parsimonious voice leading. In the passage in Example 4–29, A-major is juxtaposed with F-minor. These harmonies are hexatonic poles: they lie opposite each other in a hexatonic system and thus together exhaust the full six-note collection. The movement from which the passage is taken ends just a few measures later on F-major, another triad from the same hexatonic system.

Post-tonal progressions of triads can be lengthy, as in the opening measures of Zwilich's *Chamber Concerto* (see Example 4–30). There are eight overlapping triads here, alternating major and minor. The initial alternation of P and SLIDE results in a chain of triad roots descending by semitone: B♭–A–A♭. When A♭$^+$ has been reached, the progression moves around one of the hexatonic systems until it reaches the hexatonic pole, E$^-$.

Example 4–26 Progression of triads via SLIDE (Adams, *Harmonium*, Part I).

There is a significant group of works, by Stravinsky and others, that create some sort of centric ambiguity between triads that are related by P, L, or R. In the passage from Stravinsky's *Symphony in C* shown in Example 4–31, two L-related triads (C⁺ and E⁻) compete for priority. The accompaniment consists only of repeated Es and Gs, notes that are common to both triads. That accompaniment could support either the melodic B (producing E⁻) or C (producing C⁺), but the contour and rhythm

Example 4–27 Two progressions with a hexatonic system (Adams, *Nixon in China*, Act II).

of the melody make it hard to tell which is structural and which embellishing. A tension between C-major and E-minor triads is crucial to this passage and to the entire movement. There is no progression between the triads; rather, they are poised against each other in a state of unresolved tension.

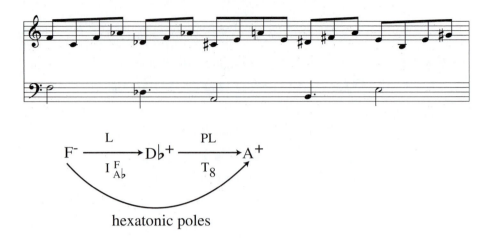

Example 4–28 Progression with a hexatonic system (Glass, *Einstein on the Beach*).

Example 4–29 Hexatonic poles (Shostakovich, String Quartet No. 4, second movement).

BIBLIOGRAPHY

Attempts to analyze post-tonal music in terms of tonal theoretical categories like key and functional harmony have produced predictably uneven results. Symptomatic of the problems inherent in such an enterprise are three published analyses of Schoenberg's Piano Piece, Op. 11, No. 1, in three different keys: Will Ogdon, "How Tonality Functions in Schoenberg's Opus 11, No. 1," *Journal of the Arnold Schoenberg Institute* 5 (1982), pp. 169–81, analyzes it in G; Reinhold Brinkmann (*Arnold Schönberg: Drei Klavierstücke Op. 11: Studien zur frühen Atonalität bei Schönberg* (Wiesbaden: Franz Steiner Verlag, 1969) analyzes it in E; William Benjamin (*Harmony in Radical European Music, 1905–20,* paper presented to the Society of Music Theory, 1984) analyzes it as a prolongation of F♯ as the dominant of B. Similar fundamental disagreements have bedeviled tonally oriented analyses of Schoenberg's Little Piano Piece,

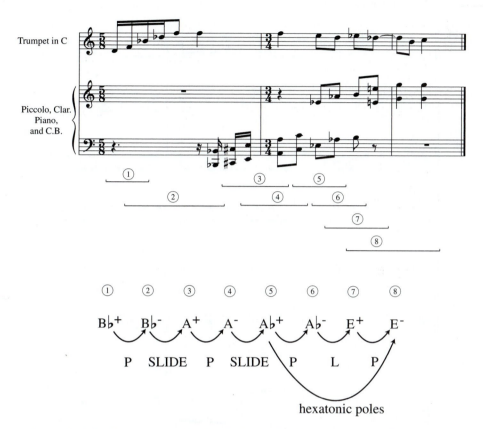

Example 4–30 Progression of triads (Zwilich, *Chamber Concerto for Trumpet and Five Players*).

Op. 19, No. 2: Hugo Leichtentritt (*Musical Form* (Cambridge, Mass.: Harvard University Press, 1951)) analyzes it in B; Hermann Erpf (*Studien zur Harmonie- und Klangtechnik der neueren Musik* (Leipzig, 1927; reprinted 1969) analyzes it in C.

Analyses rooted in the tonal theories of Heinrich Schenker have met with varying degrees of success. See Felix Salzer, *Structural Hearing: Tonal Coherence in Music* (New York: Dover, 1962); Roy Travis, "Toward a New Concept of Tonality?" *Journal of Music Theory* 3 (1959), pp. 257–84; Roy Travis, "Directed Motion in Schoenberg and Webern," *Perspectives of New Music* 4 (1966), pp. 84–88; Robert Morgan, "Dissonant Prolongations: Theoretical and Compositional Precedents," *Journal of Music Theory* 20 (1976), pp. 49–91; Paul Wilson, "Concepts of Prolongation and Bartók's Opus 20," *Music Theory Spectrum* 6 (1984), pp. 79–89; Allen Forte, "Tonality, Symbol, and Structural Levels in Berg's *Wozzeck*," *Musical Quarterly* 71 (1985), pp. 474–99; James Baker, "Voice-Leading in Post-Tonal Music: Suggestions for Extending Schenker's Theory," *Music Analysis* 9/2 (1990), pp. 177–200; James Baker, "Post-Tonal

Example 4–31 Combination of L-related triads (Stravinsky, *Symphony in C,* first movement).

Voice-Leading," in *Models of Musical Analysis: Early Twentieth Century Music,* ed. Jonathan Dunsby (Oxford: Basil Blackwell, 1993), pp. 20–41; Steve Larson, "A Tonal Model of an 'Atonal' Piece: Schoenberg's Opus 15, Number 2," *Perspectives of New Music* 25/1–2 (1987), pp. 418–33; Charles Morrison, "Prolongation in the Final Movement of Bartók's String Quartet No. 4," *Music Theory Spectrum* 13/2 (1991), pp. 179–96; David Neumeyer and Susan Tepping, *A Guide to Schenkerian Analysis* (Englewood Cliffs, NJ: Prentice Hall, 1992), pp. 117–24; Edward Pearsall, "Harmonic Progressions and Prolongation in Post-Tonal Music," *Music Analysis* 10/3 (1991), pp. 345–56; and Olli Väisälä, "Concepts of Harmony and Prolongation in Schoenberg's Op. 19/2," *Music Theory Spectrum* 21/2 (1999), pp. 230–59. The prolongational approach is critiqued in James Baker, "Schenkerian Analysis and Post-Tonal Music," in *Aspects of Schenkerian Theory,* ed. David Beach (New Haven: Yale University Press, 1983) and Joseph N. Straus, "The Problem of Prolongation in Post-Tonal Music," *Journal of Music Theory* 31/1 (1987), pp. 1–22. From a non-Schenkerian point of view, Fred Lerdahl has developed and widely applied a theory of prolongation for atonal music: *Tonal Pitch Space* (Oxford: Oxford University Press, 2001).

The centricity induced by inversional balance is a central theme of George Perle: see *Twelve-Tone Tonality* (Berkeley: University of California Press, 1977) and *The Listening Composer* (Berkeley: University of California Press, 1990). See also Elliott Antokoletz, *The Music of Bela Bartók: A Study of Tonality and Progression in Twentieth-Century Music* (Berkeley: University of California Press, 1984) and Philip Lambert, "On Contextual Transformations," *Perspectives of New Music* 38/1 (2000), pp. 45–76.

There are several prominent referential collections that are not discussed in this chapter, including the nondiatonic minor scales (melodic and harmonic minor)—see Dmitri Tymoczko, "Stravinsky and the Octatonic: A Reconsideration," *Music Theory Spectrum* 24/1 (2002), pp. 68–102.

Most discussions of the octatonic collection in Stravinsky's music, and its interaction with the diatonic collection, have taken as their point of departure Arthur Berger's seminal article "Problems of Pitch Organization in Stravinsky," *Perspectives of New Music* 2/1 (1963), pp. 11–42. The definitive treatment of this subject is Pieter van den Toorn, *The Music of Stravinsky* (New Haven: Yale University Press, 1983). See also Richard Taruskin, *Stravinsky and the Russian Traditions: A Biography of the Works Through Mavra* (Berkeley: University of California Press, 1996). For a discussion of Bartók's octatonicism, see Elliott Antokoletz, *The Music of Béla Bartók* and Richard Cohn, "Bartók's Octatonic Strategies: A Motivic Approach," *Journal of the American Musicological Society* 44/2 (1991), pp. 262–300. The octatonic collection is one of Olivier Messiaen's "modes of limited transposition." See *The Technique of My Musical Language,* trans. J. Satterfield (Paris: Alphonse Leduc, 1956), pp. 58–63.

George Perle has written extensively about interval cycles. See his "Berg's Master Array of the Interval Cycles," *Musical Quarterly* 63 (1977), pp. 1–30 and *The Operas of Alban Berg, Volume Two: Lulu* (Berkeley: University of California Press, 1985). See also Elliott Antokoletz, "Interval Cycles in Stravinsky's Early Ballets," *Journal of the American Musicological Society* 34 (1986), pp. 578–614; Dave Headlam, *The Music of*

Alban Berg (New Haven: Yale University Press, 1997); J. Philip Lambert, "Interval Cycles as Compositional Resources in the Music of Charles Ives," *Music Theory Spectrum* 12/1 (1990), pp. 43–82; and Richard Cohn, "Properties and Generability of Transpositionally Invariant Sets," *Journal of Music Theory* 35/1–2 (1991), pp. 1–32.

A concern with parsimonious voice leading and contextual inversion underpins the recent outpouring of neo-Riemannian theory. Among the foundational publications in this area are four articles by Richard Cohn: "Maximally Smooth Cycles, Hexatonic Systems, and the Analysis of Late-Romantic Triadic Progressions," *Music Analysis* 15/1 (1996), pp. 9–40; "Neo-Riemannian Operations, Parsimonious Trichords, and Their Tonnetz Representations," *Journal of Music Theory* 41/1 (1997), pp. 1–66; "Square Dances with Cubes," *Journal of Music Theory* 42/2 (1998), pp. 283–96; and "Introduction to Neo-Riemannian Theory: A Survey and Historical Perspective," *Journal of Music Theory* 42/2 (1998), pp. 167–80. The last of these introduces a special issue of the *Journal of Music Theory* dedicated to neo-Riemannian theory.

Exercises

THEORY

I.   Inversional axis: Inversionally symmetrical sets map onto themselves under T_nI. The axis of symmetry for such a set is $n/2 - n/2 + 6$.

    1.   For each of the following sets, determine if they are inversionally symmetrical. If they are, find the axis (or axes) of symmetry:
        a. [1,4,5,8]
        b. [10,0,1,2,4]
        c. [1,2,3,4,8,9]
        d. [9,10,11,3,5]
        e. [4,6,11]
        f. [1,2,5,6,9,10]

    2.   Construct at least two pitch-class sets that are symmetrical around the following axis (or axes). Give your answer in normal form.
        a. 4–10
        b. 2/3–8/9
        c. 1–7
        d. 1–7 and 4–10

II.   Referential collections:

    1.   For each of the large collections discussed in this chapter (the diatonic, octatonic, whole-tone, and hexatonic collections), do the following:
        a. Compare their interval vectors.

    b. Compare them with regard to transpositional and inversional symmetry.

    c. Compare them with regard to the trichords they contain. To do this, you will have to extract all of the trichordal subsets and identify the set classes to which they belong.

2. Write out the following scales.
    a. D-Mixolydian
    b. E♭-Phrygian
    c. G♯-Locrian
    d. $OCT_{0,1}$ beginning on G
    e. $OCT_{1,2}$ beginning on G
    f. WT_1 beginning on B
    g. $HEX_{1,2}$ beginning on A

3. Identify each of the following collections, using nomenclature presented in this chapter:

III. Triadic transformations: Major and minor triads can be connected with a variety of transformations that conjoin contextual inversion with voice-leading parsimony.

1. Apply triadic transformations as indicated:
    a. P (A^+)
    b. R ($C♯^-$)
    c. L ($F♯^-$)

     d. SLIDE (F⁺)
     e. P (F⁻)
     f. R (B♭⁺)
     g. L (A♭⁺)
     h. SLIDE (G⁻)

  2.   Construct cycles of alternating major and minor triads as follows:
       a. the hexatonic system that includes G⁺
       b. the hexatonic system that includes F♯⁻
       c. the PLR-cycle whose triads all contain pitch-class A
       d. the PLR-cycle that includes both D⁻ and D♭⁺

ANALYSIS

I.   Stravinsky, *Orpheus,* mm. 1–7. (*Hint:* The harp melody is divided into scalar tetrachords. Consider the relationship between the boundaries of these melodic tetrachords and the accompanying harmonies.)

II.   Stravinsky, *The Rake's Progress,* Act I, Scene 1, beginning to Rehearsal No. 4. (*Hint:* Despite its key signature, the piece resists traditional analysis in A major. Consider the ways in which aspects of the piece balance on a C/C♯ axis.)

III. Bartók, *Mikrokosmos* No. 109, "From the Island of Bali." (*Hint:* Consider the ways in which the octatonic collection is divided into smaller subsets, and the ways they combine to create whole collections. Think also about issues of inversional symmetry.)

IV. Bartók, *Mikrokosmos* No. 101, "Diminished Fifth." (*Hint:* Consider the ways in which the octatonic collection is divided into smaller subsets, and the ways the subsets combine to create the octatonic.)

V.   Copland, *Twelve Poems of Emily Dickinson,* No. 4, "The World Feels Dusty." (*Hint:* The harmonies are generally not triads. Identify and try to relate them to each other.)

EAR-TRAINING AND MUSICIANSHIP

I.   Stravinsky, *Orpheus,* mm. 1–7. Sing the harp part while playing the others.

II.   Stravinsky, *The Rake's Progress,* Act I, Scene 1, beginning to Rehearsal No. 4. Sing Anne's melody while accompanying yourself on the piano. You may simplify the accompaniment by playing block chords instead of moving sixteenth-notes.

III. Bartók, *Mikrokosmos* No. 109, "From the Island of Bali." Play mm. 1–10. Sing the right-hand part while playing the left hand; sing the left-hand part while playing the right hand.

IV. Bartók, *Mikrokosmos* No. 101, "Diminished Fifth." Play the piece. Sing the right-hand part while playing the left hand; sing the left-hand part while playing the right hand.

V.   Copland, *Twelve Poems of Emily Dickinson,* No. 4, "The World Feels Dusty,"
mm. 1–10. Sing the melody while playing the accompaniment.

COMPOSITION

I.   Take the first measure or two of one of the compositions listed above under the
Analysis section and, without looking ahead, continue and conclude your own
brief composition. Then compare your composition with the published piece.

II.   Write a short piece for your instrument that begins with the notes of one octatonic collection, moves to another, then returns.

Analysis 4

Stravinsky, *Oedipus Rex*, rehearsal nos. 167–70
Bartók, Sonata, first movement

Example A4–1 shows the central passage from Stravinsky's opera-oratorio *Oedipus Rex*, the moment where Oedipus realizes who he is and what he has done.

Example A4–1 The moment of Oedipus's enlightenment in Stravinsky's *Oedipus Rex*.

Analysis 4

Natus sum quo nefastum est,	I was born of whom divine law forbade,
concubui cui nefastum est,	I married whom divine law forbade,
kekidi quem nefastum est,	I killed whom divine law forbade,
Lux facta est!	All is now made clear!

In the music that precedes this passage, a shepherd and a messenger reveal to Oedipus his unhappy circumstances. They do so in a kind of static recitation that uses the D-Dorian and centers on the triad D–F–A and on pitch-class D. The first measure of Example A4.1 summarizes their music with a simple D-minor triad played by the strings. In the second measure, the woodwinds and timpani answer with a B-minor triad. Play these two measures and listen carefully—they raise a number of interesting musical issues. First, there is the idea of B versus D, an idea with symbolic resonance throughout the work. D is generally associated with moments of revelation, as when the shepherd and messenger reveal the truth about Oedipus. The B, in contrast, is associated with Oedipus's blindness, both the symbolic blindness of his ignorance and the real blindness he later inflicts upon himself.

The clash between B and D in these measures, and between the B-minor and D-minor triads, involves a further clash, between F♮ and F♯. F♮ is associated with D–F–A, while F♯ is associated with B–D–F♯. The F♮ and F♯ come into direct conflict in the measure before rehearsal no. 168, where D–F–A and B–D–F♯ are compressed into a single sonority: D–F–F♯. That sonority is a member of set class 3–3 (014), a central musical motive in this passage and throughout *Oedipus Rex*.

The entire work is spanned by a single statement of 3–3 (014), articulated by three statements of the so-called fate motive, a triplet figure that alternates notes a minor third apart. The three statements of that motive are centered on B♭, B, and G (see Example A4–2).

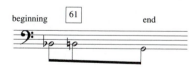

Example A4–2 A large-scale statement of 3–3 (014) that spans the entire work.

The initial B♭–B in that large statement could also have led to D, since [B♭,B,D] is also a member of set class 3–3. That implied D does, in fact, arrive in the work in precisely the passage we are discussing, the moment of Oedipus's self-revelation. When that D arrives, completing a large-scale statement of 3–3, it is immediately associated with a surface statement of another member of the same set class: [D,F,F♯] (see Example A4–3).

Analysis 4

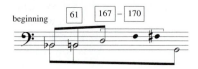

Example A4–3 An additional middleground and foreground statement of 3–3 (014), embedded within the larger work-spanning statement.

The F/F♯ clash is thus part of the large plan of the work.

The shepherd and the messenger had straightforward, diatonic music that reflected the simplicity of their characters. The intrusion of the B-minor triad as Oedipus prepares to speak immediately makes the music more complex.

The music leaves the diatonic realm of D-Dorian and moves toward $OCT_{2,3}$ on D: D, E♭, F, F♯, G♯, A, B, C. The passage does not contain all of the notes of this collection, but the central conflicts in the passage—between B and D, between B–D–F♯ and D–F–A, and between F and F♯—all take place there (see Example A4–4).

Example A4–4 Centric conflicts within an octatonic collection.

Play the music up to rehearsal no. 168 and listen carefully for the juxtaposition of B and D and the musical conflicts that result.

When Oedipus sings, he arpeggiates a B-minor triad. His melody suggests a new diatonic collection: B-Aeolian. Each of the competing centers, B and D, has both a small harmony (a minor triad) and a larger collection associated with it (see Example A4–5).

Example A4–5 A conflict between pitch-class centers, triads, and diatonic collections.

176

Analysis 4

Despite these centers, triads, and diatonic collections, however, the music is not traditionally tonal. There are no dominants and tonics, and no real sense of progression. Rather, the competing centers, triads, and larger collections are juxtaposed in a static manner.

Oedipus's melody is clearly B-centered. The harmonization of his melody, however, is ambiguous. Moments of conflict between F and F♯ and competition between B and D occur throughout. The first two times Oedipus concludes a vocal phrase on F♯, the note is harmonized by set class 3–3 (014), including both F and F♯. Sing Oedipus's melody between rehearsal nos. 168 and 169 and notice how unambiguously B-centered it seems to be. Then sing it again while playing the accompaniment. The centricity is suddenly much less clear. Listen particularly for the clash between F and F♯ and for the associated centric clash between D and B.

In the last five measures of the passage, Oedipus states his last vocal phrase, again ending on F♯. Now, however, the harmony is clarified as the symbolic light breaks in on him. Play these measures and focus particularly on the final sonority, the dyad D–F♯. The bass in these measures descends from B to D. That would seem to suggest a symbolic journey from blindness to revelation. At the same time, however, notice what happens in the top voice of the accompaniment. F♯ (spelled as E♯) trills with F♯ before definitively resolving there. The F (previously associated with D) thus moves to F♯ (previously associated with B) just at the moment the bass moves definitively from B to D. The final sonority of the passage, the dyad D–F♯, thus represents a synthesis of the competing elements. It is not really a D-major triad because there is no confirming A. It is not really a B-minor triad because there is no B. It is just a dyad, poised between the realms of B and D. It combines the F♯ (from the B-centered music) with the D (from the D-centered music). (See Example A4–6.)

Example A4–6 The conflicts between B and D, B minor and D minor, and F and F♯ are crystallized within the final D–F♯ dyad.

The musical conflicts and ambiguities are reconciled at the moment of Oedipus's illumination.

The opening of the first movement of Bartók's Sonata is shown in Example A4–7.

Analysis 4

Example A4–7 The beginning of the first theme of Bartók's Sonata (with some important pitch-class sets indicated).

With a few isolated exceptions, the pitch material for this passage is drawn from a single octatonic collection: E, F, G, G♯, A♯, B, C♯, D. Within that collection, the E has priority. It is the pitch-class center of the passage, established by several musical means. First, E occurs in the bass on the strong beat of the first thirteen measures, registrally prominent and accented. Almost every time it occurs, it is harmonized by an E-major triad, which does not function as a tonic in a tonal context, but as consonant support for the central E within an octatonic framework.

On the second beat of each of the 2/4 measures, the bass moves from an E-major triad to a form of set class 3–3 (014), consisting of D (lower neighbor to E), A♯ (upper

Analysis 4

neighbor to G♯), and B (common tone). In this way, 3–3 embellishes and reinforces the structurally superior E-major triad (see Example A4–8).

Example A4–8 An E-major triad embellished by a form of set class 3–3 (014).

Play the chords in Example A4–8 and listen to the triad being embellished by the 3–3. Both the triad and the 3–3 are subsets of the referential octatonic collection. Later in the movement, when the second theme begins, set class 3–3 will emerge from its secondary role.

While the bass is alternating between the E-major triad and the embellishing 3–3 (014), the upper voice is slowly arpeggiating from G♯ (measure 1) to B (measure 2) up through E (measure 7) to G (measure 14). This arpeggiation helps to reinforce the central E, but E major and E minor seem to be joined within a single gesture. The arpeggiation begins on G♯, but its goal is a heavily stressed G♮. When the G♮ is attained in measure 14, G♯ is heard in the bass. The clash between G♯ and G♮ (the third and fourth degrees of the octatonic scale on E) and the seeming blend of major and minor are typical of octatonic music. In fact, seeming clashes or blends of major and minor in the music of both Bartók and Stravinsky often suggest octatonic thinking and the presence of an octatonic collection. We saw an example of that in the passage from Stravinsky's *Oedipus Rex* discussed earlier. There, the D–F–A-centered music of the Shepherd and Messenger finally gave way to Oedipus's cadence on D–F♯. As we saw, that did not mean a movement from D minor to D major, but rather a synthesis of B–D–F♯ and D–F–A within an octatonic framework.

At the top of the arpeggiation in measure 14, Bartók introduces two new octatonic subsets that will be prominent throughout the movement. The notes on the downbeat of measure 14, and on the downbeats of the next four measures, form set class 4–9 (0167), a perennial favorite of Bartók's. The left-hand accompaniment in these measures, excluding the A♯ and B, focuses on set class 4–18 (0147). Example A4–9 shows the referential octatonic collection and the subsets that Bartók draws from it.

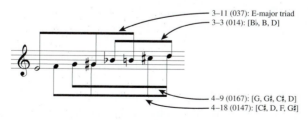

Example A4–9 The referential octatonic collection for the first theme and its most important subsets.

179

Analysis 4

This collection, these subsets, and this focus on E define a kind of tonic level for the movement. Other forms of the sets, and other pitch-class centers, will be measured with reference to this tonic level. The music centers on E, but it is not in E major. It is "in E-octatonic."

In measure 26, the transition to the second theme begins by taking the music from measure 14 and transposing it at T_5 (see Example A4–10).

Example A4–10 The transition to the second theme transposes the music from measure 14 at T_5.

That transposition results in a new octatonic collection: A, B♭, C, C♯, D♯, E, F♯, G. It also brings in transposed forms of the principal sets from the beginning of the first theme.

The second theme grows out of this new octatonic collection and begins with the music shown in Example A4–11.

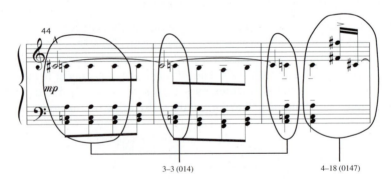

Example A4–11 The second theme.

The central pitch class here is A, established and reinforced in many of the same registral and rhythmic ways as the E in the first theme. Notice the sonority formed on the downbeats of measures 44, 45, and 46—it is set class 3–3 (014). At the beginning of the movement, 3–3 was a secondary, embellishing element; now it is primary. It

180

Analysis 4

consists of A, C, and C♯, suggesting the kind of major/minor clash typical of octatonic music. When F♯ is added at the end of measure 46, a form of set class 4–18 (0147) is created, related by T_2I to the "tonic" form back in measure 14. Play these measures and listen for their A-centricity, their use of set classes 3–3 and 4–18, and their seeming clash of major and minor.

Example A4–12 shows the referential octatonic collection for the opening of the second theme and its principal subsets. As in the first theme, these subsets include 3–3 (014) and 4–18 (0147).

3–3 (014): [A, C, C♯]
4–9 (0167): [C, C♯, F♯, G]

4–18 (0147): [F♯, A, C, C♯]
4–18: [F♯, G, B♭, C♯]

Example A4–12 The referential octatonic collection for the second theme and its most important subsets.

In a traditional sonata form, the first theme and the second theme lie in distinct harmonic areas. The first theme establishes a referential diatonic collection and pitch-class center; the second theme presents a transposition of the first collection and a new pitch-class center. Bartók's procedure is similar, but the harmonic contrast is worked out within an octatonic framework.

BIBLIOGRAPHY

On *Oedipus Rex,* see Wilfrid Mellers, "Stravinsky's Oedipus as 20th-Century Hero," *Musical Quarterly* 48 (1962), pp. 300–312, reprinted in *Stravinsky: A New Appraisal of His Work,* ed. Paul Henry Lang (New York: Norton, 1963); and Pieter van den Toorn, *The Music of Stravinsky,* pp. 299–305. Lawrence Morton discusses the moment of Oedipus's enlightenment in his "Review of Eric Walter White, *Stravinsky,*" *Musical Quarterly* 53 (1967), p. 591.

On the Bartók Sonata, see Paul Wilson, *The Music of Béla Bartók* (New Haven: Yale University Press, 1992), pp. 55–84.

Chapter 5
Basic Twelve-Tone Operations

Twelve-Tone Series

Until now, we have discussed music largely in terms of *unordered* sets of pitch classes. In what follows, we will concentrate on *ordered* sets, which we will call *series*. A series is a line, not a set, of pitch classes. A pitch-class set retains its identity no matter how its pitch classes are ordered. In a series, however, the pitch classes occur in a particular order; the identity of the series changes if the order changes.

A series can be any length, but by far the most common is a series consisting of all twelve pitch classes. A series of twelve different pitch classes is sometimes called a *set* (a usage we will avoid because of the possibility of confusion with unordered pitch-class sets) or *row*. Music that uses such a series as its basic, referential structure is known as *twelve-tone music*.

A twelve-tone series plays many musical roles in twelve-tone music. In some ways it is like a theme, a recognizable "tune" that recurs in various ways throughout a piece. In some ways it is like a scale, the basic referential collection from which harmonies and melodies are drawn. In some ways it is a repository of motives, a large design within which are embedded numerous smaller designs. But it plays a more fundamental role in twelve-tone music than theme, scale, or motive play in tonal music. In tonal music, the scales and even to some extent the themes and motives are part of the common property of the prevailing musical style. From piece to piece and from composer to composer, a great deal of musical material is shared. Tonal music is relatively communal. In twelve-tone music, however, relatively little is shared from piece to piece or composer to composer; virtually no two pieces use the same series. Twelve-tone music is thus relatively contextual. The series is the source of structural relations in a twelve-tone piece: from the immediate surface to the deepest structural level, the series shapes the music.

Basic Operations

Like unordered pitch-class sets, twelve-tone series can be subjected to various operations like transposition and inversion for the sake of development, contrast, and continuity. There is an important basic difference, however. When a set of fewer than twelve elements is transposed or inverted, the content of the set usually changes. When any member of 4–1 (0123), for example, is transposed up two semitones, two new pitch classes will be introduced. The operation of transposition thus changes the content of the collection. When a twelve-tone series is transposed, however, the content remains the same. If you transpose the twelve pitch classes, you just get the same twelve pitch classes, but in a different order. The same is true of inversion. In the twelve-tone system, the basic operations—transposition and inversion—affect order, not content.

The series is traditionally used in four different orderings: prime, retrograde, inversion, and retrograde-inversion. Some statement of the series, usually the very first one in the piece, is designated the prime ordering and the rest are calculated in relation to it. Schoenberg's String Quartet No. 4, for example, begins as shown in Example 5–1.

Example 5–1 Presenting the series—the initial statement is designated P_2 (Schoenberg, String Quartet No. 4).

The melody in the first violin presents all twelve pitch classes in a clear, forthright way. We will consider this the prime ordering for the piece. It begins on D (pitch-class 2), so we will label it P_2.

Figure 5–1 shows P_2 for Schoenberg's String Quartet No. 4 and the interval succession it describes.

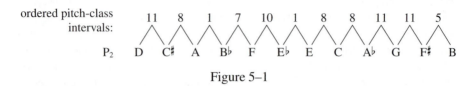

ordered pitch-class
intervals:

11   8   1   7   10   1   8   8   11   11   5

P_2 D   C♯   A   B♭   F   E♭   E   C   A♭   G   F♯   B

Figure 5–1

Let's see what happens if we transpose P_2 up seven semitones (see Figure 5–2).

ordered pitch-class
intervals:

11   8   1   7   10   1   8   8   11   11   5

P_9 A   G♯   E   F   C   B♭   B   G   E♭   D   C♯   F♯

Figure 5–2

The order of the pitch classes changes: D was first, now it is toward the end; A was third, now it is first; and so on. In fact, no pitch class occupies the same order position it did. The content, of course, is the same (both P_2 and P_9 contain all twelve pitch classes) and, more important, so is the interval succession. That particular interval succession is what defines the prime ordering of this series. We can produce that succession beginning on any of the twelve pitch classes. P_0 is the prime ordering beginning with pitch class 0; P_1 is the prime ordering beginning with pitch class 1; and so on. There are twelve different forms of the prime ordering: $P_0, P_1, P_2, \ldots, P_{11}$.

As for the other orderings (retrograde, inversion, and retrograde-inversion), we can think of them either in terms of their effect on the pitch classes or their effect on the intervals. In terms of pitch classes, the retrograde ordering simply reverses the prime ordering. What happens to the interval succession when P_2 is played backwards (an ordering called R_2)? Figure 5–3 demonstrates.

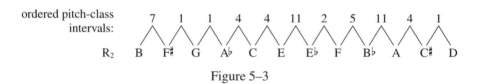

ordered pitch-class
intervals:

7   1   1   4   4   11   2   5   11   4   1

R_2 B   F♯   G   A♭   C   E   E♭   F   B♭   A   C♯   D

Figure 5–3

The interval succession is reversed and each interval is replaced by its complement mod 12 (1 becomes 11, 2 becomes 10, etc.). As with the prime ordering, there are twelve different forms of the retrograde ordering: $R_0, R_1, R_2, \ldots, R_{11}$. (Remember that R_0 is the retrograde of P_0, R_1 the retrograde of P_1, and so on. R_0 thus ends rather than begins on 0.)

The inversion of the series involves inverting each pitch class in the series: pitch class 0 inverts to 0, 1 inverts to 11, 2 inverts to 10, 3 inverts to 9, and so on.

Figure 5–4 shows the interval succession for I_7, the inverted ordering that begins on pitch class 7.

ordered pitch-class intervals:

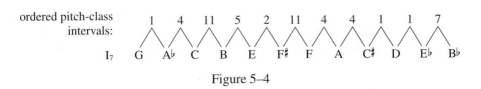

Figure 5–4

The interval succession here is the same as that of the prime ordering, but each interval is replaced by its complement mod 12. The intervals are the same as in the retrograde, but in reverse order. As with the prime and retrograde orderings, we can reproduce this interval succession beginning on any of the twelve pitch classes. The twelve resulting series-forms will be called $I_0, I_1, I_2, \ldots, I_{11}$.

The retrograde-inversion of the series is simply the retrograde of the inversion. Figure 5–5 shows the interval succession for RI_7 (I_7 played backwards).

ordered pitch-class intervals:

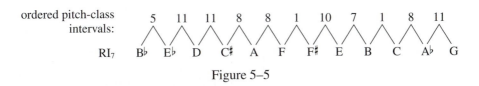

Figure 5–5

The interval succession here is similar to that of the other three transformations. It is particularly interesting to compare it to that of the prime ordering. In terms of pitch classes, the two orderings seem far apart: each is the upside-down-and-backwards version of the other. In terms of intervals, however, the two are quite similar: they have the same intervals in reverse order. Compared to the retrograde, the retrograde-inversion has the complementary intervals in the same order; compared to the inversion, it has the complementary intervals backwards. As with the other three transformations, the retrograde-inversion can begin on any of the twelve pitch classes. The resulting series-forms are named RI_0 (the retrograde of I_0), RI_1 (the retrograde of I_1), ..., RI_{11} (the retrograde of I_{11}).

For any series, we thus have a family of forty-eight series-forms: twelve primes, twelve retrogrades, twelve inversions, and twelve retrograde-inversions. All the members of the family are closely related in terms of both pitch classes and intervals. Figure 5–6 shows the intervals described by the four different orderings of the series from Schoenberg's Quartet No. 4.

	ordered pitch-class intervals										
Prime:	11	8	1	7	10	1	8	8	11	11	5
Retrograde:	7	1	1	4	4	11	2	5	11	4	1
Inversion:	1	4	11	5	2	11	4	4	1	1	7
Retrograde-Inversion:	5	11	11	8	8	1	10	7	1	8	11

Figure 5–6

Notice the predominance of intervals 1, 4, 8, and 11 and the complete exclusion of 3 and 9 in all four orderings (and thus in all forty-eight series-forms). Because of these shared intervallic features (and many other features to be discussed later), the forms of a series are closely related to one another. Each of them can impart to a piece the same distinctive sound.

Figure 5–7 summarizes the intervallic relationships among series forms.

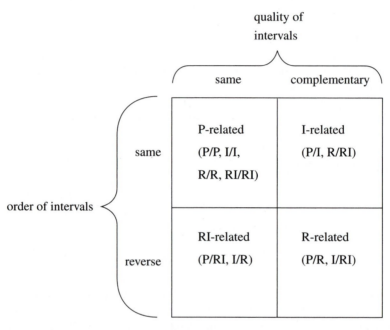

Figure 5–7

Series that have the same ordering (P and P, I and I, R and R, or RI and RI) are said to be prime-related and have the same intervals in the same order. Series that are related to each other by inversion (P and I, R and RI) have the complementary intervals in the same order. Series that are retrograde-inversionally-related (P and RI, I and R) have the same intervals in reverse order. Series that are retrograde-related (P and R, I and RI) have the complementary intervals in reverse order.

In studying a twelve-tone piece, it is convenient to have at hand a list of all forty-eight forms of the series. We could just write out all forty-eight either on staff paper or using the pitch-class integers. More simply, we could write out the twelve primes and the twelve inversions (using the musical staff, letter names, or pitch-class integers) and simply find the retrogrades and retrograde-inversions by reading backwards. The simplest way of all, however, is to construct what is known as a "12×12 matrix." To construct such a matrix, begin by writing P_0 horizontally across the top and I_0 vertically down the left side (see Figure 5–8).

0	11	7	8	3	1	2	10	6	5	4	9
1											
5											
4											
9											
11											
10											
2											
6											
7											
8											
3											

Figure 5–8

Then write in the remaining prime orderings in the rows from left to right, beginning on whatever pitch class is in the first column. The second row will contain P_1, the third row will contain P_5, and so on (see Figure 5–9).

Figure 5–9

The same matrix also could be written using letter names instead of pitch-class integers. The rows of the matrix, reading from left to right, contain all of the prime forms and, reading from right to left, the retrograde forms. The columns of the matrix reading from top to bottom contain all of the inverted forms and, from bottom to top, the retrograde-inversion forms.

The matrix thus contains an entire small, coherent family of forty-eight closely related series-forms: twelve primes, twelve retrogrades, twelve inversions, and twelve retrograde-inversions. All of the essential pitch material in a twelve-tone piece is normally drawn from among those forty-eight forms. In fact, most twelve-tone pieces use far fewer than forty-eight different forms. The material thus is narrowly circumscribed yet permits many different kinds of development. A composer builds into the original series (and thus into the entire family of forty-eight forms) certain kinds of structures and relationships. A composition based on that series can express those structures and relationships in many different ways.

One good way of getting oriented in a twelve-tone work is by identifying the series-forms. This is informally known as "twelve-counting," and it can provide a kind of low-level map of a composition. The first step in twelve-counting is to identify the series. It is usually presented in some explicit way right at the beginning of the piece, but sometimes a bit of detective work is needed. For an example, let's turn back to Webern's song "Wie bin ich froh!" discussed in Analysis 1. The melody for the passage we discussed, measures 1–5, presents the twelve-tone series for the piece, and then repeats its first four notes (see Example 5–2).

(continued)

Example 5–2 The melody presents the P_7 form of a twelve-tone series (Webern, "Wie bin ich froh!").

We will designate that form of the series as P because it is so prominent and easy to follow. Notice the usual twelve-counting procedure of identifying the order-position each pitch occupies in the series-form (G is first, E is second, and so on).

Now the problem is to identify the series-forms used in the accompaniment. We could construct a 12 × 12 matrix. Then we could take the first few notes in the accompaniment (F♯, F, D) and see which of the forty-eight forms begins like that. That would work perfectly well, but instead let's try a different, interval-oriented approach. Look at the succession of ordered pitch-class intervals described by P_7 (see Figure 5–10).

ordered pitch-class intervals:

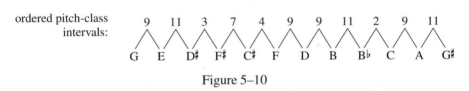

Figure 5–10

Now look at the ordered pitch-class intervals described by the first five notes of the accompaniment (see Figure 5–11).

ordered pitch-class intervals:

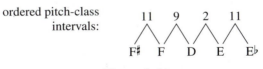

Figure 5–11

It starts out with the same intervals that P_7 ended with, but in reverse order. That means we are dealing with an RI-form. At what transposition level? Just add the first note in the accompaniment (F♯) to the last note in P_7 (G♯), the second note in the accompaniment (F) to the second-to-last note in P_7 (A), and so on. In this way, we calculate the index number that maps these series-forms onto one another. The sum in each case is 2. So the accompaniment begins with RI_7, because 7 + 7 = 2. Each note in RI_7, added to the corresponding note in P_7, sums to the index number 2.

Webern's two series forms, P_7 and RI_7, are related to each other at T_2I, and there is a strong sense in the music of balancing around the prescribed axis C♯–G. The G in particular plays a role as a center of inversional symmetry.

This passage uses only P_7 and RI_7, and the entire song uses only these two forms and their retrogrades (see Example 5–3).

Example 5–3 A "twelve-count" of melody and accompaniment.

Notice that occasionally a single note can be simultaneously the last note of one series-form and the first note of the next. The G in the accompaniment in measure 2, for example, is both the last note in RI_7 and the first note in P_7. This kind of overlap is typical of Webern. A twelve-count like this doesn't do much to help us hear the song better—the intervallic relationships discussed in Analysis 1 are probably more useful in that way—but it does give a rough structural outline of the piece. It also gives a clarifying context for those intervallic relationships.

There is nothing mechanical about either the construction of the series or its musical development in a composition. A composer of tonal music is given certain materials to work with, including, most obviously, diatonic scales and major and minor triads. The composer of twelve-tone music must construct his or her own basic materials, embedding them within the series. When it comes time to use those basic materials in a piece of music, a twelve-tone composer, like a tonal composer, does so in the way that seems musically and expressively most congenial. A good composer doesn't just lay series-forms end-to-end any more than Mozart simply strings scales together.

Once a series has been constructed, a process we will describe more later, just think how many compositional decisions are still required to turn it into music. Should the notes be sounded one at a time or should some of them be heard simultaneously? In what registers should they occur? Played by what instruments? With what durations? What articulations? It is like being given a C-major scale and told to compose some music. There are certain restrictions, but a great deal of freedom as well.

Example 5–1 showed the beginning of Schoenberg's String Quartet No. 4, where P_2 is presented as a singing melody in the first violin. Example 5–4 shows two other statements of P_2, both from the opening section of the piece.

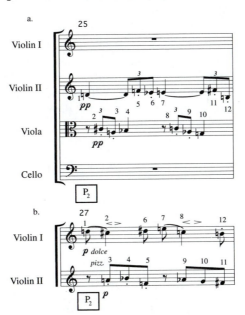

Example 5–4 Two additional statements of P_2 (Schoenberg, String Quartet No. 4).

The musical idea is recognizable in each case, but wonderfully varied. Schoenberg takes a basic shape, then endlessly reshapes it. The construction of the series, the choice of series-forms, and, most important, the presentation of the series, are musical decisions based on hearable musical relationships.

Subset Structure

A series is built up from its smaller parts, its subsets. The sound of the series, and thus the sound of a piece based on the series, is shaped by the structure of its subsets. We have already mentioned the dyads (intervals) formed by the adjacent notes. It is possible to construct series with very different intervallic characteristics. Webern, for example, prefers series that use only a few different intervals and that make particularly heavy use of interval class 1. Berg, in contrast, has a preference for series that use the triadic intervals, interval classes 3, 4, and 5. In a very rough way, those contrasting preferences account for the difference in the sound of Webern's and Berg's twelve-tone music.

In addition to the dyads, we can consider subsets of any size, but those of three, four, or six elements are usually the most important. Composers tend to embed within the series those smaller sets they are interested in using. To put it another way, they usually build up their series by combining a number of smaller sets. As listeners, most of us find it hard to grasp a series as a whole and pretty much impossible to recognize when a series is being turned upside down and backwards, for example. Luckily for us, most twelve-tone music does not require that we be able to hear things like that. Instead, all we have to listen for are the smaller collections, the intervals and subsets embedded within the series.

Remember that every form of a series will have the same subset structure. If, for example, the first three notes of P_0 are a member of set class 3–9 (027), then so will the first three notes of all the P-forms and I-forms, and the last three notes of all the R-forms and RI-forms. That is because set-class membership is not affected by transposition, inversion, or retrograde. We will look at the subset structure of the series from Schoenberg's String Quartet No. 4 and then suggest briefly some of the ways that structure is reflected musically.

It is shown in Figure 5–12 with various subsets identified.

Figure 5–12

As you can see, the organization of the series features certain sets. These features become important musical motives. The trichord 3–4 (015), for example, occurs many times within the series. In the beginning of the Quartet, the music divides the series into its four *discrete* trichords. (The discrete subsets are the ones that divide the series into nonoverlapping portions. There are four discrete trichords, three discrete tetrachords, and two discrete hexachords in every series.) Each trichord in the melody is accompanied by the remaining three trichords in the other instruments. While the first violin plays the first trichord (D–C♯–A), the remaining instruments play the second (B♭–F–D♯), third (E–C–A♭), and fourth (G–F♯–B). When the first violin plays the second trichord, the other instruments play the first, third, and fourth, and so on. Each trichord thus occurs four times in the passage, once in the melody and three times in the accompaniment. Since two of the discrete trichords are members of set class 3–4 (015), and since that set class also occurs in two other places in the series, the passage can be heard, in part, as the varied presentations of that musical idea (see Example 5–5).

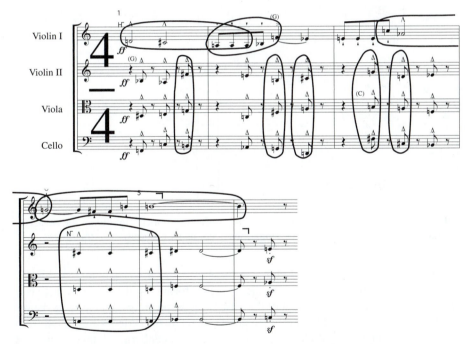

Example 5–5 The trichord 3–4 (015), a subset of the series.

As for the tetrachords, let's focus our attention on a single set class, 4–19 (0148), that occurs three times in the series (and therefore three times in the first violin melody in measures 1–6). We have seen that this passage involves a melody accompanied by three-note chords. But how does Schoenberg choose which melody note will sound with each chord? In measure 1, for example, why does the melodic C♯ come with the second chord instead of, say, the third chord? In measure 2, the melodic A might more logically have been heard back in measure 1 with the third chord. Why does it occur where it does?

In both cases, the answer seems to be that, with this particular vertical alignment, Schoenberg is able to reproduce set classes from series (see Example 5–6).

Example 5–6 The vertical alignment of tones that are not contiguous in the series produces a set class, 4–19 (0148), that does occur as a linear subset of the series.

The melodic C♯ and the second chord in measure 1 are *not* contiguous within P_2. When they sound together, however, they create a form of 4–19 (0148), a set class that *does* occur as a linear segment of the series. The same thing happens in measures 2 and 6. These vertical alignments are not determined by the series—they result from independent compositional choices. In this piece, Schoenberg has taken care that both the linear dimension and the relatively free vertical dimension express the same musical ideas, ideas that he has embedded in his series. In this way, the series achieves an even deeper influence on the music.

A series is a repository of musical ideas, its subsets. In writing a series, a composer chooses preferred intervals, trichords, tetrachords, etc., and embeds them in the series. Because different composers have different kinds of preferences, series vary enormously in their internal characteristics. It is possible to write series that use each of the eleven ordered pitch-class intervals once, and series that confine themselves to only one or two different intervals. It is possible to write series in which each of the ten segmental trichords represents a different set class, and series in which all of the segmental trichords are of the same type. In every case, the subset structure of the series will profoundly shape the sound and structure of a work based on it.

Invariants

When we listen to twelve-tone music, we don't need to be able to identify the forms of the series. Instead, we need to hear the musical consequences of the series, the musical results of its ongoing transformations. Any musical quality or relationship preserved when the series is transformed is called an *invariant*. As we hear our way through a piece, our ear is often led via a chain of invariants.

We have already studied or alluded to a number of musically significant invariants. For example, we noticed that when you transpose a series, the succession of intervals remains the same. In other words the intervallic succession is held invariant under transposition. You don't have to be able to identify the level at which the series has been transposed to hear that the same intervals are coming back in the same order. We also discussed the subset structure of a series. That structure remains invariant under inversion and transposition. If all the discrete trichords of P_0 are members of 3–3 (014), for example, then that will also be true for the other forty-seven series-forms. No matter how the series is transposed or inverted or retrograded, one will be able to hear the constant presence of those subsets. There are so many different kinds of invariants that it would be impossible to give a survey here. What we will do instead is to confine our discussion to invariants under inversion and content ourselves with just two specific instances: preserving a small collection and maintaining vertical dyads in note-against-note counterpoint.

To begin with, recall that inversion always involves a double mapping: if T_nI maps x onto y then it also will map y onto x. To take an example: $T_5I(1) = 4$ and $T_5I(4) = 1$. We can use this relationship not only for individual pitch classes, but for larger collections as well. Let's say we have within a series a subset (its actual notes, not just its set class) that we want to keep intact (although possibly reordered) even when we move to a new form of the series. It's not hard to do, as long as there is an equivalent subset, one related by transposition or inversion, somewhere else in the series. If the two subsets are related by T_nI, inverting the series as a whole by the same T_nI will cause the two subsets to map onto each other, and both will remain intact. If the subset is inversionally symmetrical, at some level of inversion it will remain intact by mapping onto itself.

The subset in question can be as small as a dyad. In Figure 5–13, you will see the familiar series from Schoenberg's String Quartet No. 4, written in pitch-class integers and transposed to start on C.

$$\underline{0 \ \ 11} \ \ 7 \ \ 8 \ \ 3 \ \ 1 \ \ 2 \ \ 10 \ \ \underline{6 \ \ 5} \ \ 4 \ \ 9$$

Figure 5–13

The series begins with the dyad (0, 11). If we want to keep 0 and 11 next to each other while we transform the series, we will want to select a transformation that will map 0 and 11 onto themselves or onto some other semitone dyad in the series. Let's try to map it onto (6, 5), although we could just as easily have mapped it into any of the other semitones in the series. It would be easy to do that under transposition, but it is also possible under inversion. We are looking for the index number of [11,0] and [5,6]. The index number is 5 (0 + 5 = 6 + 11). T_5I will thus map 0 and 11 onto 6 and 5 (and vice versa). Compare P_0 with I_5 (see Figure 5–14).

$$
\begin{array}{lllllllllllll}
P_0: & \overline{0} & \overline{11} & 7 & 8 & 3 & 1 & 2 & 10 & \overline{6} & \overline{5} & 4 & 9 \\
I_5: & \underline{5} & \underline{6} & 10 & 9 & 2 & 4 & 3 & 7 & \underline{11} & \underline{0} & 1 & 8
\end{array}
$$

Figure 5–14

The transformation of P_0 into I_5 moves the (0, 11) into the place formerly occupied by (6, 5) and moves the (6, 5) into the place formerly occupied by the (0, 11).

Notice, in Example 5–7, how Schoenberg uses this kind of invariance to create an associative path through the music.

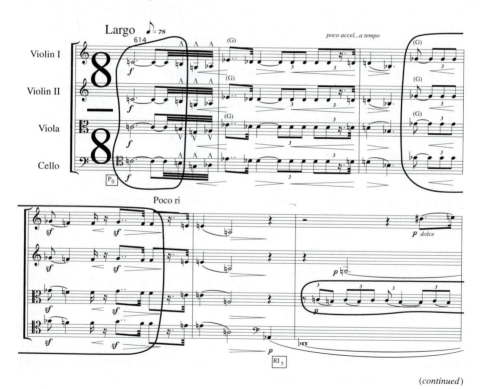

(continued)

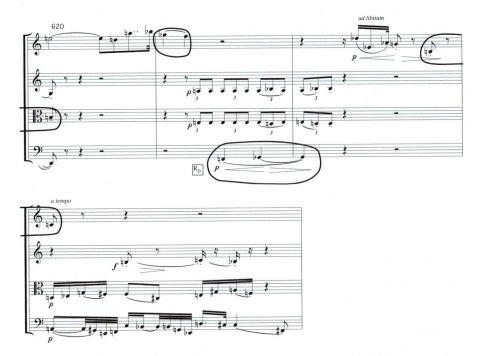

Example 5–7 Invariant dyads (Schoenberg, String Quartet No. 4, third movement).

In P₀, C–B is the first thing heard, while G♭–F is the only dyad to be repeated. The next series-form is RI₅ (I₅ backwards). The C and B are still together, now repeated (as the G♭–F was before), and the G♭ and F are also still together, now at the end of the series. As the music continues with R₀, the G♭–F is picked up in the cello with the same rhythmic values, and the statement of R₀ ends, of course, with B–C. It is difficult, and musically unrewarding, to hear the piece as a P₀ followed by an RI₅ and an R₀. It is easy, and musically rewarding, to hear the chain of invariants moving through the music. The dyad is the simplest collection to hear and discuss, but the same principles apply to holding larger collections invariant as well.

The series from Berg's Violin Concerto is interesting in a number of respects (see Figure 5–15).

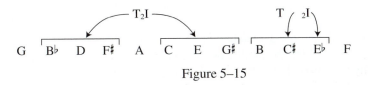

Figure 5–15

First, many of its segmental subsets are major or minor triads. Berg often enjoyed producing a quasitonal sound in his twelve-tone works, and this series makes it easy for him to do so. The series also contains two occurrences of the augmented triad,

3–12 (048), and, as Figure 5–15 shows, these map onto one another at T_2I. [B,C♯,E♭], a member of set-class 3–6 (024), occurs later in the series and maps onto itself at T_2I. As a result, if we perform T_2I on the series as a whole, the two augmented triads will map onto each other and the 3–6 will map onto itself. Performing T_2I on P_7 produces I_7, because 2 is the index number that relates the two series, and $7 + 7 = 2$. Figure 5–16 compares P_7 and I_7, and shows the segmental invariance.

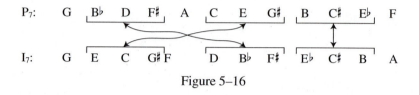

Figure 5–16

Let's see how Berg makes use of these invariants. After a slow introduction, the solo violin states the rising figure shown in Example 5–8a, followed, after a brief inter- lude, by the descending figure shown in Example 5–8b.

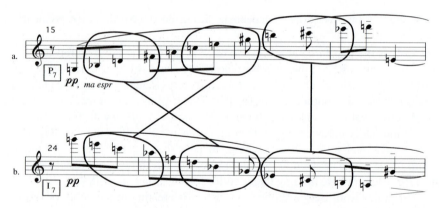

Example 5–8 Trichords held invariant between two series-forms (Berg, Violin Concerto).

The rising figure is P_7 and the descending one is I_7. Notice that the second figure is the pitch inversion as well as the pitch-class inversion of the first—the ordered pitch intervals are simply reversed. The two forms of set class 3–12 (048) change places and the form of 3–6 (024) stays in the same place. The two melodic lines are thus associated not only by their clear inversional relationship, but by their shared seg- mental subsets as well. Segmental associations of this kind provide a nice way of hearing a path through twelve-tone music.

For a different kind of invariant under inversion, consider what happens when a series sounds note-against-note with an inversionally related form. We will use the series from Webern's Piano Variations, Op. 27, as our example, although the property we discuss will be true of any series. Figure 5–17 shows P_8 sounding note-against-note with I_{10}.

$$
\begin{array}{lcccccccccccc}
P_8\text{:} & 8 & 9 & 5 & 7 & 4 & 6 & 0 & 1 & 2 & 10 & 11 & 3 \\
I_{10}\text{:} & 10 & 9 & 1 & 11 & 2 & 0 & 6 & 5 & 4 & 8 & 7 & 3
\end{array}
$$

Figure 5–17

The pitch-class dyads between the series-forms are held invariant. If 8 sounds with 10 once, it will sound with 10 again. 1 sounds only opposite 5, 2 sounds only opposite 4, and so on. There are only seven different pitch-class dyads and each of them occurs twice, except for the unison 9s and 3s, each of which occurs once. To understand why this is so, you must remember about index numbers. The index number of these two inversionally related series-forms is 6. The sum of each element in the first series with the corresponding element in the inversionally related series must be 6. But there are not that many different ways of summing to 6. If there is a 7 in one series, there must be a corresponding 11 in the other because no other pitch class can be added to 7 to make 6.

If we transpose one of the two series above, we can still keep those invariant pitch-class dyads, as long as we keep the index number the same. For example, if we transpose P_8 up five semitones we get:

$$
\begin{array}{lcccccccccccc}
P_1\text{:} & 1 & 2 & 10 & 0 & 9 & 11 & 5 & 6 & 7 & 3 & 4 & 8
\end{array}
$$

What inversionally related series-form will we need to keep those invariant pitch-class dyads? We want to keep the index as 6, so we will need I_5 ($1 + 5 = 6$). (See Figure 5–18.)

$$
\begin{array}{lcccccccccccc}
P_1\text{:} & 1 & 2 & 10 & 0 & 9 & 11 & 5 & 6 & 7 & 3 & 4 & 8 \\
I_5\text{:} & 5 & 4 & 8 & 6 & 9 & 7 & 1 & 10 & 11 & 3 & 2 & 10
\end{array}
$$

Figure 5–18

We have transposed both series (one went up five semitones and one went down five semitones), but we have kept the index number the same. As a result, the pitch-class dyads are still invariant.

Webern exploits this invariant relationship throughout the second movement of his Piano Variations. Example 5–9 shows the first six measures of that movement, where P_8 in the right hand is heard with I_{10} in the left (the series switch hands in measure 5).

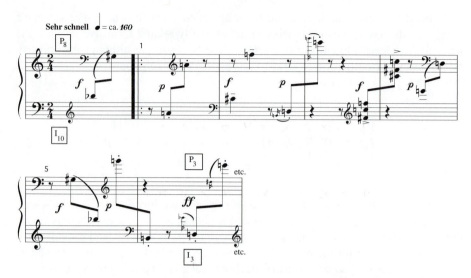

Example 5–9 Inversionally related series-forms transposed to keep the index number the same (Webern, Piano Variations, Op. 27, second movement).

As the movement continues, a prime form of the series in one hand is always heard with an inverted form in the other. Beginning in measure 6, P_3 is paired with I_3, then P_{10} is paired with I_8, and finally P_1 is paired with I_5. Between these pairs of forms, the index number is always the same, 6. As a result, there are only seven different pitch-class dyads in the movement (see Figure 5–19).

1	2	3	4	5	6	7
G♯–B♭	A–A	F–C♯	G–B	E–D	F♯–C	E♭–E♭

Figure 5–19

These seven dyads sound repeatedly, giving the movement a unity that is easy to hear.

At the same time, a nice rhythmic variety is provided since the dyads do not always occur in the same order. As with other invariant relationships, these fixed pitch-class dyads help us to hear our way through the piece. Because the index number remains constant, the two series and all of the dyads can be heard to balance on the same axis, namely A–E♭. The A above middle C is particularly audible as a pitch center. It is always heard as a unison between the series forms, and all the other notes are arranged pitch-symmetrically around it.

What is important here, as in all twelve-tone music, is not the mere presence of the series, but its audible musical content and the chain of associations created by its transformations. In analyzing twelve-tone music, it can be useful to start by identifying the series. But that is only the barest beginning. The series is not a static object that is mechanically repeated again and again, but a rich network of musical relationships that are expressed and developed in a multitude of ways.

BIBLIOGRAPHY

Virtually all modern work in twelve-tone theory stems from the writing and teaching of Milton Babbitt. He has written a series of seminal articles, including: "Some Aspects of Twelve-Tone Composition" (1955), "Twelve-Tone Invariants as Compositional Determinants" (1960), and "Set Structure as a Compositional Determinant" (1961), all reprinted in *The Collected Essays of Milton Babbitt.* Some of this material is presented more informally in *Milton Babbitt: Words About Music,* ed. Stephen Dembski and Joseph N. Straus (Madison: University of Wisconsin Press, 1987).

Pedagogical discussion of basic twelve-tone concepts can be found in Robert Gauldin, "A Pedagogical Introduction to Set Theory," *Theory and Practice* (1978), pp. 3–14; and Charles Wuorinen, *Simple Composition* (New York: Longman, 1979). See also Schoenberg's own presentation of the topic: "Composition with Twelve Tones," in *Style and Idea* (Berkeley and Los Angeles: University of California Press, 1975).

Robert Morris's "Set-type Saturation among Twelve-tone Rows," *Perspectives of New Music* 22/1–2 (1983–84), pp. 187–217, is a study of the subset structure of twelve-tone series. His *Composition with Pitch Classes, Class Notes for Atonal Music Theory,* and *Class Notes for Advanced Atonal Music Theory* cover a variety of topics in serial and twelve-tone theory.

For material on twelve-tone invariants, see David Beach, "Segmental Invariance and the Twelve-Tone System," *Journal of Music Theory* 20 (1976), pp. 157–84; David Lewin, "A Theory of Segmental Association in Twelve-Tone Music," *Perspectives of New Music* 1/1 (1962), pp. 89–116 (reprinted in *Perspectives on Contemporary Music Theory,* ed. Boretz and Cone (New York: Norton, 1972)); and a series of articles by Andrew Mead: "Some Implications of the Pitch-Class/Order-Number Isomorphism Inherent in the Twelve-Tone System," Part One: *Perspectives of New Music* 26/2 (1988), pp. 96–163; Part Two: *Perspectives of New Music* 27/1 (1989), pp. 180–233; "Twelve-Tone Organizational Strategies: An Analytical Sampler," *Integral* 3 (1989), pp. 93–170; "'Tonal' Forms in Arnold Schoenberg's Twelve-Tone Music," *Music Theory Spectrum* 9 (1987), pp. 67–92; "Large-Scale Strategy in Arnold Schoenberg's Twelve-Tone Music," *Perspectives of New Music* 24/1 (1985), pp. 120–57; "'The Key to the Treasure. . . .,'" *Theory and Practice* 18 (1993), pp. 29–56.

Exercises

THEORY

I.   Basic operations: A series is traditionally used in four different orderings: prime (P), inversion (I), retrograde (R), and retrograde-inversion (RI). Each of these four orderings may begin on any of the twelve pitch classes. Use the following twelve-tone series in answering the succeeding questions.

a. 2 1 9 t 5 3 4 0 8 7 6 e

b. 7 e t 3 2 6 4 5 1 0 8 9

c. 5 4 0 9 7 2 8 1 3 6 t e

d. t 5 0 e 9 6 1 3 7 8 2 4

1. For each of the notated series, write the following series forms. (Give your answer both in integers and in staff notation.)
   a. P_7
   b. R_{10}
   c. RI_6
   d. I_5

2. Each of the following series is a transformation of one of the four given above. Identify the series and the transformation.
   a. 7, 6, 2, 11, 9, 4, 10, 3, 5, 8, 0, 1
   b. 3, 4, 8, 7, 0, 2, 1, 5, 9, 10, 11, 6
   c. 4, 6, 0, 1, 5, 7, 2, 11, 9, 8, 3, 10
   d. 8, 7, 11, 0, 4, 3, 5, 1, 2, 9, 10, 6
   e. 9, 10, 6, 5, 1, 2, 0, 4, 3, 8, 7, 11
   f. 10, 5, 6, 7, 11, 3, 2, 4, 9, 8, 0, 1

3. For each of the notated series, construct a 12 × 12 matrix. Using the matrix, check your answers to the previous questions.

4. Indicate whether the following statements are true or false. (If false, make the necessary correction.)
   a. The prime and retrograde-inversion have the same intervals in reverse order.
   b. The inversion and retrograde-inversion have complementary intervals in reverse order.
   c. The retrograde and inversion have complementary intervals in the same order.

II. Subset structure: The constituent groupings within a series are its subsets.

  1. For each of the notated series, identify the set classes to which the following belong:
   a. the discrete trichords; the remaining trichords
   b. the discrete tetrachords; the remaining tetrachords
   c. the discrete hexachords; the remaining hexachords

  2. Construct at least one twelve-tone series for each of the following characteristics:
   a. Its hexachords are related to each other by inversion, and two of its discrete tetrachords are members of the same set class.
   b. As many segmental subsets as possible are members of set class 3–3 (014).
   c. It uses each of the eleven ordered pitch-class intervals once.
   d. Every other interval is a member of interval class 1.
   e. Its first and fourth trichords are members of the same set class, as are its second and third trichords.
   f. It has the same ordered pitch-class intervals as its retrograde.

III. Invariants: Any musical object or relationship preserved under some operation is an invariant.

  1. For the series from Schoenberg's String Quartet No. 4, (D–C♯–A–B♭–F–E♭–E–C–A♭–G–F♯–B), identify the series-forms that preserve the following segments:
   a. (G, F♯, B)
   b. (B♭, F, E♭)
   c. (D, C♯, A, B♭)

  2. For the series from Webern's Concerto for Nine Instruments, Op. 24, (G–B–B♭–E♭–D–F♯–E–F–C♯–C–A♭–A), identify the series-forms that preserve the discrete trichords.

  3. Construct at least one series for each of the following characteristics:
   a. All of the discrete trichords of P_0 are preserved at I_7.
   b. The first tetrachord of P_0 has the same content as the last tetrachord of I_3.
   c. The first five notes of P_0 become the last five of I_{10}.
   d. The collection [E,F♯,B] is a segmental subset of at least four different series-forms.
   e. [F♯,G] and [C♯,D] are segmental subsets of at least four different series-forms.

ANALYSIS

I.   Webern, Quartet, Op. 22, mm. 1–15. (*Hint:* The series is C♯–B♭–A–C–B–E♭–
     E–F–F♯–G♯–D–G, and the passage contains a canon in inversion around the F♯
     above middle C.)

II. Dallapiccola, *Goethe Lieder,* No. 2, "Die Sonne kommt!" (*Hint:* Think about
     motivic relations within each melodic line, and about the intervals and sets
     formed between the lines.)

III. Stravinsky, *Epitaphium.* (*Hint:* The series is C♯–A♯–D♯–E–C–B–F♯–F–D–G–
     G♯–A. Stravinsky commented that "the constructive problem that first attracted
     me was the harmonic one of minor seconds." Think about the ways in which
     intervals representing ic1 are expressed and related.)

EAR-TRAINING AND MUSICIANSHIP

I.   Webern, Quartet, Op. 22, mm. 1–5. Play these measures, accurately and in
     tempo, on the piano.

II. Dallapiccola, *Goethe Lieder,* No. 2, "Die Sonne kommt!": Sing the vocal part
     using pitch-class integers in place of solfege syllables. Sing the vocal part
     while playing the clarinet accompaniment.

III. Stravinsky, *Epitaphium.* In the flute-clarinet duets (mm. 2, 4, and 6), sing the
     flute part while playing the clarinet part on the piano, then switch.

COMPOSITION

I.   Take the first measure or two of one of the compositions listed above in the
     Analysis section and, without looking ahead, continue and conclude your own
     brief composition. Then compare your composition with the published piece.

II. Take one of the series you wrote under Theory Exercise II.2 and use it as the
     basis for a short composition for your instrument. The composition should
     consist of a statement of the series followed by its retrograde and should fea-
     ture in some way the structural characteristic for which it was created.

Analysis 5

Schoenberg, Suite for Piano, Op. 25, Gavotte
Stravinsky, *In Memoriam Dylan Thomas*

The Gavotte from Schoenberg's Suite for Piano, Op. 25 is based on a twelve-tone series. But rather than beginning with the series, let's plunge right into an examination of the first phrase of music, shown in Example A5–1, to discover what sorts of musical ideas Schoenberg is working with.

Example A5–1 First phrase of the Gavotte from Schoenberg's Suite for Piano, Op. 25.

Play the phrase and think about what is gavottelike about it. A gavotte is a Baroque dance in duple meter that usually begins and ends in the middle of the bar and places some stress on the second beat of the measure. It is usually quite simple rhythmically. Schoenberg's gavotte exhibits each of these aspects. Its simple two-voice texture also recalls familiar Baroque models. At the same time, of course, the melodies, motives, and harmonies have little in common with those of a Baroque work. Schoenberg has been severely criticized, by the composer Pierre Boulez among others, for mixing old forms with a new musical language. In this critical view, it would have been more consistent and more convincing if Schoenberg had devised new forms that grew organically from his new language. Schoenberg's defenders have responded that, far from a sign of weakness, his use of old forms shows the power of his new musical language both to create musical coherence and, at the same time, to remake the old forms. He creates beautiful new works that subtly, and ironically, imitate old ones.

Now play the phrase again and listen particularly to the intervallic and motivic structure of the melodic line in the right hand. That melody is divided into two groups of four notes. Those two groups balance one another in duration and shape, and each ends on a tritone: G–D♭ for the first group and A♭–D for the second. The tritones are rhythmically similar—the second note of each tritone is a half-note on the downbeat of a measure. The second tritone, with its wide intervallic span, sounds like an expansion of the first one. Between the tritones, connecting them, is the descending 3 from G♭ to E♭. Those two pitch classes form, with each of the tritones, a member of set class 4–Z15 (0146). (See Example A5–2.)

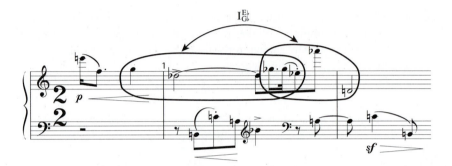

Example A5–2 Two tritones linked by a 3 to create two overlapping forms of 4–Z15 (0146).

The two forms of 4–Z15 are related by inversion, specifically by the inversion that maps E♭ and G♭ onto each other: $I_{G♭}^{E♭}$. One can hear the first tritone, D♭–G, flipping around the E♭–G♭ to map onto the second tritone, A♭–D. The dyad G♭–E♭ thus draws the tritones together and balances them. Play the melodic line and listen for this.

The first tritone, G–D♭, is preceded by a member of interval class 1, E–F. Similarly, the second tritone, A♭–D, is followed, in the left hand, by another 1, C–B. In both cases, the combination of interval class 1 with the tritone creates a form of set class 4–12 (0236). As with the statements of 4–Z15 (0146), these two statements of 4–12 enhance the sense of melodic balance in the phrase. (See Example A5–3.)

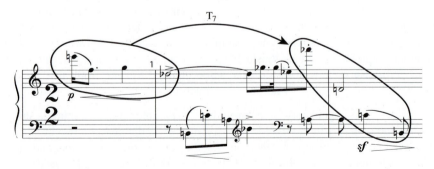

Example A5–3 Two tritones preceded and followed by a semitone to create two balancing forms of 4–12 (0236).

Analysis 5

The sets are related at T_7, which one can hear in the interval between the first and highest note of the first set (E) and the last and lowest note of the second set (B) as well as between the last and lowest note of the first set (D♭) and the first and highest note of the second set (A♭).

The first three notes in the phrase, E–F–G, and the last three notes in the phrase, D–C–B, both form members of 3–2 (013). In addition, other forms of the same set class are embedded in the left-hand part. That part begins with B–C–A, overlapped with C–A–B♭. When the B♭ is reached, the pitches are stated in reverse order: B♭–A–C is overlapped with A–C–B. All of these are members of 3–2. (See Example A5–4.)

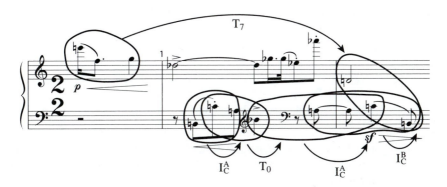

Example A5–4   Six forms of set class 3–2 (013).

The first and last forms are related at T_7, just as their superset 4–12s were. In the left hand, the first and second forms are related at I_C^A. That operation causes the low B to flip around A–C and map onto the high B♭. The process is reversed when I_C^A recurs. The last two forms of 3–2, [A, B, C] and [B, C, D], are related at I_C^B. That causes us to hear the perfect fourth A–D divided right in half by the final two notes, B–C.

Notice also that the last four notes in the left hand, B♭–A–C–B, spell out the name of Bach (in German nomenclature, B = B♭ and H = B). This motive has been used by many composers as an homage to Bach. (We will see another example of it in Webern's String Quartet, Op. 28, in Chapter 6.) It seems particularly appropriate here where Schoenberg is so clearly evoking the musical style of the eighteenth century. The retrograde-symmetry in the left hand—it is the same from right to left as it is from left to right—and the melodic balance in both parts help to unify the phrase. Play the phrase again and listen for the sense of musical balance.

The musical ideas we have been discussing are embedded in the twelve-tone series for this piece. As Example A5–5 shows, the series is built up from the interaction of its subsets.

Analysis 5

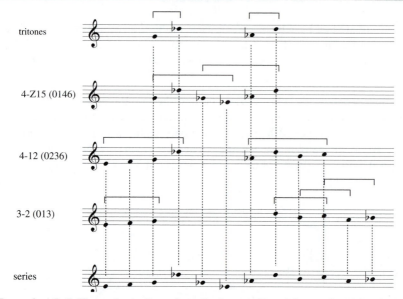

Example A5–5 The series built up from the interaction of the musical ideas it contains.

Far from being an arbitrary or mechanical listing of notes, a twelve-tone series is the embodiment of interrelated musical ideas. A piece of music based on a series will be concerned with the musical ideas contained in the series.

In principle, forty-eight forms of the series are available and could be summarized in a 12×12 matrix. In practice, however, most twelve-tone pieces use far fewer than forty-eight forms, and Schoenberg's Gavotte uses only four: P_4, P_{10}, I_4, and I_{10}. These are written out in Example A5–6.

Example A5–6 Four forms of the series.

As we've already noted, one way of getting oriented in a twelve-tone piece is to do a "twelve-count," identifying the forms of the series being used and the order position in the series of each pitch class. A twelve-count for measures 1–8 of the Gavotte is provided in Example A5–7. Occasionally, a single pitch will be simultaneously the last note of one series-form and the first note of the next.

Example A5–7 A "twelve-count."

Analysis 5

But while such a twelve-count can help us to get oriented, it hardly begins to answer the kinds of musical questions that normally concern us—questions of harmonic and motivic organization, questions of rhythm and phrase structure, questions of contour and shape. We have already tried to approach these questions in the discussion of measures 1–2. Now let's see how the musical ideas presented there are developed in the subsequent music.

The second phrase, measures 2–4, balances the first in a kind of antecedent-consequent formation. Just as the first phrase is balanced within itself, the second phrase balances the first to form a larger musical unit. Play the second phrase, and notice, as in the first, the two tritones separated by an interval 3, preceded and followed by an interval class 1, accompanied by a retrograde-symmetrical line in the left hand consisting of overlapping forms of 3–2 (013). Of the two tritones in the second phrase, one of them, G–D♭, is the same as in the first phrase. In fact, all four of the series-forms that Schoenberg uses—P_4, I_4, P_{10}, and I_{10}—have that tritone as their third and fourth notes. Figure out why this is so. One of the reasons that Schoenberg uses the series-forms he does is precisely to feature this particular interval. As you listen to the rest of the piece, you will certainly notice how prominent the interval G–D♭ is throughout.

So far, we have been concerned mainly with the melodic progress of each line, but the lines combine in interesting and significant ways. Consider, for example, what happens at the barline of measure 2, when the melody in the first phrase leaps from A♭ to D, and at the same time the left hand states A and C. These four notes together make up yet another form of 4–Z15 (0146). This form of 4–Z15, however, unlike the others in the first phrase, is not a linear segment of P_4. Rather, it consists of the seventh, eighth, tenth, and eleventh notes of P_4. This form of 4–Z15 does, however, occur as a linear segment of P_{10}, where it comprises the fifth, sixth, seventh, and eighth notes. The same sort of thing happens in the second phrase. There, the melodic G♭–C combines with F–D in the bass to create a form of 4–Z15 that occurs later as a linear segment of I_4 (see Example A5–8).

This example demonstrates two important principles of Schoenberg's twelve-tone music, and of twelve-tone music generally. The first principle is that the vertical combinations of notes, even when they don't follow the strict linear order of the series, still tend to express musical ideas that are found directly in the series. In the Gavotte, 4–Z15 (0146) is a linear subset of the series (it occurs twice). The vertical form in measures 1–2 reflects those linear forms. Tones that are not adjacent in the series are combined to create sets equivalent to those that do occur as contiguous segments of the series. Second, the sets formed by tones that are not adjacent in the series frequently come back later as contiguous segments of other series-forms; that is, they are secondary at one point in a piece, then they become primary later on. In this way, Schoenberg is able to direct the music from place to place. The vertical form of 4–Z15 in the first phrase gets a full linear statement later when the music moves to

Analysis 5

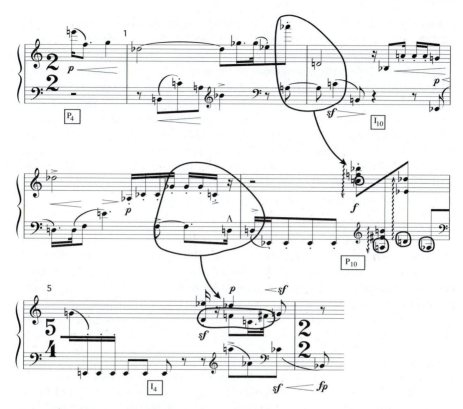

Example A5–8 Nonlinear subsets of P_4 and I_{10} direct the motion toward P_{10} and I_4, where the same collections occur as linear segments.

P_{10}. In that way, the music is directed from P_4 to P_{10} (and, in similar fashion, from I_{10} to I_4).

The first section of the piece comes to an end with a big cadence on the downbeat of measure 8. Let's consider some of the musical factors that make it sound cadential. Partly, it's simply a matter of tempo; the music slows down right at that point and then resumes its former tempo. It's also partly a matter of texture and contour; after a passage in which two or three lines move with great independence, all the parts come together here in a homophonic descent culminating in a single low note. There are also some pitch-related factors, as there must be to make a truly convincing cadence. For one thing, the music at this point returns to P_4 for the first time since the beginning of the piece. The melody, E–F–G–Db, recalls the first four notes of the piece and thus seems to return us to our starting point.

Analysis 5

There is more. In this piece, phrases frequently begin and end a tritone apart. If you look back at the structure of the series, you will notice that its first and last notes are a tritone apart. (This is true for all forms of the series.) Since the phrases of the piece frequently coincide with a statement of the series, this phrase-spanning tritone is often in evidence. Look, for example, at the third phrase of the piece, beginning in measure 4 with a high B♭ and ending in measure 5 with the low, repeated Es. The same sort of thing happens over the course of the entire first section of the piece. The first note of the piece is E, in a high register. The section ends on the downbeat of measure 8 with the low, cadential B♭. That very large-scale statement of E–B♭ reflects many briefer statements of that tritone and other tritones. The same musical idea we started with in discussing the melody of the first phrase is thus used over a larger span to link the beginning and end of an entire section of music.

During much of the twentieth century, Schoenberg and Stravinsky were considered antithetical. Schoenberg's new twelve-tone language and Stravinsky's neoclassical return to traditional textures and sonorities seemed to place them in opposing camps of progressives and conservatives. But more recently the connections and similarities between them have become more and more apparent. We have already gotten a hint, in his Gavotte, of Schoenberg's immersion in traditional music and musical forms. As for Stravinsky, close examination of many of his neoclassical works reveals an almost Schoenbergian concern with motivic saturation and manipulation.

Any gap between the two composers was bridged further in the early 1950s when Stravinsky underwent what he called his second "crisis" as a composer. His first crisis, back around 1920, marked his abandonment of the "Russian" idiom of his early ballets for the more intensive engagement with eighteenth-century models that defined his second, "neoclassical" period. His second crisis led to his embrace of twelve-tone serialism. For some observers, this change seemed an inexplicable capitulation to an alien force. For others, more sensitive to the musical continuities underlying the stylistic change, it came to seem a logical outgrowth of what had come before.

Stravinsky's transition to twelve-tone composition unfolded gradually and was marked by a number of short, experimental pieces. Some of these use a series of fewer than twelve pitch classes. *In Memoriam Dylan Thomas,* a setting of Thomas's well-known poem "Do Not Go Gentle into That Good Night," uses a series of five notes: E–E♭–C–C♯–D (see Example A5–9).

Example A5–9 The five-note series for Stravinsky's *In Memoriam Dylan Thomas.*

Analysis 5

Notice the intense intervallic concentration. All the intervals except one are members of interval class 1. The series as a whole comprises a chromatic pentachord, 5–1 (01234). Its first four notes state set class 4–3 (0134), a longtime favorite of Stravinsky's. (As we saw in Chapter 4, this set class was the basic idea for his *Symphony of Psalms*.) The fifth note of the series then fills in the gap in the middle of the set. This idea of creating a chromatic gap and then filling it, or of filling out a chromatic space, is an important one in this work. With a five-note series, a 12×12 matrix is obviously out of the question. Instead, the prime and inverted forms of the series are listed below. (The retrograde and retrograde-inversion forms can simply be read backwards.) Notice that for each prime ordering there is an inverted ordering with the same pitch-class content listed across from it.

P_4	E	E♭	C	C♯	D		I_0	C	C♯	E	E♭	D
P_5	F	E	C♯	D	E♭		I_1	C♯	D	F	E	E♭
P_6	F♯	F	D	E♭	E		I_2	D	E♭	F♯	F	E
P_7	G	F♯	E♭	E	F		I_3	E♭	E	G	F♯	F
P_8	A♭	G	E	F	F♯		I_4	E	F	A♭	G	F♯
P_9	A	A♭	F	F♯	G		I_5	F	F♯	A	A♭	G
P_{10}	B♭	A	F♯	G	A♭		I_6	F♯	G	B♭	A	A♭
P_{11}	B	B♭	G	A♭	A		I_7	G	A♭	B	B♭	A
P_0	C	B	A♭	A	B♭		I_8	A♭	A	C	B	B♭
P_1	C♯	C	A	B♭	B		I_9	A	B♭	C♯	C	B
P_2	D	C♯	B♭	B	C		I_{10}	B♭	B	D	C♯	C
P_3	E♭	D	B	C	C♯		I_{11}	B	C	E♭	D	C♯

In Stravinsky's setting of Thomas's poem, the singer (a tenor) is accompanied by a string quartet. The setting has a purely instrumental prelude and postlude, scored for string quartet and trombone quartet, which Stravinsky calls "Dirge-Canons." ("Dirge" refers to the emotional quality of the music, and "canons" to the contrapuntal relationships among the parts.) Example A5–10 contains the first phrase of the instrumental prelude.

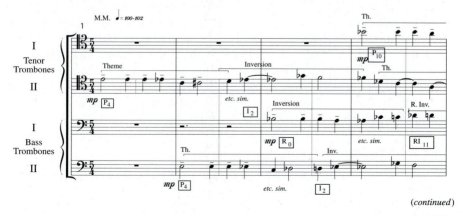

(continued)

Analysis 5

Example A5–10 First phrase with series-forms marked.

Stravinsky himself identified the orderings of the series using his own personal vocabulary: "Theme" = prime, "Riversion" = retrograde, "Inv." = inversion, and "R. Inv." = retrograde inversion. The modern labels of the series-forms, including their transposition levels, are also given on the example. Sing each of the parts. You will immediately hear their mournful chromatic winding. Now listen for the contrapuntal relationship among the parts. Play just the parts for Tenor Trombone 2 and Bass Trombone 2, and notice that they have a canon at the octave. Now add Tenor Trombone 1 and hear how it imitates the other two a tritone higher. The contrapuntal relationship of Bass Trombone 1 is harder to hear, since it begins with the retrograde ordering of the series. Still, because of the intervallic concentration of the series, it sounds imitative and thickens the contrapuntal web. It also participates in filling out the chromatic space that defines the passage. Each voice fills in all the pitch classes within some span. The four voices together fill in the entire chromatic space from the low C in Bass Trombone 2 up to the high B♭ in Tenor Trombone 1 (with a single missing note). Play all four parts and listen for both the contrapuntal imitations and the filling in of the chromatic space.

Now play it again and listen to the vertical sonorities. Unlike Schoenberg's practice, they do not seem to duplicate set classes formed by subsets of the series. Instead, they are not entirely consistent. (Stravinsky did not solve to his own satisfaction the problem of creating meaningful simultaneities until several years later.) The sonorities used most often are 3–7 (025) and 3–11 (037), the major or minor triad. These diatonic references are by-products of the serial voice leading. The most striking simultaneity is the one that ends the passage. It is an F♭-major (or E-major) triad. Its emergence from the chromatic haze is arresting and dramatic. It is related to the frequent melodic emphasis on pitch class E in this work. Stravinsky here generally prefers series-forms that either begin or end on E; in this way, he creates a sense of centric focus within a serial texture.

The same sorts of musical concerns inform the song itself, the first two phrases of which are shown in Example A5–11.

Analysis 5

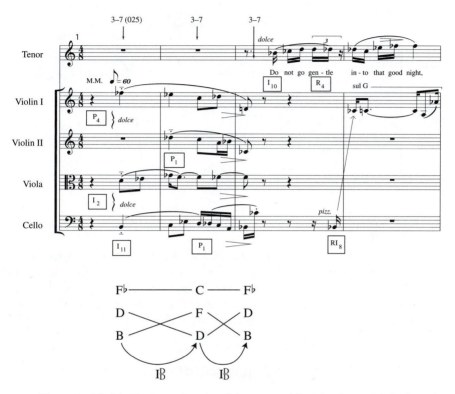

Example A5–11 First two phrases of the song, with series-forms marked.

The series continues to be developed, now with frequent octave expansions of its intervals. The series-forms used by the instruments are just those from the first phrase of the prelude: P_4, P_1, I_2, and I_{11}. The texture is not overtly imitative, but the parts are still quite independent rhythmically. The simultaneities are formed more consistently than in the prelude. In the first instrumental phrase, the first and last sonorities are members of set class 3–7 (025). These come about because the first violin moves from E to D while the viola moves from D to E. At each end of this voice exchange, the D–E dyad is accompanied by a B in the other instruments. Another member of the same set class is formed in the middle of the passage. The only note common to all three forms, D, is the fulcrum on which the progression among them turns, as each inverts around D onto the next.

When the voice comes in, it overlaps two series forms, I_{10}, and R_4. As a result, it fills in the chromatic span of a tritone and reaches up to an arrival point on E, reinforcing that pitch class as a point of centric focus. The motivic ideas in the voice part, particularly the dyads B♭–B and E♭–E, are echoed in the instrumental introduction and in the accompaniment (see Example A5–12).

Analysis 5

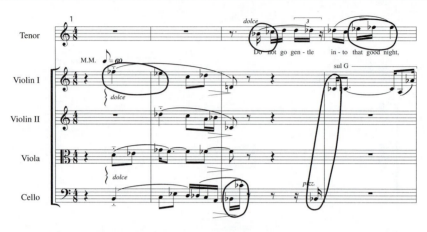

Example A5–12 Motivic interplay between voice and accompaniment.

The first melodic dyad in the instrumental introduction, E–E♭ (first violin, measure 1) becomes the last melodic dyad in the voice. The last melodic dyad in the instrumental introduction, B♭–B (cello, measure 3) becomes the first melodic dyad in the voice. That same dyad is also stated at the beginning of the accompaniment in measures 3–4. This kind of interweaving of the vocal line with the instrumental accompaniment continues throughout the song.

BIBLIOGRAPHY

Schoenberg's Suite for Piano, Op. 25, is discussed in Martha Hyde, "Musical Form and the Development of Schoenberg's Twelve-Tone Method," *Journal of Music Theory* 29/1 (1985), pp. 85–144. Hyde has analyzed the harmonic dimension of Schoenberg's music in a series of studies, including: *Schoenberg's Twelve-Tone Harmony: The Suite Op. 29 and the Compositional Sketches* (Ann Arbor: UMI Research Press, 1982); "The Roots of Form in Schoenberg's Sketches," *Journal of Music Theory* 24/1 (1980), pp. 1–36; and "The Telltale Sketches: Harmonic Structure in Schoenberg's Twelve-Tone Method," *Musical Quarterly* 66/4 (1980), pp. 560–80. Another valuable source of information is Ethan Haimo, *Schoenberg's Serial Odyssey: The Evolution of His Twelve-Tone Method, 1914–1928* (London: Oxford University Press, 1990). Boulez criticizes Schoenberg in his famous essay "Schoenberg Is Dead," *The Score* 6 (1952), pp. 18–22.

There have been several published studies of Stravinsky's *In Memoriam Dylan Thomas*. See W. R. Clemmons, "The Coordination of Motivic and Harmonic Elements in the 'Dirge-Canons' of Stravinsky's *In Memoriam Dylan Thomas*," *In Theory Only* 3/1 (1977), pp. 8–21; Hans Keller, "*In Memoriam Dylan Thomas*: Stravinsky's Schoenbergian Technique," *Tempo* 35 (1955), pp. 13–20; Robert Gauldin and Warren Benson, "Structure and Numerology in Stravinsky's *In Memoriam Dylan Thomas*," *Perspectives of New Music* 23/2 (1985), pp. 166–85; and Joseph N. Straus, *Stravinsky's Late Music* (Cambridge: Cambridge University Press, 2001).

Chapter 6

More Twelve-Tone Topics

Twelve-tone music is not a uniform or monolithic enterprise. Twelve-tone composers share a premise—that interesting and expressive music can be written with reference to a precomposed ordering of the twelve pitch classes—but when they actually get down to writing music, they do so in unique and individual ways. Twelve-tone composition is a world of musical possibilities, and within that world, each composer has discovered or created a new country or province with its own distinctive landscape. In this chapter we will survey six of the many kinds of twelve-tone music.

Webern and Derivation

Webern's music is highly concentrated motivically. It tends to make intensive use of just a few intervals or sets. Indeed, one of the reasons that Webern's works are so short is that their generating materials tend to be so restricted. In writing twelve-tone music, Webern often guaranteed a high degree of motivic concentration by employing a *derived* series. A derived series is one in which the discrete segmental trichords or tetrachords are all members of the same set class.

Figure 6–1 shows the series for Webern's *Concerto for Nine Instruments,* Op. 24, and identifies its discrete segmental trichords.

3–3 (014)	3–3 (014)	3–3 (014)	3–3 (014)
G B B♭	D♯ D F♯	E F C♯	C A♭ A

Figure 6–1

All four of the discrete trichords are members of the same set class. A series like this is said to be derived from 3–3 (014); that set class is the *generator* of the series. Any trichord (except 3–10 (036)) can act as a generator. It is also possible to derive a series from a tetrachord. In that case, all three discrete tetrachords must be members

of the same set class. Any tetrachord that excludes interval class 4 can act as generator. A derived series makes possible an extraordinary motivic unity. As an added
bonus, Webern has ordered each trichord so that if the first trichord is considered to
be in a prime ordering (P_7), the second is the retrograde-inversion (RI_6), the third the
retrograde (R_1), and the fourth the inversion (I_0). (See Figure 6–2.)

$$\underbrace{\text{G B B}\flat}_{P_7} \quad \underbrace{\text{D}\sharp\ \text{D F}\sharp}_{RI_6} \quad \underbrace{\text{E F C}\sharp}_{R_1} \quad \underbrace{\text{C A}\flat\ \text{A}}_{I_0}$$

Figure 6–2

The operations of the system are thus reflected even at this micro-level. This permits
a particularly intense kind of motivic development. Let's see how Webern writes
music using this series.

Example 6–1 shows the first nine measures of the second movement of
Webern's Concerto, with the series-forms and the discrete trichords marked. All of
them, of course, are members of 3–3 (014).

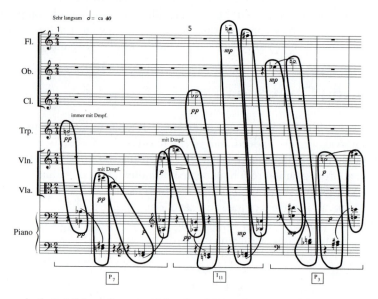

Example 6–1 All four discrete trichords of the series are members of the same set
class, 3–3 (014) (Webern, Concerto for Nine Instruments, Op. 24).

As always, we will fare better as listeners if we focus not on the series as a whole but
on the smaller units—in this case, on the highly concentrated development of set
class 3–3 (014). Every time a form of the series is stated, we are assured of hearing
four statements of that set class.

We thus have three levels of structure unfolding at the same time: the motions
from note to note, from trichord to trichord, and from series to series. One of the
advantages of the serial idea, from Webern's point of view, was that it enabled him to

shape the motivic and intervallic flow at each of these levels of structure. It also was possible to project the same musical ideas simultaneously at each of these levels. For example, the first two notes of the series are four semitones apart, and so are the first and third series of the movement (see Figure 6–3a).

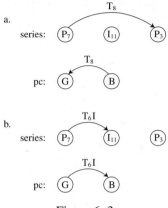

Figure 6–3

Similarly, the first two notes of the series can be thought of as related at T_6I, and so can the first two series of the movement (see Figure 6–3b). For the early twelve-tone composers, like Webern, and for their successors, the twelve-tone approach was attractive, in part, because it permitted them to write music that not only had a rich, engaging motivic surface, but had structural depths as well.

The influence of the series (and its prominent 3–3s) goes far beyond simple, direct statements. Consider the organization of the melodic line (that is, all the instruments except the accompanying piano). (See Example 6–2.)

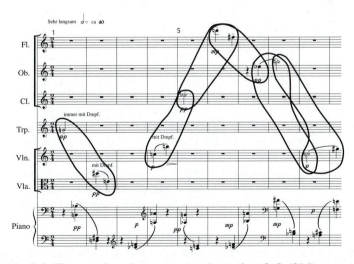

Example 6–2 The set class that generates the series, 3–3 (014), permeates the melodic line.

The notes in this line are by no means all contiguous within the series. The first circled trichord, for example, contains the first, fourth, and seventh notes of P_7. Yet this and all the other circled trichords in the melody are members of 3–3 (014), a set class that does occur directly in the series. What is more, Webern has linked these forms of 3–3 to each other by the same transpositions and inversions that also can be found within them (see Figure 6–4).

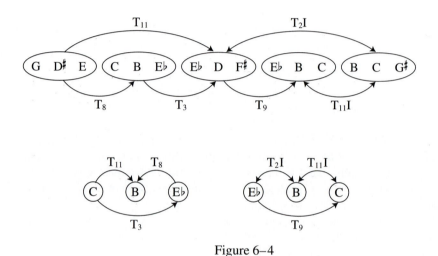

Figure 6–4

From this point of view, it appears that 3–3 not only generates the series but shapes many dimensions of the music that do not fall under any kind of direct serial control.

The influence of the series and its trichords extends even to the instrumentation, registers, and articulations of the passage (see Example 6–3). The viola, for example, plays two notes in measure 2 (the fourth and seventh notes of P_7) and then is silent until measure 13, when it plays two more notes (the first and fourth notes of P_4). These four notes together (the E is repeated), associated by instrumentation, create a 3–3 (014), the very set class from which the series is derived. The same sort of thing happens in the violin part.

The registers and articulations are similarly influenced by the series. In measures 2, 4, and 6, a melodic instrument plays a pair of notes. The highest notes of each pair, taken together, again create 3–3 (014). This is easy and rewarding to hear and shows the profound role of the series in shaping all aspects of the musical structure.

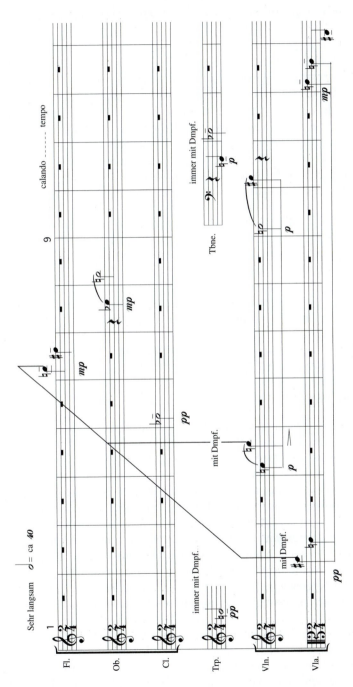

Example 6–3 The trichord that generates the series, 3–3 (014), also influences the instrumentation, register, and articulation.

Schoenberg and Hexachordal Combinatoriality

Just as Webern constructs series that are motivically concentrated, and often derived, Schoenberg, in his mature twelve-tone music, always constructs series in which the two hexachords are related by inversion. To understand the extraordinary significance of this relationship for the structure of his music, we will have to begin by recalling some general points about hexachords from Chapter 3. First, since complementary hexachords have the same interval content, the hexachords of a twelve-tone series have the same interval content. Second, some hexachords are self-complementary: they and their complements are members of the same set class. Such hexachords can map onto their complements under either transposition or inversion. In Appendix 1, self-complementary hexachords have nothing written across from them. If a hexachord is not self-complementary, then it must be Z-related to its complement. Remember that the Z-relation holds between sets that are not members of the same set class but that nonetheless have the same interval vector. Such hexachords are not related to their complements by transposition or inversion.

In short, some hexachords can map onto their complements under either transposition or inversion, and some cannot. Furthermore, like sets of other sizes, some hexachords can map onto themselves and some cannot. We thus have a simple way of classifying any hexachord by posing four questions:

1. Can it map onto its complement under transposition?
2. Can it map onto its complement under inversion?
3. Can it map onto itself under transposition?
4. Can it map onto itself under inversion?

The answers to these questions define a hexachord's most basic structural properties. For some hexachords, the answer to all four questions is no (except insofar as every set maps onto itself at T_0); for others, the answer to all four questions is yes; and for still others, the answer is yes to some questions and no to others.

The *aggregate*—a collection consisting of all twelve pitch classes—is the basic harmonic unit in twelve-tone music, so it is not surprising that composers find various ways of combining collections to create it. *Combinatoriality* is the general term for combining a collection with one or more transposed or inverted forms of itself (or its complement) to create an aggregate. Not all collections are capable of being combined in that way (except insofar as any collection can combine with its complement at T_0 to create an aggregate). Those that are, are called *combinatorial* collections. Composers have been particularly interested in combinatorial hexachords, so we will concentrate on them.

There are four kinds of combinatoriality: *prime-, inversional-, retrograde-,* and *retrograde-inversional-combinatoriality.* If a hexachord can combine with a transposed form of itself to create an aggregate, then it is prime- (or P-) combinatorial. In Figure 6–5, a hypothetical P_0 contains two complementary hexachords, called H_1 and H_2, while some other prime ordering of the series contains the same hexachords in reverse order.

$$P_0: \quad H_1 \qquad H_2$$
$$P_x: \quad \underline{H_2} \qquad \underline{H_1}$$
$$\qquad \text{agg.} \qquad \text{agg.}$$

Figure 6–5

Notice that we are only talking about the content of the hexachords. H_1 in P_0 may have a different order from H_1 in P_x. What defines H_1 (or H_2) is the content, not the order. This is true for all the kinds of combinatoriality.

What kind of hexachord has this P-combinatorial property? As the diagram shows, at the combinatorial transposition level H_1 maps onto H_2 and H_2 maps onto H_1. That means that H_1 and H_2 must be related by T_n. We already know that H_1 and H_2 are complementary. So, to be P-combinatorial, a hexachord must be transpositionally related to its complement. In other words, a P-combinatorial hexachord is one for which the answer to question 1 is yes. You will notice in Appendix 1 that all the prime-combinatorial hexachords have a 0 somewhere in their interval vector. Try to figure out why this is so. Only seven of the 50 hexachords are P-combinatorial, and only one of them, 6–14 (013458), is P-combinatorial without also being I-combinatorial.

Inversional combinatoriality involves combining a hexachord with an inverted form of itself to create an aggregate. With an I-combinatorial hexachord, combining inversionally related forms of the series at the proper transposition level will result in aggregates, as shown in Figure 6–6.

$$P_0: \quad H_1 \qquad H_2$$
$$I_x: \quad \underline{H_2} \qquad \underline{H_1}$$
$$\qquad \text{agg.} \qquad \text{agg.}$$

Figure 6–6

To create aggregates in this way, the hexachord must be inversionally related to its complement. In other words, an inversional-combinatorial hexachord is one that maps onto its complement under inversion (and for which the answer to question 2 is yes).

If you look at the set list in Appendix 1, you will see that I-combinatoriality is much more common than P-combinatoriality. Only one hexachord is P-combinatorial without also being I-combinatorial, but many hexachords are I-combinatorial without also being P-combinatorial. Schoenberg virtually always constructed his series with inversionally combinatorial hexachords.

Retrograde-combinatoriality involves combining a collection with a transposed form of its complement. With an R-combinatorial hexachord, combining retrograde-related forms of the series at the proper transposition level will result in aggregates (see Figure 6–7).

$$P_0: \quad H_1 \qquad H_2$$
$$R_x: \quad \underline{H_2} \qquad \underline{H_1}$$
$$\qquad \text{agg.} \qquad \text{agg.}$$

Figure 6–7

Every hexachord is R-combinatorial in that it can combine with its complement at T_0. In other words, P_0 is always combinatorial with R_0 (see Figure 6–8).

$$P_0: \quad H_1 \qquad H_2$$
$$R_0: \quad \underline{\;H_2\;} \quad \underline{\;H_1\;}$$
$$\text{agg.} \quad \text{agg.}$$

Figure 6–8

There are four hexachords, however, that can combine with their complements at transposition levels other than 0 to make an aggregate. To be R-combinatorial, the answer to question 3 must be yes—the hexachord must map onto itself under transposition. It is easy to find such hexachords in the set list. Just look for interval-vector entries of 6 (or 3 in the tritone column). If a hexachord has six of some interval (or three tritones), it will be R-combinatorial at that transposition level.

Retrograde-inversional-combinatoriality involves combining a hexachord with an inverted form of its complement. With such an RI-combinatorial hexachord, combining retrograde-inversionally related forms of the series at the proper transposition level will result in aggregates, as in Figure 6–9.

$$P_0: \quad H_1 \qquad H_2$$
$$RI_x: \quad \underline{\;H_2\;} \quad \underline{\;H_1\;}$$
$$\text{agg.} \quad \text{agg.}$$

Figure 6–9

Such a hexachord must be self-inversional, able to map onto itself under inversion—the answer to question 4 must be yes. Figure 6–10 summarizes the four kinds of combinatoriality.

	maps onto itself	maps onto its complement
under T_n	R-combinatorial	P-combinatorial
under T_nI	RI-combinatorial	I-combinatorial

Figure 6–10

Some hexachords have more than one kind of combinatoriality but only six have all four kinds. Those six hexachords are *all-combinatorial,* and they are listed in Figure 6–11.

6–1	(012345)
6–8	(023457)
6–32	(024579)
6–7	(012678)
6–20	(014589)
6–35	(02468T)

Figure 6–11

The first three hexachords have all four types of combinatoriality at one transposition level each (they are R-combinatorial only at R_0). The fourth hexachord has each type of combinatoriality at two levels; the fifth is all-combinatorial at three levels; and the sixth, the whole-tone scale, is all-combinatorial at six levels. These hexachords thus have remarkable properties from a twelve-tone point of view. They constitute a rich resource that has been exploited by more recent generations of twelve-tone composers.

Combinatoriality is musically important for two reasons, one having to do with small-scale succession and the other with large-scale organization. First, combinatoriality gives composers a good way of combining series-forms simultaneously (say, in two different instruments or voices) or of progressing from one series-form to another. In both circumstances, combinatoriality will create aggregates. It may also bring about other kinds of important musical associations.

Let's see how inversional-combinatoriality works in a familiar passage, the beginning of the third movement of Schoenberg's String Quartet No. 4 (see Example 6–4).

(continued)

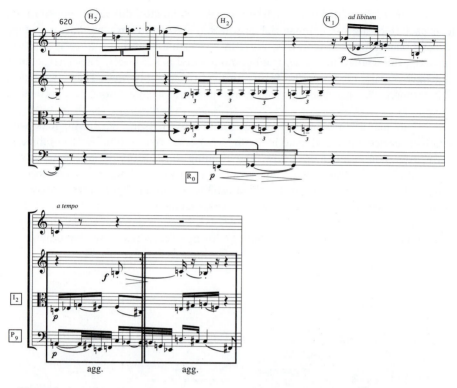

Example 6–4 Combinatoriality permits common-tone links from phrase to phrase as well as the creation of aggregates (Schoenberg, String Quartet No. 4, third movement).

In measures 614–20, P_0 is followed by RI_5; Figure 6–12 summarizes the progression. H_1 contains [G,A♭,B,C,D♭,E♭]; H_2 contains the remaining six pitch classes. Because of combinatoriality, the second hexachord of P0 and the first hexachord of RI_5 together create an aggregate. This provides a link between these two series-forms.

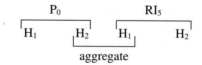

Figure 6–12

Another kind of connection occurs in measures 620–21. RI_5 (beginning at the end of measure 618) and R_0 are combinatorially related, so the second hexachord of RI_5 has the same pitch-class content as the first hexachord of R_0. As a result, Schoenberg is able to make a nice, smooth connection. The dyads in the first violin in measures 620–21 are simply distributed among the other three instruments in the music that immediately follows. Like the aggregate formed between the end of P_0 and the beginning of RI_5, this sharing of pitch classes creates a strong link between RI_5 and R_0.

For another example of combinatoriality at work on the small scale, look at the viola and cello parts in measure 623. The series forms are I_2 and P_9. If P_0 and I_5 are combinatorially related, then so are P_1 and I_6, P_2 and I_7, and so on even though the index number that maps the hexachords onto each other differs. P_9 and I_2 are thus combinatorially related and, as a result, aggregates are created by combining them. Combinatoriality, with the aggregates and common-tone links it provides, thus gives twelve-tone composers a way of getting from series to series and of combining series.

Combinatoriality also influences the large-scale organization of twelve-tone pieces. It does so by taking the forty-eight series-forms and dividing them into twelve or fewer closely knit groups of series-forms. Each of these groups constitutes an *area* that functions like the tonicized keys in a tonal piece. In the case of Schoenberg's String Quartet No. 4, P_0, I_5, and their retrogrades, R_0 and RI_5, constitute a single area which we will designate A_0. The four series-forms in this area all have the same hexachordal content. With an I-combinatorial series like this one, there will be twelve such areas, each containing four series-forms. A_1 will contain P_1, I_6, R_1, and RI_6; A2 will contain P_2, I_7, R_2, and RI_7; and so on (see Figure 6–13).

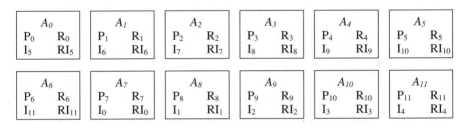

Figure 6–13

Because of combinatoriality, Schoenberg and other twelve-tone composers are able to "modulate" from area to area, creating a sense of harmonic motion at the highest levels of structure.

Of course a twelve-tone area is significantly different from a traditional tonal harmonic area. The diatonic collection changes its content when it is transposed. We can discern motion from tonal area to tonal area (or from key to key) because of the changing pitch-class content. In twelve-tone music, however, the referential collection (the twelve-tone series) contains all twelve pitch classes. When it is transposed or inverted, the content remains the same, as we noted earlier. As a result, harmonic areas cannot be created on the same basis as before. Combinatoriality provides a solution to this problem because it groups together families of series-forms based not on their total content (which is always the same) but on the content of their hexachords. For Schoenberg in particular, these twelve-tone areas are something like the keys in a tonal piece. Large-scale motion in his music often involves movement from area to area.

The first thirty-one measures of his String Quartet No. 4 (first movement) use only P_2, the combinatorially related I_7, and the retrogrades of these. In other words, the movement begins in A_2. Some time later, the passage shown in Example 6–5 occurs.

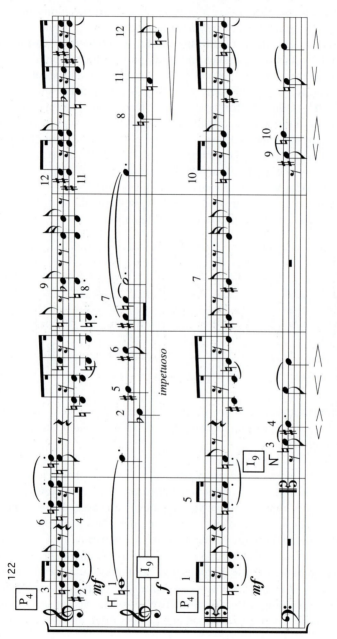

Example 6–5 "Modulation" to A4.

The melody in this passage (divided between the second violin and cello) states I_9 while the accompaniment states P_4. These combinatorially related series define a new area, A_4. The music has effectively "modulated" up a step. It is heading toward its eventual goal, A_8, which it reaches in measure 165. That is the climactic moment where the opening melody comes back a tritone away from its starting point. A_4 is thus part of the large-scale path that leads onward to A_8.

At the same time, A_4 recalls important events from A_2. Notice that I_9, part of A_4, preserves the tetrachords from P_2 (see Figure 6–14).

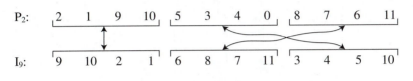

P_2: 2 1 9 10 5 3 4 0 8 7 6 11

I_9: 9 10 2 1 6 8 7 11 3 4 5 10

Figure 6–14

This is because the second and third tetrachords of the series are related to one another at $T_{11}I$, while the first tetrachord maps onto itself at $T_{11}I$. Earlier, we talked about the possibility of keeping a dyad or trichord intact when the series-form changed. Now we see that larger collections, in this case tetrachords, can be treated in the same way. Compare P_2 as it occurs at the beginning of the movement with I_9 as it occurs in measures 122–25 (see Example 6–6). The two are associated by their shared tetrachords. By "modulating" to A4, Schoenberg thus simultaneously points ahead to where he is going and recalls where he has been.

The more combinatorial the hexachord, the fewer the areas. If the hexachord is 6-1 (012345), for example, there will be only six areas, as shown in Figure 6–15.

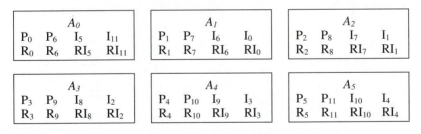

A_0			
P_0	P_6	I_5	I_{11}
R_0	R_6	RI_5	RI_{11}

A_1			
P_1	P_7	I_6	I_0
R_1	R_7	RI_6	RI_0

A_2			
P_2	P_8	I_7	I_1
R_2	R_8	RI_7	RI_1

A_3			
P_3	P_9	I_8	I_2
R_3	R_9	RI_8	RI_2

A_4			
P_4	P_{10}	I_9	I_3
R_4	R_{10}	RI_9	RI_3

A_5			
P_5	P_{11}	I_{10}	I_4
R_5	R_{11}	RI_{10}	RI_4

Figure 6–15

Each area contains eight series-forms, all with the same hexachordal content. The most combinatorial of the hexachords, the whole-tone hexachord, has only a single area—all forty-eight series-forms have the same hexachordal content. Because there is no possibility of contrast between areas with this hexachord, most twelve-tone composers have avoided it.

Example 6–6 P_2 (within A_2) shares its tetrachords with I_9 (within A_4).

Stravinsky and Rotational Arrays

When Stravinsky started writing serial and twelve-tone music late in his life, he brought to bear the full force of his vigorous and highly individual musical personality. Beginning with *Movements* in 1960 and ending with *Requiem Canticles* in 1966, he settled on a reasonably stable twelve-tone practice based on rotational arrays, like the one in Figure 6–16.

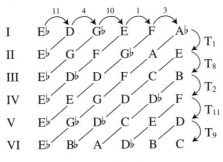

Figure 6–16

Stravinsky normally used only four, untransposed forms of the series: a prime (P), an inversion starting on the same first note (I), the retrograde of the prime (R), and the inversion of the retrograde, starting on the same first note (IR). In Figure 6–16, the first hexachord of the I-form of the series for *A Sermon, A Narrative, and A Prayer* is written across the top row. The second line of the array takes that hexachord (E♭–D–G♭–E–F–A♭), rotates it to start on its second note (D–G♭–E–F–A♭–E♭), then transposes it up a semitone to start on E♭. The third line of the array rotates the hexachord to start on its third note (G♭–E–F–A♭–E♭–D) and transposes it down a minor third to start on E♭. The remaining lines proceed in similar fashion.

Each line of the array rotates the first hexachord and transposes the rotation to start on E♭. Each of the rows thus describes the same succession of intervals (allowing for wraparound), but begins one note earlier than the row directly above it. As a result, the lines create a kind of six-voice canon.

The lines of the array are all related by transposition, and the intervals of transposition are the complements mod 12 of the intervals within the original hexachord. As a result, when Stravinsky writes music that moves systematically through an array like this from top to bottom, he will compose-out the inversion of the generating hexachord.

Example 6–7 reproduces a passage based on the array from Figure 6–16.

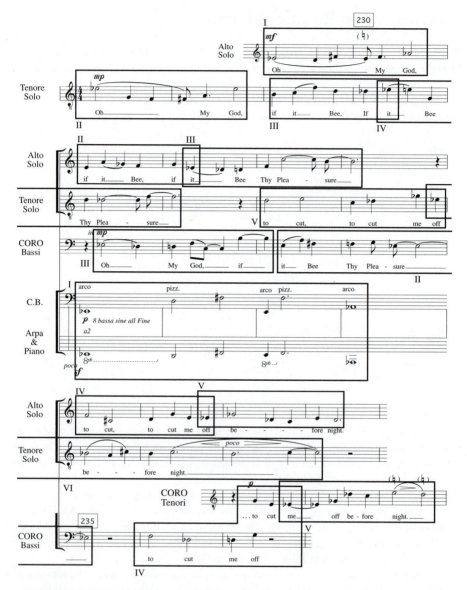

Example 6–7 Three cycles through a rotational array (Stravinsky, *A Sermon, A Narrative, and A Prayer,* mm. 227–39).

Stravinsky presents the notes in each of the rows of the array either from first to last or last to first. The passage contains three distinct cycles through the array: in the alto solo (I–II–III–IV–V); in the tenor solo (II–III–IV–V–VI); and in the choral basses and tenors together with the instrumental accompaniment (I–III–II–IV–V). Within each cycle, the transpositional levels compose-out the inversion of the original hexachord.

The rows of the array often have common tones. The first note of each of the rows is always the same and often plays a centric role. That is certainly true of the E♭, so frequently a point of arrival and departure in this passage. Other notes also recur from row to row, although less frequently. The result is an intensive melodic focus, with a relatively small group of notes in circulation. This is typical of Stravinsky's melodies throughout his career. His twelve-tone music, very unlike the Schoenbergian variety, is not generally based on the aggregate. Stravinsky's late music often traces melodic pathways through his rotational arrays.

Although Stravinsky generally used the rows of the arrays to create melodies, he also sometimes used the columns (or "verticals") of the arrays to write harmonies. Example 6–8 shows another rotational array and a cadential passage from *Requiem Canticles* based on it.

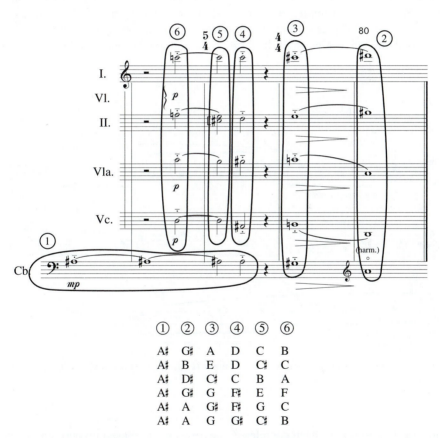

①	②	③	④	⑤	⑥
A♯	G♯	A	D	C	B
A♯	B	E	D	C♯	C
A♯	D♯	C♯	C	B	A
A♯	G♯	G	F♯	E	F
A♯	A	G♯	F♯	G	C
A♯	A	G	G♯	C♯	B

Example 6–8 A rotational array and its verticals (Stravinsky, *Requiem Canticles,* "Exaudi," mm. 76–80).

Vertical No. 1 consists of a single pitch class, A♯, which forms an axis of symmetry for the rest of the verticals. Verticals No. 6 and No. 2 are related at $I_{A\sharp}^{A\sharp}$ as are Verticals

No. 3 and No. 5. Vertical No. 4 maps onto itself at I$_{A\sharp}^{A\sharp}$. In that sense, the A$\sharp$ is a centric note for the passage. That sense of centricity, together with the frequent pitch-class doublings, both in the array and in the passage, impart a sense of weightedness and focus. In that way, Stravinsky's twelve-tone music is about as different from the twelve-tone musics of Schoenberg and Webern as it can be.

Crawford and Her "Triple Passacaglia"

Of Ruth Crawford Seeger's small but distinctive body of works, five follow multilay-ered serial plans of rotation and transposition. In the third movement of *Diaphonic Suite No. 1,* for example, a seven-note series stated in the first measure (G–A–G$\sharp$–B–C–F–C$\sharp$) is systematically rotated in the measures that follow, so that the second measure begins on A, the third on G$\sharp$, and so on (see Example 6–9).

Example 6–9 Series projected at two levels (Crawford, *Diaphonic Suite No. 1,* mm. 1–8).

When the rotations have been completed, the series is transposed up two semitones, and that new series-form is rotated in the same manner. The new series-form begins, of course, on A, the second note of the original series. As the piece progresses, each new series-form begins in turn with the next note of the series, thus projecting, on this highest structural level, the pitch-class succession of the original series (see Example 6–10).

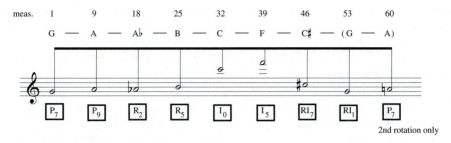

Example 6–10 Series projected at a third level (Crawford, *Diaphonic Suite No. 1*).

Thus the series is projected at three levels: in eighth notes within each measure, from downbeat to downbeat, and from section to section. That three-fold projection is what Crawford had in mind when she referred to this movement as a "triple passacaglia."

The progression from series-form to series-form recalls the progression from note to note within the series (see Example 6–11).

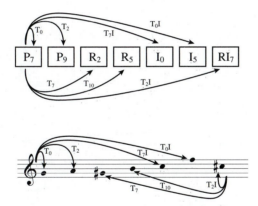

Example 6–11 Transformations that connect the forms of the series also connect the notes of the series (Crawford, *Diaphonic Suite No. 1*).

This is not twelve-tone music exactly, but it is serial music from its surface details to its structural depths.

Boulez and Multiplication

In the years immediately following World War II, many composers sought new ways of coordinating all aspects of music with twelve-tone pitch organization. In traditional tonal music, the form, rhythm, dynamics, register, and instrumentation are not arbitrary, but are closely integrated with the harmony and voice leading. Many twelve-tone composers yearned for a similar kind of integration. Milton Babbitt describes "the desire for a completely autonomous conception of the twelve-tone system, and for works in which all components, in all dimensions, would be determined by the relations and operations of the system." By an interesting historical coincidence, this desire was felt simultaneously by American and European composers, even though they had had virtually no contact with one another because of the war. Although their aims were similar, however, their approaches were different.

The European approach, as exemplified in the music of Pierre Boulez, was to construct twelve-element series of durations, dynamics, or articulations, and then to manipulate them as though they were series of pitch classes. Durations, for example, can be arranged in a twelve-element "scale," from one thirty-second-note through twelve thirty-second-notes. Then those twelve durations can be ordered into a twelve-element rhythmic series. Example 6–12 shows the first piano part in the opening passage from Boulez's *Structures 1a,* a passage that involves serialized pitches and rhythms.

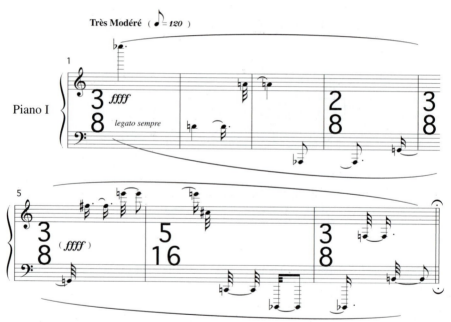

Example 6–12 Serialization of pitch and rhythm (Boulez, *Structures 1a*).

The piano states a series of pitches (E♭–D–A–A♭–G–F♯–E–C♯–C–B♭–F–B) and a series of durations (see Figure 6–17).

Figure 6–17

In a similar fashion, one can devise a series of dynamics by constructing another twelve-element "scale," ranging from *pppp* to *ffff,* and then ordering those elements into a series. Even articulations can be serialized in this way; just take twelve different modes of attack (staccato, sforzando, legato, etc.) and arrange them into a series.

In the pitch domain, Boulez often made use of pitch-class *multiplication.* This is a way of generating material from a series by the transposition of its segmental subsets to levels defined by its segmental subsets. Here is how it works in *Le Marteau sans Maître,* Boulez's most famous piece.

Boulez begins with a twelve-tone series, divided into five segments (see Example 6–13).

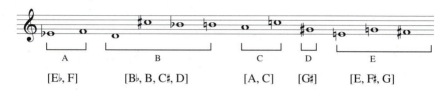

A	B	C	D	E
[E♭, F]	[B♭, B, C♯, D]	[A, C]	[G♯]	[E, F♯, G]

Example 6–13 Series divided into five segments (Boulez, *Le Marteau sans Maître*).

The segments can then be multiplied by each other. Multiplication involves transposing the notes of one segment to the pitch levels defined by another segment. Let's multiply Segment A by Segment B to see how this works. Segment A consists of the whole-tone [E♭, F] and Segment B consists of [B♭, B, C♯, D]. Multiplying A by B means transposing A (a whole-tone) to start on each of the notes of Segment B. That gives us four whole-tones: [B♭, C], [B, C♯], [C♯, D♯] and [D, E]. Combining those four sets and eliminating duplicates, we get [B♭, B, C, C♯, D, D♯, E] (see Figure 6–18).

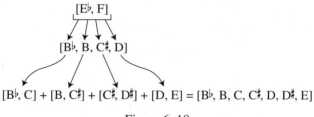

[B♭, C] + [B, C♯] + [C♯, D♯] + [D, E] = [B♭, B, C, C♯, D, D♯, E]

Figure 6–18

If we had done it the other way around, multiplying B by A, we would have gotten another member of the same set class, related by transposition to the one we did get.

Segments can also be multiplied by themselves. For example, to multiply Segment B by itself, we transpose Segment B to begin on each of the notes of Segment B, giving us [B♭, B, C♯, D] + [B, C, D, D♯] + [C♯, D, E, F] + [D, D♯, F, F♯] = [B♭, B, C, C♯, D, D♯, E, F, F♯] (see Figure 6–19).

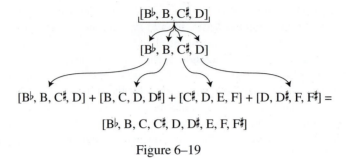

$$[B\flat, B, C\sharp, D] + [B, C, D, D\sharp] + [C\sharp, D, E, F] + [D, D\sharp, F, F\sharp] =$$

$$[B\flat, B, C, C\sharp, D, D\sharp, E, F, F\sharp]$$

Figure 6–19

Figure 6–20 shows the results of multiplying each of the five segments of the series by Segment B.

A	B	C	D	E
[E♭, F]	[B♭, B, C♯, D]	[A, C]	[G♯]	[E, F♯, G]

BA = [B♭, C] + [B, C♯] + [C♯, D♯] + [D, E] = [B♭, B, C, C♯, D, D♯, E]

BB = [B♭, B, C♯, D] + [B, C, D, D♯] + [C♯, D, E, F] + [D, D♯, F, F♯] = [B♭, B, C, C♯ D, D♯ E, F, F♯]

BC = [B♭, C♯] + [B, D] + [C♯, E] + [D, F] + [B♭, B, C♯, D, E, F]

BD = [B♭] + [B] + [C♯] + [D] = [B♭, B, C♯, D]

BE = [B♭, C, C♯] + [B, C♯, D] + [C♯, D♯, E] + [D, E, F] = [B♭, B, C, C♯, D, D♯, E, F]

Figure 6–20

The five *multiplicands* embed one or more subsets related by transposition to each of the relevant *multipliers*. For example, the multiplicand BA embeds four forms of A and two forms of B. In fact, B is present as a literal subset of all five multiplicands. Possibly in order to ensure greater harmonic variety, Boulez does one more thing. He transposes each of the five multiplicands by the interval between a constant, in this case F (always the last note of the first segment), and the first note of each segment (see Figure 6–21).

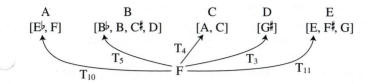

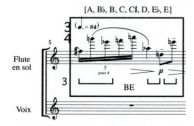

	Multiplicands from Figure 6–19		Transposed by predetermined interval
BA	[B♭, B, C, C♯, D, D♯, E]	T_{10}	[A♭, A, B♭, B, C, C♯, D]
BB	[B♭, B, C, C♯, D, D♯, E, F, F♯]	T_5	[E♭, E, F, F♯, G, G♯, A, A♯, B]
BC	[B♭, B, C♯, D, E, F]	T_4	[D, D♯, F, F♯, G♯, A]
BD	[B♭, B, C♯, D]	T_3	[C♯, D, E, F]
BE	[B♭, B, C, C♯, D, D♯, E, F]	T_{11}	[A, B♭, B, C, C♯, D, D♯, E]

Figure 6–21

The five transposed multiplicands of Figure 6–21 provide the pitch-class content for the first five measures of the third movement of *Le Marteau* (see Example 6–14, and notice that the flute is written in G).

Example 6–14 Multiplication (Boulez, *Le Marteau sans Maître*, third movement, "L'Artisanat furieux," mm. 1–5).

At each stage in the journey from series to score—the division of the series into segments, the multiplication of segments by each other, the transposition of the resulting products—different compositional decisions might have been made and, indeed, Boulez varies each stage over the course of the work. The result is a musical surface of dazzling variety, but all with its roots in the original twelve-tone series. The series is no longer an explicit part of the music—it's never presented as a tune. Rather, it exerts its influence on the music from a structural distance.

Babbitt and Trichordal Arrays

Babbitt was and remains the preeminent figure in American serialism. He has sought to compose rhythms, dynamics, and other nonpitch elements in a way that would reinforce his pitch structures. Look, for example, at the first nine measures of his String Quartet No. 2 (see Example 6–15).

Example 6–15a Dynamics used to reinforce intervallic ideas (Babbitt, String Quartet No. 2).

Example 6–15b Dynamics used to reinforce intervallic ideas (Babbitt, String Quartet No. 2).

In the first three measures, we hear six pairs of notes: A–C, B–D, F–Ab, G–Bb, C#–E, and Eb–Gb. Each pair projects ordered pitch-class interval +3. Measures 4–6 have a somewhat more varied surface, but we are still hearing mainly pairs of notes. Now, however, a new ordered pitch-class interval, −4 (or 8) is projected: D–Bb, E–C, Bb–Gb, C–Ab, G–Eb, A–F, B–G, and F–Db. In measure 7 those two intervals, +3 and −4, are combined into a trichord that generates a twelve-tone series.

Babbitt uses dynamics to reinforce these intervallic ideas. In measures 1–3, for example, three pitch classes occur at each of four dynamic levels. Notice the succession of ordered pitch-class intervals at each dynamic level (see Figure 6–22).

pp: B–D–Bb = +3, −4
mp: A–C–Ab = +3, −4
mf: G–Eb–Gb = −4, +3
ff: F–C#–E = −4, +3

Figure 6–22

The surface of the music in these measures projects only +3, but the dynamics point ahead to the later combination of that interval with −4.

Something similar happens in measures 4–6. Again, there are four dynamic levels and three pitch classes at each, and, with two small exceptions, intervallic patterns involving +3 and −4 are stated at each level. The dynamics thus reinforce and enrich the pitch structure. They are not serialized independently, but integrated within a larger unified structure.

At this relatively early stage in his career (1947–60), these larger structures emerge from *trichordal arrays*. A typical trichordal array consists of four lines (see Figure 6–23).

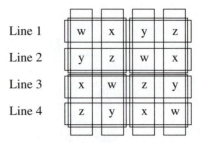

Line 1	w	x	y	z
Line 2	y	z	w	x
Line 3	x	w	z	y
Line 4	z	y	x	w

Figure 6–23

All four lines contain a derived series: trichords W, X, Y, and Z are all members of the same set class, and are presented in the four serial orderings (P, I, R, and RI). Aggregates are formed within each line, between pairs of lines (hexachordal combinatoriality) and, in the columns of the array, among all four lines (trichordal combinatoriality). Babbitt's trichordal array thus represents a synthesis of Schoenbergian combinatoriality and Webernian derivation. Mm. 7–9 realize the first half of a trichordal array (see Figure 6–24).

Vln. 1	A – C – A♭	E – C♯ – F	etc.
Vln. 2	B – G – B♭	D – F♯ – D♯	etc.
Vla.	E – C♯ – F	A – C – G♯	etc.
Cel.	D – F♯ – E♭	B – G – B♭	etc.

Figure 6–24

The twelve tones are ordered in so many different ways in this passage—within individual instruments, within pairs of instruments, within dynamic levels—that one may well ask, "Which one is the series?" The answer is that no one of these orderings may be taken as *the* series for the piece. There is a generating series, but it emerges only interval by interval, and doesn't receive explicit musical presentation until measure 266, when the piece is almost over. Until then, its intervals are heard one or two at a time. The intervals combine to form trichords and tetrachords that generate the series that give rise to the gradually evolving trichordal arrays. In Babbitt's music, the series is no longer necessarily a thematic element of the musical surface. Rather, it may operate at some structural distance, spawning the arrays that shape the surface.

Like dynamics, register and articulation also can be integrated within a twelve-tone structure. Groupings created by shared register or mode of attack can duplicate, in those musical dimensions, the musical ideas of the pitch surface. In the theme of Babbitt's *Semi-Simple Variations,* for example, the music projects, in register, the four lines of the first half of a trichordal array (see Example 6–16).

Example 6–16 Register, articulation, and dynamics used to project intervallic ideas (Babbitt, *Semi-Simple Variations*).

Aggregates are formed among all four lines, between pairs of lines, and (as the music continues beyond the example) within each line.

Consider the trichords contained as subsets within the soprano hexachord (see Example 6–17).

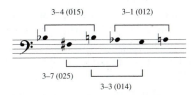

Example 6–17 The hexachord and its subsets.

Four different trichords are stated—3–4 (015), 3–7 (025), 3–3 (014), and 3–1 (012)—and, of course, the other three registral hexachords contain the same trichords. These same trichords are projected by articulation and dynamics. The first three notes of the piece, for example, are drawn from three different registral voices, but share a legato articulation and a *pp* dynamic level. That trichord, B♭–D–A, is a member of set class 3–4, simultaneously undergoing a linear statement in the outer voices. The next trichord, C♯–A–B♭, also cuts across the registral lines and also shares articulation (nonlegato) and dynamic level (*mf*). These notes form trichord 3–3, also a linear subset of the series. Throughout the passage and the work, groupings created by dynamics and articulation reinforce the pitch structure of the work as a whole.

The rhythm is also serialized in *Semi-Simple Variations*. If the sixteenth-note is the basic rhythmic unit, there are sixteen different ways of partitioning (carving up) a quarter-note into attacks and silences. The theme in measures 1–6 is sixteen quarter-notes long, and each quarter-note is partitioned differently. Figure 6–25 shows the rhythmic series projected by the theme.

Figure 6–25

That rhythmic series can be transformed in the usual serial manner: it can be played in retrograde, it can be inverted (its attacks replaced by rests and vice versa), and it can be retrograde-inverted. As the work progresses, each section is articulated by a transformation of the rhythmic series. In that way, the rhythmic serialization reinforces the form of the work.

Over the course of his career, Babbitt has approached rhythm in a variety of ways. In some works, he uses *duration rows*. These involve patterns of durations, measured in relation to a fixed rhythmic unit. For example, the durational pattern 1–4–3–2 (where 1 is, say, an eighth-note, 4 is a half-note, 3 is a dotted quarter-note, and 2 a quarter-note), might be established as a prime ordering, which could then be inverted (4–1–2–3), retrograded (2–3–4–1), or retrograde-inverted (3–2–1–4). The pattern of durations might replicate the ordering of pitch classes in a series. For example, if we number the pitch classes 1 through 12 (instead of 0 through 11) and assign 1 to B♭, the series for the String Quartet No. 2 is: 11–2–10–3–12–1–7–9–4–8–6–5 (or G♯–B–G–C–A–B♭–E–F♯–C♯–F–E♭–D). In measure 260, when that pitch-class series is heard explicitly for the first time, it is associated with that duration series (the G♯ lasts for eleven thirty-second notes; the B lasts for two thirty-second notes; the G lasts for ten thirty-second notes; and so on).

Later in his career, Babbitt developed a new way of serializing rhythm, one based on *time points*. This newer system is concerned with the time interval between the downbeat of the measure and the point of attack of each note in the rhythmic series. The series 0–3–11–4–1–2–8–10–5–9–7–6, for example, could be realized either in pitches or in rhythms, as shown in Example 6–18 (from Babbitt's own discussion of time points).

Example 6–18 A time-point series.

The first attack occurs right on the downbeat, time point 0; the second attack occurs at time point 3 (after three sixteenth-notes have elapsed); the third attack occurs at time point 11 (after eleven sixteenth-notes); and so on. The same series could be realized rhythmically in other ways—Example 6–18 shows it in its shortest possible representation. For example, eight beats elapse between the attacks at time points 3 and 11. That time span could equally well be realized by a measure plus eight beats or five measures plus eight beats. Just as the octave is the modulus among pitch classes, the measure is the modulus among time points. Furthermore, only the attack points, not the durations, are specified by the system. In the example, the attacks could initiate notes of shorter duration, with rests filling out the necessary time until the next attack. If the same series were used to shape the pitches, the result would be a remarkable coordination of pitch and rhythm.

BIBLIOGRAPHY

The definitive discussions of Schoenbergian combinatoriality may be found in the articles by Milton Babbitt cited in the bibliography for Chapter 5. Ethan Haimo provides a useful summary of this and other aspects of Schoenberg's mature style in *Schoenberg's Serial Odyssey: The Evolution of His Twelve-Tone Method, 1914–1928* (Oxford: Oxford University Press, 1990).

The idea of twelve-tone areas is developed in studies by David Lewin. See his "Inversional Balance as an Organizing Force in Schoenberg's Music and Thought," *Perspectives of New Music* 6/2 (1968), pp. 1–21; "*Moses and Aron:* Some General Remarks, and Analytic Notes for Act I, Scene 1," *Perspectives of New Music* 6/1 (1967), pp. 1–17; and "A Study of Hexachord Levels in Schoenberg's Violin Fantasy," *Perspectives of New Music* 6/1 (1967), pp. 18–32.

On Stravinsky's rotational arrays, see Milton Babbitt, "Stravinsky's Verticals and Schoenberg's Diagonals: A Twist of Fate" (1987), in *The Collected Essays of Milton Babbitt;* Robert Morris, "Generalizing Rotational Arrays," *Journal of Music Theory* 32/1 (1988), pp. 75–132; John Rogers, "Some Properties of Non-duplicating Rotational Arrays," *Perspectives of New Music* 7/1 (1968), pp. 80–102; and Joseph N. Straus, *Stravinsky's Late Music.*

On Crawford, see Joseph N. Straus, *The Music of Ruth Crawford Seeger* (Cambridge: Cambridge University Press, 1995).

The serial organization of Boulez's *Le Marteau sans Maître* is described in Lev Koblyakov, *Pierre Boulez: A World of Harmony* (Chur, Switzerland: Harwood Academic

Publishers, 1990). See also Stephen Heinemann, "Pitch-Class Set Multiplication in Theory and Practice," *Music Theory Spectrum* 20/1 (1998), pp. 72–96. The idea of "multiplication" relates closely to Cohn's "transpositional combination," discussed in Chapter 3.

The literature on Babbitt is voluminous. The best single source is Andrew Mead, *An Introduction to the Music of Milton Babbitt* (Princeton: Princeton University Press, 1994). See also a trilogy of articles by Joseph Dubiel: "Three Essays on Milton Babbitt," Part 1: *Perspectives of New Music* 28/2 (1990), pp. 216–61; Part 2: *Perspectives of New Music* 29/1 (1991), pp. 90–123; Part 3: *Perspectives of New Music* 30/1 (1992), pp. 82–131. Babbitt describes his time-point system in "Twelve-Tone Rhythmic Structure and the Electronic Medium" in *The Collected Essays of Milton Babbitt.*

Exercises

THEORY

I. Derivation: A derived series is one whose discrete segmental trichords or tetrachords are all members of the same set class.

  1. The following series by Webern are derived. Identify the generating trichord or tetrachord and the transformations (transposition, inversion, retrograde) that connect it with the other segmental subsets of the series.
      a. C♯–C–E♭–D–F♯–G–E–F–A–A♭–B–B♭ (String Quartet, Op. 28)
      b. E♭–B–D–C♯–F–E–G–F♯–B♭–A–C–A♭ (Cantata I, Op. 29)

  2. Construct series as indicated.
      a. Its discrete trichords are all members of same set class, ordered as P, I, R, and RI. Use a set class other than 3–1 (012).
      b. Its discrete tetrachords are all members of the same set class, ordered as P, I, and R. Use a set class other than 4–1 (0123), and remember that any tetrachord containing ic4 will not work.

II. Combinatoriality: Some collections can combine with transpositions or inversions of themselves (or their complements) to create aggregates.

  1. For each of the following hexachords, name the kinds of combinatoriality it possesses and identify the level (or levels) of transposition.
      a. 6–30 (013679)
      b. 6–20 (014589)
      c. 6–14 (013458)
      d. 6–Z37 (012348)

2.   Construct series as indicated.

   a. Its hexachords are I-combinatorial but not P-combinatorial.

   b. Its hexachords are P-combinatorial but not I-combinatorial.

   c. Its hexachords are RI-combinatorial but not I-combinatorial.

   d. Its hexachords are all-combinatorial and its discrete trichords are all members of the same set class.

ANALYSIS

I.   Webern, *Concerto for Nine Instruments,* Op. 24, second movement, mm. 1–28. (*Hint:* Mm. 1–11 are discussed in the text.)

II.   Schoenberg, *Piano Piece,* Op. 33b (*Hint:* The series is B–C♯–F–E♭–A–G♯–F♯–B♭–G–E–C–D, and it is hexachordally I-combinatorial.)

III.   Stravinsky, *Requiem Canticles,* "Lacrimosa," mm. 229–65. (*Hint:* This movement is based on one of the two series for the work (F–G–D♯–E–F♯–C♯–B–C–D–A–G♯–A♯) but uses only the first hexachord of R (A♯–G♯–A–D–C–B), the first hexachord of I (F–D♯–G–F♯–E–A), the two hexachords of IR (A♯–C–B–F♯–G♯–A and G–D–E–F–C♯–D♯), and rotational arrays derived from each.)

IV.   Crawford, *Three Songs,* "Prayers of Steel." (*Hint:* The oboe part makes use of a rotational plan and can be understood to provide material for the other parts.)

V.   Babbitt, *Du,* mm. 1–5. (*Hint:* The trichordal array is formed by the voice part and three registral lines in the piano.)

VI.   Babbitt, *The Widow's Lament in Springtime,* mm. 1–6. (*Hint:* The trichordal array is formed by the voice part and three registral lines in the piano.)

VII.   Wuorinen, *Twelve Short Pieces,* No. 3 (*Hint:* One series form is played by the right hand and another by the left. Look closely at the relationships within and among the hexachords.)

EAR-TRAINING AND MUSICIANSHIP

I.   Webern, *Concerto for Nine Instruments,* Op. 24, second movement, mm. 1–11 (first beat): Play this passage on the piano. (It may help to write it out first on two staves. The piano part can be played by the left hand, while the melody [shared by all of the other instruments] can be played by the right.) Then sing the melody (transposing by octave as necessary) while playing the piano part with two hands.

II.   Schoenberg, *Piano Piece,* Op. 33b, mm. 1–5 (downbeat only): Sing the right-hand melody while playing the left-hand accompaniment.

III.   Stravinsky, *Requiem Canticles,* "Lacrimosa," mm. 229–65. Sing the vocal part.

IV.   Crawford, *Three Songs,* "Prayers of Steel." Sing the vocal part.

V.   Babbitt, *Du,* mm. 1–5. Sing the vocal part.

VI.   Babbitt, *The Widow's Lament in Springtime,* mm. 1–6. Sing the vocal part.

VII. Wuorinen, *Twelve Short Pieces,* No. 3, mm. 1–4. Sing the right-hand melody while playing the left-hand melody, then switch.

COMPOSITION

Write short works for your own instrument (or piano) based on any of the series or arrays described in Chapter 6 or constructed in response to the exercises.

Analysis 6

Webern, String Quartet, Op. 28, first movement
Schoenberg, Piano Piece, Op. 33a

The first movement of Webern's String Quartet, Op. 28, consists of a theme (measures 1–15) and six variations. Listen to the movement and try to identify the large sections; usually they are distinguished by changes in tempo and articulation and separated by rests. Actually, the formal designation "theme and variations" is a bit too cut-and-dried. The theme itself contains intensive development of a small number of underlying ideas, and the process of variation sweeps through the entire movement. In addition to a constant process of motivic development, a two-part canon begins in measure 16 and continues until the end of the movement, cutting across the sectional divisions. Webern was fond of canons—they are a constant feature of his music. He seems to have enjoyed them both for their own sake and for their association with traditional tonal and modal practices.

Example A6–1 shows the series for this movement and illustrates three important properties.

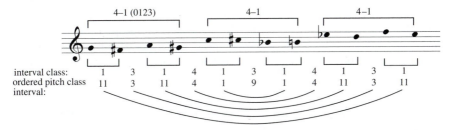

Example A6–1 The series from Webern's String Quartet, Op. 28, and some of its properties.

Notice first the extraordinary intervallic concentration. All of the discrete dyads (the six two-note groups) are members of the interval class 1. The remaining intervals are all members of either interval class 3 or 4. This kind of intensive focus on a small number of intervals is typical of Webern. Economy and concentration are hallmarks of his style. Sing the series and listen to its intervallic makeup.

Not only are the intervals concentrated, but they are arranged in retrograde-symmetrical order. They are the same reading from right to left as they are reading from left to right. This means that for every P-form of the series, there will be an RI-form that presents the twelve pitch classes in exactly the same order. Similarly, for every I-form there will be an identical R-form. Write out the RI_4 form of the series, for example, and you will see that it is identical to P_7. Better yet, write out an entire 12×12 matrix for Webern's series. Because of the retrograde-symmetry of the series, there are only twenty-four rather than the usual forty-eight distinct orderings. Retrograde-symmetry,

249

Analysis 6

like intervallic concentration, is a characteristic of Webern's style. It applies not only to the construction of the series but, as we will see, to the organization of musical phrases and sections as well.

A third important property of Webern's series is that all three discrete tetrachords are members of the same set class, 4–1 (0123). In other words, the series is derived from that tetrachord. Sing the first tetrachord, then compare it to the others. The second tetrachord relates to the first as either its inversion or its retrograde. The third tetrachord relates to the first as either its transposition or its retrograde-inversion. Derivation helps ensure the kind of intervallic economy that Webern prefers. It also guarantees that the generating set class (4–1 in this case) will be the basic musical motive of the composition.

Let's study the fourth variation of the movement (measures 66–78) to see what kind of music Webern writes using his intervallically concentrated, retrograde-symmetrical, and derived series (see Example A6–2).

Play each part individually and notice how Webern articulates each occurrence of interval class 1. The bowed notes always come in slurred pairs, spanning pitch intervals 11 or 13. The pizzicato notes also come in pairs, often alternating with the bowed pairs, and also state various forms of interval class 1. Over the course of the passage, all twelve members of interval class 1 (C–C♯, C♯–D, D–E♭, etc.) are stated exactly three times each—once toward the beginning of the passage, once in the middle, and once toward the end. The concentration on interval class 1 is striking, as is the variety of gestures and shapes possible within that exclusive focus.

(continued)

Analysis 6

Example A6–2 The fourth variation.

Because of the intervallic redundancy of the series, there are many different possible twelve-counts of this passage. The twelve-count provided in Example A6–3 shows the two-part canon that runs through the passage. The series-forms are divided among the instruments, usually moving to a new instrument after completing one of the tetrachords. Curved lines trace the progress of the series.

P_{10} is the leading voice. Three beats later, P_7 enters as the following voice. P_{10} contains six distinct pitch-class dyads, all members of interval class 1. Because the interval of imitation is odd, the following voice (P_7) contains six different pitch-class dyads, again all members of interval class 1. This is how, as we noted above, all twelve members of interval class 1 come to be present. Notice that, for the most part, this is a pitch canon as well as a pitch-class canon.

Work through the canon carefully, listening to the imitations. The canon begins with the first tetrachord of P_{10}: B♭–A–C–B. This, of course, is the B–A–C–H motive, a musical version of Bach's name. (In German notation, B♭ = B and B = H.) Because the series is derived from 4–1 (0123), the B–A–C–H motive—transposed, inverted, retrograded, and retrograde-inverted—is omnipresent. Play these four notes as they occur in the first violin together with their canonic imitation in the viola. Notice that the leading voice (P_{10}) moves only on beats 2 and 4, the weak beats of the measure, while the following voice (P_7) moves only on beats 1 and 3, the strong beats. This rhythmic contrast between the parts makes the canon easier to hear. Continue to work through the canon, playing first the off-beat tetrachords of P_{10}, then the on-beat imitation in P_7.

Analysis 6

Example A6–3 Twelve-count of the fourth variation (a canon between P_{10} and P_7).

Analysis 6

By measure 71, P_{10} and P_7 have both been stated. At that point, each tetrachord is stated for a second time, now in reverse order. In measure 73, the opening music returns (with a few slight alterations of register and rhythm). This formal layout, ABA, is retrograde-symmetrical and thus recalls the retrograde-symmetry of the series. Notice that the exact midpoint of the passage, in measure 72, is marked by the resumption of the tempo after a ritardando.

An extraordinary wealth of motivic detail is crowded into this brief passage. Let's pluck out just a single thread from the fabric for closer inspection. Example A6–4 shows a melodic/rhythmic figure that occurs four times in the lower strings in the passage.

Example A6–4 A melodic/rhythmic figure and the transpositional path it describes.

This figure occurs twice in the cello, then once in the viola, then again in the cello. The fourth statement is articulated staccato and its third note is only a quarter-note long. This helps give a feeling of gradual fragmentation or dissolution to the end of the passage. Each four-note figure represents one of the discrete tetrachords of P_{10}, the leading voice of the canon. They are arranged as pitch transpositions of one another. The four-note motive is projected through a descending 4-cycle, ending where it began. Play the four figures and listen for that transpositional path. Each of the tetrachords of the series is related to the other two by T_4 or T_8. Through repetition of a single identifiable melodic/rhythmic figure, a long-range path through the passage reflects the structure of the series itself.

Schoenberg's Piano Piece, Op. 33a, begins with the six chords shown in Example A6–5.

Example A6–5 The first six chords of Schoenberg's Piano Piece, Op. 33a.

Analysis 6

Play these chords and listen to them. Their contour (moving upward to a high point and then descending) and rhythm (with the last chord longer than the others) make them sound like a single musical gesture. Now compare the first and sixth chords. The sixth chord has the same pitch intervals from top to bottom that the first chord has from bottom to top. In other words, the two chords are both pitch-class and pitch inversions of each other. The same is true of the second and fifth chords and the third and fourth chords. Play these pairs of chords (1 + 6, 2 + 5, and 3 + 4) and listen for the inversional relationships. Each chord in measure 2 is related by T_1I to the corresponding chord in measure 1. Listen also for the retrograde symmetry that results in the phrase as a whole (see Example A6–6).

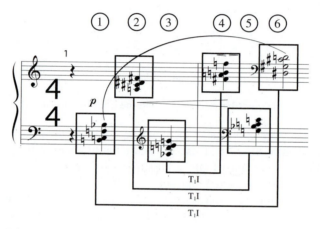

Example A6–6 The first, second, and third chords relate by T_1I to the sixth, fifth, and fourth chords.

Measures 1 and 2 each contain all twelve pitch classes. If measure 1 states P, then measure 2 states the retrograde of T_1I (P). Of course, we don't yet know the proper order of the pitch classes within each tetrachord. In measures 3–5, we find out.

In measures 3–5, the chords from measures 1–2 are linearized, with chords 4, 5, and 6 above and chords 3, 2, and 1 below (see Example A6–7). Because of the inversional relationship among the chords established in measures 1–2, we can infer a serial ordering for all of the notes from what we hear in measures 3–5. Chords 4 and 3 are related at T_1I, so if Chord 4 is ordered as A–B–F–G♭, then Chord 3 should be E–D–A♭–G. Similarly, Chord 5 is B♭–C–G–E and Chord 2 is E♭–D♭–G♭–A, while Chord 6 is D–C♯–G♯–D♯ and Chord 1 is B–C–F–B♭. The lower part states a twelve-note series (E–D–A♭–G–E♭–D♭–G♭–A–B–C–F–B♭) that is the retrograde of the series in measure 1. So measure 1 is P_{10} and the lower part in measures 3–5 is R_{10}. And measure 2, like the upper part in measures 3–5, is RI_3 (A–B–F–G♭–B♭–C–G–E–D–C♯–G♯–D♯).

254

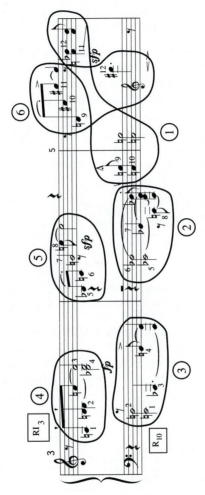

Example A6–7 Two series-forms stated linearly and partitioned into tetrachords.

Analysis 6

Play the melodic tetrachords of RI_3 and compare them to their chordal counterparts in measure 2. Then do the same for the melodic tetrachords of R_{10} and the chords of measure 1.

When Schoenberg says, "The two-or-more-dimensional space in which musical ideas are presented is a unit," this is the kind of situation he has in mind. His musical ideas retain their identity regardless of whether they are presented harmonically, melodically, or in some combination of these.

Schoenberg has a particular reason for combining R_{10} with RI_3. The first hexachord of R_{10} has the same pitch-class content as the second hexachord of RI_3 (and vice versa). The same is true, of course, of the hexachords of P_{10} and I_3. In other words, Schoenberg's series is hexachordally combinatorial (see Example A6–8).

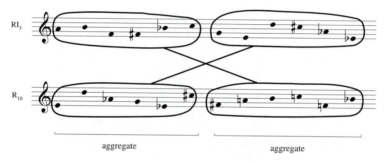

Example A6–8 R_{10} is combinatorial with RI_3 (the first hexachord of R_{10} has the same pitch-class content as the second hexachord of RI_3, and vice versa).

Notice how this works in the music. By the middle of measure 4, we have heard the first hexachord of RI_3 and the first hexachord of R_{10}. As a result, all twelve pitch classes (an aggregate) are already present. At the end of measure 5, when the two linear series statements come to an end, a second aggregate is also completed (see Example A6–9).

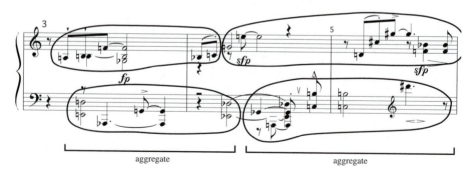

Example A6–9 Hexachordal combinatoriality used to create aggregates.

Analysis 6

The aggregate is a basic harmonic unit in Schoenberg's twelve-tone music. Completion of an aggregate frequently coincides with, or articulates, the end of a phrase or section of music. Play this passage and listen for a kind of large voice exchange, where the first six pitch classes from the right hand become the last six pitch classes in the left hand, and vice versa.

Combining P_{10} (or R_{10}) with I_3 (or RI_3) has another important effect that Schoenberg exploits throughout this work. He combines dyads from each series-form to create tetrachords (see Example A6–10).

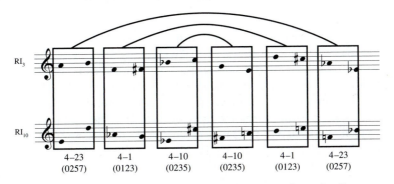

Example A6–10 Tetrachords formed between the series-forms.

The result is a layout very like that of measures 1–2: six tetrachords arranged symmetrically. The first and sixth tetrachords are members of the same set class, 4–23 (0257), as are the second and fifth tetrachords (4–1 (0123)) and the third and fourth tetrachords (4–10 (0235)). Let's see how this idea plays out in measures 3–5 (see Example A6–11).

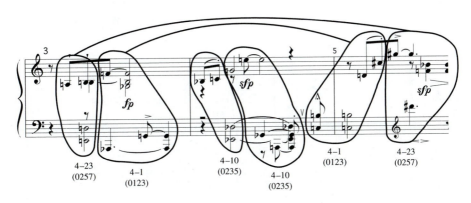

Example A6–11 The between-series tetrachords.

Analysis 6

Play this passage and try to hear this symmetrical arrangement. The easiest thing to hear is probably that the passage begins and ends on 4–23 (0257). In fact, 4–23 acts as a kind of phrase-marker throughout this piece. Listen for it when you listen to the piece as a whole. 4–23 can be thought of either as two 2s related by T_5 or as two 5s related by T_2. (Any inversionally symmetrical set can be thought of in two ways like this.) Notice that in measure 3 Schoenberg presents the 2s, and in measure 5 he presents the 5s. He gets a similar kind of variety in his presentation of the third and fourth tetrachords and, to a lesser extent, the second and fifth tetrachords. Play the pairs of tetrachords (1 + 6, 2 + 5, and 3 + 4) and listen to their shared set-class membership, the varied manner of their presentation, and the symmetrical balance that results, unifying the passage.

In the first twenty-three measures of this piece, the only series-forms used are P_{10}, I_3, and their retrogrades. Since P_{10} is combinatorial with I_3 (and R_{10} with RI_3), these four series-forms constitute a single twelve-tone area, A_{10}. But the entire piece does not remain within A_{10}. The middle section of the piece (measures 23–32) contains motions to A_0 (beginning at the end of measure 27) and A_5 (beginning in the middle of measure 29, with an earlier premonition in measure 28). The final section (measures 32–39) then returns to A_{10}. The moment when A_5 leads back to A_{10} is shown in Example A6–12.

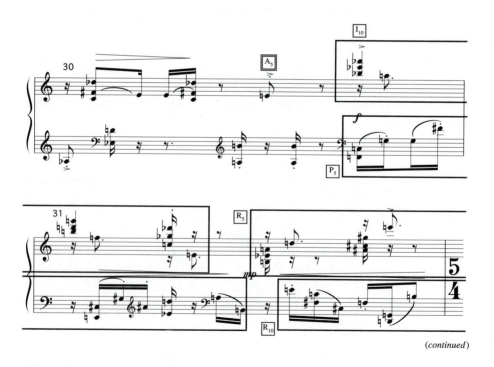

(continued)

Analysis 6

Example A6–12 Motion from A_5 to A_{10}.

The large-scale progression of the piece, then, is A_{10}–A_0–A_5–A_{10}. In traditional terms, that is a motion up a whole-step, then up a perfect fourth, then a final descent by perfect fifth. Obviously Schoenberg has in mind some kind of analogy to the tonal motion I–II–V–I. But there is more than an analogy at work here. Look again at the first three notes of the series: B♭–F–C, or 10–5–0. They form set class 3–9 (027), as does the set of areas, A_{10}, A_0, and A_5. The large-scale motion from area to area thus composes-out the initial melodic idea.

BIBLIOGRAPHY

Webern's own discussion of his String Quartet, Op. 28, can be found in Hans Moldenhauer, *Anton von Webern: A Chronicle of His Life and Work* (New York: Knopf, 1979), pp. 751–56. See also Arnold Whittall, "Webern and Multiple Meaning," *Music Analysis* 6/3 (1987), pp. 333–53, and Kathryn Bailey, *The Twelve-Note Music of Anton Webern* (Cambridge: Cambridge University Press, 1991).

On Schoenberg's Piano Piece, see Eric Graebner, "An Analysis of Schoenberg's Klavierstück, Op. 33a," *Perspectives of New Music* 12/1–2 (1973–74), pp. 128–40. See also *Milton Babbitt: Words About Music,* ed. Stephen Dembski and Joseph N. Straus (Madison: University of Wisconsin Press, 1987), pp. 75–79.

Appendix 1
List of Set Classes

The following list shows all the set classes containing between three and nine pitch classes. The first and last columns contain prime forms. (Those in the first column are in ascending numerical order.) In the prime forms, the letters T and E stand for the integers 10 and 11 respectively. The second and second-to-last columns provide the names of the set classes, according to Allen Forte's *The Structure of Atonal Music*. The third and third-to-last columns give the interval vector for each set class. For each set class with a Z in its name, there is another with an identical interval vector. In the middle column, the first number gives the degree of transpositional symmetry—that is, the number of levels at which both sets on that line will map onto themselves under transposition. (This number is always at least 1, since every set maps onto itself at T_0.) The second number gives the degree of inversional symmetry—that is, the number of levels at which a set maps onto itself under inversion. Complementary set classes are listed across from each other.

TRICHORDS						NONACHORDS
(012)	3–1	210000	1, 1	876663	9–1	(012345678)
(013)	3–2	111000	1, 0	777663	9–2	(012345679)
(014)	3–3	101100	1, 0	767763	9–3	(012345689)
(015)	3–4	100110	1, 0	766773	9–4	(012345789)
(016)	3–5	100011	1, 0	766674	9–5	(012346789)
(024)	3–6	020100	1, 1	686763	9–6	(01234568T)
(025)	3–7	011010	1, 0	677673	9–7	(01234578T)
(026)	3–8	010101	1, 0	676764	9–8	(01234678T)
(027)	3–9	010020	1, 1	676683	9–9	(01235678T)
(036)	3–10	002001	1, 1	668664	9–10	(01234679T)
(037)	3–11	001110	1, 0	667773	9–11	(01235679T)
(048)	3–12	000300	3, 3	666963	9–12	(01245689T)

List of Set Classes

TETRACHORDS

(0123)	4–1	321000	1, 1	765442	8–1	(01234567)
(0124)	4–2	221100	1, 0	665542	8–2	(01234568)
(0125)	4–4	211110	1, 0	655552	8–4	(01234578)
(0126)	4–5	210111	1, 0	654553	8–5	(01234678)
(0127)	4–6	210021	1, 1	654463	8–6	(01235678)
(0134)	4–3	212100	1, 1	656542	8–3	(01234569)
(0135)	4–11	121110	1, 0	565552	8–11	(01234579)
(0136)	4–13	112011	1, 0	556453	8–13	(01234679)
(0137)	4-Z29	111111	1, 0	555553	8-Z29	(01235679)
(0145)	4–7	201210	1, 1	645652	8–7	(01234589)
(0146)	4-Z15	111111	1, 0	555553	8-Z15	(01234689)
(0147)	4–18	102111	1, 0	546553	8–18	(01235689)
(0148)	4–19	101310	1, 0	545752	8–19	(01245689)
(0156)	4–8	200121	1, 1	644563	8–8	(01234789)
(0157)	4–16	110121	1, 0	554563	8–16	(01235789)
(0158)	4–20	101220	1, 1	545662	8–20	(01245789)
(0167)	4–9	200022	2, 2	644464	8–9	(01236789)
(0235)	4–10	122010	1, 1	566452	8–10	(02345679)
(0236)	4–12	112101	1, 0	556543	8–12	(01345679)
(0237)	4–14	111120	1, 0	555562	8–14	(01245679)
(0246)	4–21	030201	1, 1	474643	8–21	(0123468T)
(0247)	4–22	021120	1, 0	465562	8–22	(0123568T)
(0248)	4–24	020301	1, 1	464743	8–24	(0124568T)
(0257)	4–23	021030	1, 1	465472	8–23	(0123578T)
(0258)	4–27	012111	1, 0	456553	8–27	(0124578T)
(0268)	4–25	020202	2, 2	464644	8–25	(0124678T)
(0347)	4–17	102210	1, 1	546652	8–17	(01345689)
(0358)	4–26	012120	1, 1	456562	8–26	(0134578T)
(0369)	4–28	004002	4, 4	448444	8–28	(0134679T)

OCTACHORDS

PENTACHORDS   SEPTACHORDS

(01234)	5–1	432100	1, 1	654321	7–1	(0123456)
(01235)	5–2	332110	1, 0	554331	7–2	(0123457)
(01236)	5–4	322111	1, 0	544332	7–4	(0123467)
(01237)	5–5	321121	1, 0	543342	7–5	(0123567)
(01245)	5–3	322210	1, 0	544431	7–3	(0123458)
(01246)	5–9	231211	1, 0	453432	7–9	(0123468)
(01247)	5-Z36	222121	1, 0	444342	7-Z36	(0123568)
(01248)	5–13	221311	1, 0	443532	7–13	(0124568)
(01256)	5–6	311221	1, 0	533442	7–6	(0123478)
(01257)	5–14	221131	1, 0	443352	7–14	(0123578)
(01258)	5-Z38	212221	1, 0	434442	7-Z38	(0124578)
(01267)	**5–7**	310132	1, 0	532353	7–7	(0123678)
(01268)	**5–15**	220222	1, 1	442443	7–15	(0124678)
(01346)	**5–10**	223111	1, 0	445332	7–10	(0123469)
(01347)	**5–16**	213211	1, 0	435432	7–16	(0123569)
(01348)	**5-Z17**	212320	1, 1	434541	7-Z17	(0124569)
(01356)	**5-Z12**	222121	1, 1	444342	7-Z12	(0123479)
(01357)	**5–24**	131221	1, 0	353442	7–24	(0123579)
(01358)	**5–27**	122230	1, 0	344451	7–27	(0124579)
(01367)	**5–19**	212122	1, 0	434343	7–19	(0123679)
(01368)	**5–29**	122131	1, 0	344352	7–29	(0124679)
(01369)	**5–31**	114112	1, 0	336333	7–31	(0134679)
(01457)	**5-Z18**	212221	1, 0	434442	7-Z18	(0145679)
(01458)	**5–21**	202420	1, 0	424641	7–21	(0124589)
(01468)	**5–30**	121321	1, 0	343542	7–30	(0124689)
(01469)	**5–32**	113221	1, 0	335442	7–32	(0134689)
(01478)	**5–22**	202321	1, 1	424542	7–22	(0125689)
(01568)	**5–20**	211231	1, 0	433452	7–20	(0125679)
(02346)	**5–8**	232201	1, 1	454422	7–8	(0234568)
(02347)	**5–11**	222220	1, 0	444441	7–11	(0134568)
(02357)	**5–23**	132130	1, 0	354351	7–23	(0234579)
(02358)	**5–25**	123121	1, 0	345342	7–25	(0234679)
(02368)	**5–28**	122212	1, 0	344433	7–28	(0135679)
(02458)	**5–26**	122311	1, 0	344532	7–26	(0134579)
(02468)	**5–33**	040402	1, 1	262623	7–33	(012468T)
(02469)	**5–34**	032221	1, 1	254442	7–34	(013468T)
(02479)	**5–35**	032140	1, 1	254361	7–35	(013568T)
(03458)	**5-Z37**	212320	1, 1	434541	7-Z37	(0134578)

HEXACHORDS

The first column in this list of hexachords describes the combinatoriality of each set class. The four entries in the column provide the number of transpositional levels at which each hexachord is P-combinatorial, R-combinatorial, I-combinatorial, and RI-combinatorial. (Every hexachord is R-combinatorial at least at R_0.) Hexachords, like sets of other sizes, are listed across from their complements. Hexachords with nothing listed across from them are self-complementary.

P	R	I	RI						
1	1	1	1	(012345)	6–1	543210	1, 1		
0	1	1	0	(012346)	6–2	443211	1, 0		
0	1	0	0	(012347)	6-Z36	433221	1, 0	6-Z3	(012356)
0	1	0	1	(012348)	6-Z37	432321	1, 1	6-Z4	(012456)
0	1	1	0	(012357)	6–9	342231	1, 0		
0	1	0	0	(012358)	6-Z40	333231	1, 0	6-Z11	(012457)
0	1	1	0	(012367)	6–5	422232	1, 0		
0	1	0	0	(012368)	6-Z41	332232	1, 0	6-Z12	(012467)
0	1	0	1	(012369)	6-Z42	324222	1, 1	6-Z13	(013467)
0	1	0	1	(012378)	6-Z38	421242	1, 1	6-Z6	(012567)
0	1	1	0	(012458)	6–15	323421	1, 0		
0	1	1	0	(012468)	6–22	241422	1, 0		
0	1	0	0	(012469)	6-Z46	233331	1, 0	6-Z24	(013468)
0	1	0	0	(012478)	6-Z17	322332	1, 0	6-Z43	(012568)
0	1	0	0	(012479)	6-Z47	233241	1, 0	6-Z25	(013568)
0	1	0	0	(012569)	6-Z44	313431	1, 0	6-Z19	(013478)
0	1	1	0	(012578)	6–18	322242	1, 0		
0	1	0	1	(012579)	6-Z48	232341	1, 1	6–Z26	(013578)
2	2	2	2	(012678)	6–7	420243	2, 2		
0	1	0	0	(013457)	6-Z10	333321	1, 0	6-Z39	(023458)
1	1	0	0	(013458)	6–14	323430	1, 0		
0	1	1	0	(013469)	6–27	225222	1, 0		
0	1	0	1	(013479)	6-Z49	224322	1, 1	6-Z28	(013569)
0	1	1	0	(013579)	6–34	142422	1, 0		
0	2	2	0	(013679)	6–30	224223	2, 0		
0	1	0	1	(023679)	6-Z29	224232	1, 1	6-Z50	(014679)
0	1	1	0	(014568)	6–16	322431	1, 0		
0	1	1	0	(014579)	6–31	223431	1, 0		
3	3	3	3	(014589)	6–20	303630	3, 3		
1	1	1	1	(023457)	6–8	343230	1, 1		
0	1	1	0	(023468)	6–21	242412	1, 0		
0	1	0	1	(023469)	6-Z45	234222	1, 1	6-Z23	(023568)
0	1	1	0	(023579)	6–33	143241	1, 0		
1	1	1	1	(024579)	6–32	143250	1, 1		
6	6	6	6	(02468T)	6–35	060603	6, 6		

[Handwritten margin note, pointing to the (013458) row:] Only hexachord that is transp. comb. but not inv. comb.

Appendix 2
Index Vectors

This list gives index vectors for each set class. The first and second columns give the prime form and set name for each set class. The third column gives the index vector for the prime form of the set class. The fourth column gives the index vector for the set related by T_0I to the prime form. For members of the set class related to the prime form by T_n, rotate the prime form's index vector 2n places to the right, wrapping around the end. For example, each entry in the index vector for a set related by T_3 to its prime form will be six places farther to the right than the same entry in the index vector for the prime form. The number of occurrences of index 2 in the vector for the prime form will be the number of occurrences of index 8 in the vector for the set related by T_3; the number of occurrences of index 10 in the vector for the prime form will be the number of occurrences of index 4 in the vector for the set related by T_3; and so on. For members of the set class related to the prime form by T_nI, rotate the index vector for T_0I 2n places to the right, wrapping around the end.

012	3-1	123210000000	100000001232		0125	4-4	123212220010	101002221232
013	3-2	121220100000	100000102212		0126	4-5	223210222000	200022201232
014	3-3	121022001000	100010022012		0127	4-6	124210022200	100222001242
015	3-4	121002200010	101000220012		0134	4-3	121242121000	100012124212
016	3-5	221000220000	200002200012		0135	4-11	121222302010	101020322212
024	3-6	102030201000	100010203020		0136	4-13	221220320200	200202302212
025	3-7	102012020010	101002021020		0137	4-Z29	122220122020	102022102222
026	3-8	202010202000	200202201020		0145	4-7	121024201210	101210242012
027	3-9	103010020200	100202001030		0146	4-Z15	221022221020	202012222012
036	3-10	200200300200	200200300200		0147	4-18	122022023002	120032022022
037	3-11	101200120020	102002100210		0148	4-19	321032003200	300230023012
048	3-12	300030003000	300030003000		0156	4-8	221002420012	221002420012
					0157	4-16	322002222010	301022220022
0123	4-1	123432100000	100000123432		0158	4-20	141012202210	101220221014
0124	4-2	123232201000	100010223232		0167	4-9	242000242000	200024200024

0235	4-10	102214122010	101022141220
0236	4-12	202212302200	200220321220
0237	4-14	103212120220	102202121230
0246	4-21	202030403020	202030403020
0247	4-22	103030221202	120212203030
0248	4-24	302040203020	302030204020
0257	4-23	303012040210	301204021030
0258	4-27	122022022030	103022022022
0268	4-25	204020204020	202040202040
0347	4-17	101220141022	122014102210
0358	4-26	120212104012	121040121202
0369	4-28	400400400400	400400400400
01234	5-1	123454321000	100012345432
01235	5-2	123434322010	101022343432
01236	5-4	223432322200	200222323432
01237	5-5	124432122220	102222123442
01245	5-3	123234421210	101212443232
01246	5-9	223232423020	202032423232
01247	5-Z36	124232223202	120232223242
01248	5-13	323242203220	302230224232
01256	5-6	223212442012	221024421232
01257	5-14	324212242210	301224221242
01258	5-Z38	143222222230	103222222234
01267	5-7	244210244200	200244201244
01268	5-15	225220224220	202242202252
01346	5-10	221242341220	202214324212
01347	5-16	122242143022	122034124222
01348	5-Z17	321252123202	320232125212
01356	5-Z12	221222522212	221222522212
01357	5-24	322222324030	303042322222
01358	5-27	141232304212	121240323214
01367	5-19	242220342220	202224302224
01368	5-29	223230322402	220422303232
01369	5-31	421420420420	402402402412
01457	5-Z18	322024223212	321232242022
01458	5-21	341034203414	301430243014
01468	5-30	423032223220	402232223032
01469	5-32	241222321240	204212322214
01478	5-22	322232025202	320252023222
01568	5-20	243012422212	221222421034
02346	5-8	202232523220	202232523220
02347	5-11	103232341222	122214323230
02357	5-23	303214142230	303224141230
02358	5-25	122224124032	123042142222
02368	5-28	204222304222	222240322240
02458	5-26	322042223230	303232224022
02468	5-33	404040405040	404050404040
02469	5-34	222230503222	222230503222
02479	5-35	123050321404	140412305032
03458	5-Z37	320232125212	321252123202
012345	6-1	123456543210	101234565432
012346	6-2	223454543220	202234545432
012347	6-Z36	124454343222	122234345442
012348	6-Z37	323464323222	322232346432
012356	6-Z3	223434544212	221244543432
012357	6-9	324434344230	303244343442
012358	6-Z40	143444324232	123242344434
012367	6-5	244443234444	202444323444
012368	6-Z41	225442324422	222442324452
012369	6-Z42	423632422422	422422423632
012378	6-Z38	124642124442	124442124642
012456	6-Z4	223234643232	223234643232
012457	6-Z11	324234443412	321434443242
012458	6-15	343244423340	303432444234
012467	6-Z12	244232445222	222254423244
012468	6-22	425242425240	404252424252
012469	6-Z46	243432523242	224232523434
012478	6-Z17	324442225422	322452224442
012479	6-Z47	144252323424	142432325244
012567	6-Z6	444212464212	421246421244
012568	6-Z43	245222444232	223244422254
012569	6-Z44	225412542234	243224521452
012578	6-18	344422244430	303444222444
012579	6-Z48	326232342432	323424323262
012678	6-7	246420246420	202464202464
013457	6-Z10	322244345232	323254344222
013458	6-14	341254325412	321452345214
013467	6-Z13	242242363242	224236324224
013468	6-Z24	423252343422	422434325232
013469	6-27	441442441440	404414424414
013478	6-Z19	322452145224	342254125422
013479	6-Z49	342262243242	324234226224
013568	6-Z25	243232524414	241442523234
013569	6-Z28	423422622432	423422622432
013578	6-Z26	342432325232	323262323424
013579	6-34	524242424250	505242424242
013679	6-30	442440442440	404424404424
014568	6-16	443034423432	423432443034
014579	6-31	344044323432	323432344044
014589	6-20	363036303630	303630363036
014679	6-Z50	262242343242	224234324226
023457	6-8	303234363432	323436343230
023458	6-Z39	322244345232	323254344222
023468	6-21	404242525242	424252524240
023469	6-Z45	422432623422	422432623422
023568	6-Z23	224224326234	243262342242
023579	6-33	505234242432	523424243250
023679	6-Z29	423432422622	422622423432
024579	6-32	325052341614	341614325052
02468T	6-35	606060606060	606060606060
0123456	7-1	223456765432	223456765432
0123457	7-2	324456565432	323456565442
0123458	7-3	343466545432	323455666434
0123467	7-4	244454565442	224456545444
0123468	7-9	425464545442	424454546452
0123469	7-10	443654643442	424434645634
0123478	7-6	324664345444	344454346642
0123479	7-Z12	344474443444	344434447444
0123567	7-5	444434566432	423466543444
0123568	7-Z36	245444546434	243464544454
0123569	7-16	425634644434	443444643432
0123578	7-14	344644346452	325464344644
0123579	7-24	526454444452	525444445462
0123678	7-7	266642346642	224664324664
0123679	7-19	444652444642	424644425494
0124568	7-13	445244645452	425454644254
0124569	7-Z17	245434743454	245434743454
0124578	7-Z38	544444445632	523654444444
0124579	7-27	346254543634	343634545264
0124589	7-21	365246523652	325632564256
0124678	7-15	446442447442	424474424464
0124679	7-29	264452545444	244454525446
0124689	7-30	445444525462	426452544442
012468T	7-33	627262626262	626262626272
0125679	7-20	446432564434	443446523464
0125689	7-22	247424544454	245444542474
0134568	7-11	443254545634	443654545234
0134578	7-Z37	542454347434	543474345424
0134579	7-26	544264445452	525454446244
0134679	7-31	462462463462	426436426426
0134689	7-32	643454443432	624634445434
013468T	7-34	445272544444	444444527254
0135679	7-28	644442644452	625444624444
013568T	7-35	263452725436	263452725436
0145679	7-18	464244543454	445434544246
0234568	7-8	424244547454	445475544242
0234579	7-23	525254463634	543636445252
0234679	7-25	443452643644	444634625434
01234567	8-1	444456787654	445678765444
01234568	8-2	445466767654	445676766454
01234569	8-3	445656865654	445656865654
01234578	8-4	544666567654	545676566644
01234579	8-11	546476665654	545656667464
01234589	8-7	565468645654	545654686456

01234678	8-5	446664567664	446676546664	01345679	8-12	664464665674	647656646446
01234679	8-13	464674665664	446656647646	01345689	8-17	665456645854	645854665456
01234689	8-Z15	645666645664	646654666654	0134578T	8-26	564656548456	565484565646
0123468T	8-21	647484746464	646464748474	0134679T	8-28	484484484484	448448448448
01234789	8-8	544686445666	566654468644	02345679	8-10	645454665856	665856645454
01235678	8-6	466644568654	445686544666				
01235679	8-Z29	646654666654	645666645664	012345678	9-1	666666789876	667898766666
01235689	8-18	447646646656	465664664674	012345679	9-2	666676887876	667878867666
0123568T	8-22	465664747456	465474746656	012345689	9-3	667668867876	667876886676
01235789	8-16	546664446674	547664466664	01234568T	9-6	667686968676	667686968676
0123578T	8-23	564846547474	547474564846	012345789	9-4	766688667876	767876688666
01236789	8-9	446864446864	446864446864	01234578T	9-7	766868768676	767686786866
01245679	8-14	466454765656	465656745466	012346789	9-5	666886667886	668876668866
01245689	8-19	467446745674	447654764476	01234678T	9-8	668686768686	668686768686
0124568T	8-24	647464846474	647464846474	01234679T	9-10	686696686686	668668669668
01245789	8-20	566466545854	545854546466	01235678T	9-9	686866769676	667696766868
0124578T	8-27	746646646654	745664664664	01235679T	9-11	866876687676	867678667866
0124678T	8-25	648464648464	646484646484	01245689T	9-12	669666966696	669666966696

Index